The New Comparative Mythology

C. Scott Littleton

The New
Comparative Mythology

An Anthropological Assessment
of the Theories of Georges Dumézil

University of California Press
Berkeley and Los Angeles   1966

University of California Press
Berkeley and Los Angeles, California
Cambridge University Press
London, England

for
Leslie Ann

Preface

I should like to emphasize at the outset that this book is not intended to be an intellectual biography. I do not intend to do for Professor Dumézil what Alpert (1939) did for Émile Durkheim or what Bendix (1960) did some years ago for Max Weber. Such books can be written only when all is said and done, and this is certainly not true of Dumézil. His theories are still evolving, and it would be presumptuous in the extreme to treat them as if they were complete. I should also like to emphasize that my approach to this subject is that of a social anthropologist. As I am not by training primarily an Indo-Europeanist, I must rely upon the judgment of others more competent than myself in the more technical aspects of Indo-European philology. Yet the fact that Dumézil's comparative mythology is so heavily based upon sociological and anthropological assumptions rather than upon purely philological ones—indeed, it is this fact, as much as anything else, which sets Dumézil apart from his predecessors—renders it thoroughly amenable to assessment by one whose training and experience has been that of a social anthropologist specializing in mythology, folklore, and general linguistics.

The plan of the book is as follows: After a brief discussion of the general significance of Dumézil's work and of some of the reasons that it is not so familiar as it might be to my fellow anthropologists, the introduction focuses upon an overview of his theory as it stands today and the nature of the evidence used to support it. Part I is concerned with a review of the theory's linguistic, culture-historical, comparative mythological, and sociological background. Part II deals with the evolution of the theory from 1924 to the

Preface

present. Part III is concerned with the contributions made to the theory over the years by disciples and colleagues of Dumézil, with the many criticisms that have been lodged against it, and with an overall assessment of its worth to the social anthropology of myth and folklore, to say nothing of social anthropology per se.

No book of this sort could possibly have been written without the generous assistance, in one form or another, of a host of institutions and persons. The bulk of the research was done with the aid of a research-assistantship (1961–62) under the auspices of the Center for the Study of Comparative Folklore and Mythology, University of California, Los Angeles. I should like to express my thanks to all those concerned with the Center, especially its director, Dr. Wayland D. Hand, for providing this opportunity. Thanks are also due to Occidental College and the John Randolph Haynes and Dora Haynes Foundation, Los Angeles, California, for providing me with a summer faculty fellowship (1963), which in no small measure facilitated the writing of the pages that follow.

Among those individuals to whom I am indebted, Professor Georges Dumézil, of the Collège de France, should, of course, head the list. In addition to providing the stimulus for the present work, he has also contributed to its present form through his invaluable comments and clarifications. Even though there remain a few matters upon which we disagree, the extent of my debt cannot be overestimated. Special thanks are also due Dr. Jaan Puhvel, professor of Indo-European linguistics and director of the Center for Research in Languages and Linguistics, University of California, Los Angeles, for introducing me to Professor Dumézil's theories and for guiding me through the intricacies of comparative Indo-European mythology and philology. On the anthropological side I should like first of all to express my sincerest gratitude to Professor William A. Lessa, of the Department of Anthropology, University of California, Los Angeles, not only for invaluable suggestions and criticisms relative to earlier drafts of the book, but also for advice and encouragement throughout the course of my research. I am also grateful to Professors John T. Hitchcock and Henry B. Nicholson, of the Department of Anthropology, University of California, Los Angeles, for their many helpful suggestions; to Mr. James Kubeck, Mrs. Sherri Butterfield, and Mrs. Grace Stimson, of the University of California Press, for their invaluable editorial assistance; to Mrs. Marilyn Askary for her skill as a typist; and last, but by no means least, to my wife Mary Ann for her help, patience, and understanding during a long and sometimes difficult period. Here, too, the extent of my debt cannot be overestimated.

C. S. L.

Occidental College
Los Angeles, California

Contents

Contents

Contents

Introduction

This book is concerned with the theories and methods developed
by perhaps the most original, and at the same time most contro-
versial, student of comparative Indo-European mythology since
the turn of the century: Georges Dumézil, professor of Indo-European civilization in the Collège de France and for many years a
director of studies in the Section des Sciences Religieuses of the
École des Hautes Études of the Sorbonne.

Trained under the great French Indo-Europeanist Antoine Meillet, and thoroughly exposed to the sociology of Émile Durkheim,
Marcel Mauss, and others who in the early years of the twentieth
century were shaping a functional approach to the study of primitive religion, Professor Dumézil has developed an approach to
comparative mythology which is unique, to say the least. In adding
a functionally oriented sociological and anthropological dimension
to the traditional comparative study of the myths, epics, ritual, and
folktales of the ancient Indo-European-speaking peoples, he has
forged a wholly new conception of the relationship among language,
myth, and social organization. As I see it, the conception has profound implications not only for social anthropology, but also for
the social sciences as a whole.

Yet with a very few exceptions, this new comparative mythology
has been almost totally ignored by British and American anthropologists, even by those primarily concerned with the analysis of
myth and folklore. The principal reason for their neglect—aside

1

from the fact that as yet none of Dumézil's works has been translated into English—would seem to lie in the history of the relationship between comparative mythology, especially comparative I-E[1] mythology, and anthropology. In the earlier phases of this history, before 1900, the efforts of such scholars as Adalbert Kuhn and Max Müller usually commanded the attention, if not always the respect, of anthropologists, sociologists, social philosophers, and the like. But after the turn of the century, largely as a result of the conflict between Andrew Lang and Müller over the adequacy of naturistic[2] interpretations of myth, and the subsequent growth of a more rigorous and sophisticated body of theory in the social sciences as a whole, anthropological interest in comparative Indo-European mythology rapidly waned. The new spirit of empiricism, fostered by Boas in the United States and by Malinowski and others in Britain, precluded an interest in matters of this sort. Save for Frazer and a few others whose outlook remained essentially that of the nineteenth century, anthropological interest, as far as mythology is concerned, came to be focused almost exclusively upon the myths and folktales of living primitive peoples.

This shift in emphasis on the part of anthropologists came to be reflected in a host of allied disciplines. Among the scholars concerned with the various I-E mythologies—Greek, Germanic, and so on—comparativism, associated as it was with the discarded naturism of Kuhn, Müller, and others, became something to be avoided at all costs.

The last few decades, however, have seen a resurgence of comparative I-E studies, a phenomenon largely if not wholly stimulated by the efforts of Dumézil and his school. This school, with its insistence upon a sociological (or at least Durkheimian) interpretation of mythical data, has aroused both the respect and the ire of a generation of European linguists, classicists, folklorists, mythologists, and "historians of religion," if not anthropologists. Since the advent of this new comparative mythology, many regional specialists, in criticizing what sometimes appear to be gross oversimplifications or misinterpretations on the part of Dumézil and his

---

[1] Wherever possible, and in accordance with long-established linguistic usage, the abbreviation "I-E" is substituted for "Indo-European."

[2] The term "naturistic" refers to the widely held nineteenth-century view that all mythical personages (gods, heroes, etc.) are in the last analysis symbolic representations of natural phenomena of one sort or another (e.g., sun, moon, fire, storms).

students, have had to come to terms once more with the idea that particular problems in the mythologies of particular I-E-speaking regions can perhaps be solved by viewing them against a broad, comparative background. What is more, such specialists have been forced to consider the proposition that this background includes a common set of myths functionally interrelated to a common set of social institutions, to a common ideology, whether in ancient Italy, Scandinavia, Iran, or even Greece.

In short, the advent of Dumézilian mythology has precipitated what amounts to a revolution in most of the disciplines that impinge upon the ancient I-E-speaking domain. No longer is it possible for a student of any one of the I-E religions to view the character of that religion as wholly unique. Even if one totally rejects Dumézil's specific interpretations of the principal myths and divinities involved, he must indeed take cognizance of the fundamental assumptions upon which these interpretations are based.

Another aspect of this revolution is a renewed interest in structure or system. It is fair to say that Dumézil has become one of the leading contemporary exponents of structuralism—an opinion shared by no less an exponent of structural analysis than the eminent French social anthropologist Claude Lévi-Strauss (1953, p. 535)—for Dumézil's concern is not with isolated events or episodes, but rather with, as he puts it, "le système, explicite ou implicite," in terms of which the myths and social patterns of the ancient (and, as shall become apparent, not so ancient) I-E-speaking communities tend to organize themselves. Here, too, students of the various I-E religions have had to come to terms. The advent of the new comparative mythology has fostered the development of more systematic models on the part of Latinists, Germanists, Indologists, and the like, even when Dumézil's comparative framework itself has not been adopted. This shift in the direction, at least, of structural analysis has been made not only by those who agree with Dumézil, but also by those who, in endeavoring to prove him wrong, have been forced to confront him on his own ground (e.g., the work of Frye and Kuiper, to be discussed in a later chapter).

Yet another, albeit closely related, effect of the new comparative mythology has been to awaken an interest in the idea that myths, sagas, and so on, I-E and otherwise, are best viewed in terms of the extent to which they reflect a common, underlying ideol-

3

ogy, an ideology manifest not only in myth and religion, but also in the very nature of social organization. This has been especially true in the instance of the discipline that in Europe is termed the "history of religion."[3] As we shall see later on, perhaps the leading figure in this field, Mircea Eliade, has indeed taken Dumézil's theories into consideration in his studies of the idea of the sacred (cf. Eliade, 1961).

All of this should, of course, be of interest to anthropologists, even if no general theoretical principles were involved. But the fact that such principles are indeed involved in the Dumézilian "revolution" makes it imperative that we assess this new comparative mythology in the light of contemporary anthropological theory, that we forget the prejudices of our immediate intellectual forebears and take a long look at what Dumézil has to say about the nature of I-E myth.

In applying the fundamental Durkheimian principle—that the persons, places, events, and situations that receive expression in myths are inevitably representations of important social and cultural realities—to his analysis of I-E materials, Dumézil has sought to demonstrate that the earliest I-E-speaking societies of India, Europe, and elsewhere shared a common set of such "collective representations." Most if not all of these early I-E societies, he asserts, were characterized, at least in their earliest known periods, by a hierarchically ordered, tripartite social organization, each stratum of which was collectively represented in myth and epic by an appropriate set of gods and heroes. These three social strata, which included, in order of precedence, a priestly stratum, a warrior stratum, and a herder-cultivator stratum, together with their mythical counterparts, each made a specific contribution to the maintenance of the whole social and/or supernatural system, and, apparently for this reason, Dumézil has chosen to refer to them as *fonctions* or "functions." The first or most important function (i.e., the priestly stratum and its mythical representations) was

---

[3] The term "history of religion," just beginning to gain currency in the United States, refers to studies aimed at understanding the essential similarities and differences among the world's religious systems. It is not so much concerned with "history" in the limited sense of the word as it is with the evolution of religious ideas across a broad historical spectrum. The term is synonymous with German *Religionswissenschaft*, as employed by Rudolf Otto and others.

concerned with the maintenance of magico-religious and juridical sovereignty or order; the second function (i.e., the warrior stratum and its representations) was concerned with physical prowess; and the third or least important function as far as the Indo-Europeans were concerned (i.e., the herder-cultivator stratum and its representations) was charged with the provision of sustenance, the maintenance of physical well-being, plant and animal fertility, and other related activities. Underlying this functionally interrelated, tripartite social and supernatural system or structure was a tripartite ideology, a tendency to conceive of phenomena in general as divided into three interrelated categories, defined in terms of the three above-mentioned functions.

There is, of course, a problem for anthropologists in Dumézil's use of the term "function," which, despite his exposure to sociological theory, or at least that form of it espoused by Durkheim and his school, is somewhat ambiguous. He uses the term to refer not only to what most anthropologists and sociologists would consider the functions served by the three I-E social and supernatural strata—the ways in which they contribute to the maintenance of the social and supernatural system—but also to the strata themselves. The concept of function here employed deviates rather sharply from long-accepted British, American, and, indeed, French usage (cf., for example, Radcliffe-Brown, 1953; Eggan, 1955; Spencer, 1965; Lévi-Strauss, 1949), and at first glance this somewhat misleading use of the term in question tends to weaken the effectiveness of Dumézil's arguments. There is, however, some logic to his usage.

The unfortunate discrepancy between the conventional and Dumézil's use of the term "function" would seem to stem from his emphasis upon the importance of the I-E ideology. As Dumézil sees it, this ideology is the sum of three fundamental classificatory principles—sovereignty, force, and nourishment—each of which is, in the mathematical sense, a function of the others. Together they form a functionally integrated whole, "le système, implicite ou explicite," which Dumézil has isolated in the several ancient I-E traditions. The term "function," as Dumézil uses it, refers in the last analysis to neither the social strata, the behavior of their occupants, nor their divine representations. Rather, it refers to the principles in terms of which these phenomena are defined. The labels "first," "second," and "third" refer to the hierarchical order in which these principles usually manifest themselves. Therefore, given Dumézil's framework, it is perhaps correct to say that any phenomenon asso-

5

ciated, say, with the principle of sovereignty, be it a social class, the obligations and expectations of such a class, or a corresponding stratum of divine beings, belongs to the "first function." I do feel, however, that it would have been better had he followed the more usual usage of the term in question.

I should add here that this criticism of Dumézil's use of the term "function" is a relatively minor one. It does not materially affect the overall assessment of the validity of his conclusions. My reason for raising it at this point is simply to ensure that the reader clearly understands what Dumézil means by the term in question and the extent to which his meaning differs from the one ordinarily encountered in sociological and social anthropological works.

In sum, on the basis of his comparative analysis of the varied social and mythological forms presented by the ancient I-E-speaking world, Dumézil has concluded (1) that the parent or Proto-I-E society, before it broke up, was characterized by a tripartite ideology; (2) that elements of this ideology were carried by the inheritors of that society across the length and breadth of what was to become the historic I-E domain; and (3) that these elements can be discovered in most, but by no means all, of the early I-E mythical and epical literature, from the *Vedas* of ancient India to the *Eddas* of pre-Christian Iceland, from the *Mahābhārata* to the *Heimskringla*. Moreover, this ideology, whether expressed in myth, epic, or social organization, is asserted to be uniquely I-E, having no parallels among the ancient civilizations of the Near East, the Nile Valley, China, or any other region of the Old World prior to the I-E migrations in the second millennium B.C.

These, then, are the fundamental assumptions upon which Dumézil has constructed the new comparative I-E mythology. Among the regional specialists who have utilized these assumptions in their own work may be included, for example, the late Jan de Vries, until his death last year perhaps the leading specialist in Germanic religion, Celticists Françoise Le Roux and Alwyn and Brinley Rees, and Iranianists Stig Wikander, J. Duchesne-Guillemin, and Kaj Barr.

There are, of course, those who, like the eminent British classicist H. J. Rose, strongly question the efficacy of this new comparativism. Others, while not necessarily hostile to comparativism itself, seem to resent the avowedly structural, and by extension sociological and social-anthropological, assumptions that underlie most of

6

Dumézil's interpretations. Still others, notably John Brough and Paul Thieme, have accused him of being highly selective in the data used to support his tripartite system and have asserted that the latter is not uniquely I-E. In subsequent chapters I analyze in detail both sides of the argument relative to Dumézil's work, and offer some of my own conclusions as to its merit.

A more immediate task, however, is to take a closer, more detailed look at Dumézil's theory against a background of the data he uses to support it.

THE TRIPARTITE SYSTEM: AN OVERVIEW

Perhaps the best way to introduce Georges Dumézil's system is to consider it in context and to begin, as he often begins, with the ancient I-E-speaking communities of northern India. As is well known, classical Indian social organization was composed of four main castes: the *Brāhmanas* (more commonly rendered *Brahmans*), or priests; the *Kṣatriyas*, or warriors; the *Vaiśyas*, or cultivators; and the *Śūdras*, or those whose obligation it was to serve all the rest. Of these castes, only the first three were defined as *Arya*, a description which, like many contemporary ethnic self-identification terms,[4] seems originally to have meant simply "people";[5] the *Śūdras*, thus, were "out-castes" in the most basic sense of the term and, in theory at least, included the conquered, indigenous population. In its broad outlines, this system still obtains, despite the proliferation of sub-castes within each major group and the fact that today the line between *Vaiśya* and *Śūdra* is by no means clearly defined in many regions, especially in South India.

If one analyzes the ancient Sanskrit religious literature, Dumézil claims, one can see that the earliest Indian pantheon reflected this stratified social organization, especially the three *Arya* castes. Even in the oldest of all Indian texts, the *Rig Veda*,[6] there can be found

---

[4] The ethnic self-identification terms *Yun* (south China) and *Navaho* both mean simply 'the people.'

[5] Or perhaps 'free men' (see Laroche, 1960). Dumézil and Thieme have engaged in a long, running debate over the meaning of the root *ari-*. Thieme (1938) has suggested that it means 'foreigner' or 'stranger,' whereas Dumézil has maintained that it is simply an ethnic self-identification term of the kind mentioned in note 4.

[6] The hymns of the *Rig Veda* do not present a fully developed picture of the classical Hindu castes or *Varna*, although the roots of the words later used as caste designations (e.g., *Brahman*, from *brh-*, 'be great') are indeed present (see Dumézil, 1941a, 1948a).

7

three hierarchically ranked, functionally differentiated strata of gods—a pattern that appears over and over again in the later *Vedas* and *Brāhmanas*, and indeed persists, in a somewhat altered form, in the great Indian epic, the *Mahābhārata*.

At the highest of these three divine levels appear the sovereign gods, Mitra and Varuna. In Dumézil's opinion, the characteristics of these two deities are such that they are projections, or collective representations, of the *Brahman* caste, which, of course, is at the apex of the mortal social system. Moreover, Dumézil has concluded that there exists between these two gods a definite division of supernatural labor as regards the management of the universe. On the one hand, Mitra is concerned with the rational and legal aspects of sovereignty; indeed, Meillet, as early as 1907, had suggested that Mitra might be the personification of the idea of Contract. Varuna, on the other hand, represents the awesome and sometimes terrible magico-religious aspects of sovereignty. Thus, respectively, Mitra and Varuna reflect the two basic functions of the *Brahman*: (1) to serve as an arbiter of legal and contractual disputes, and (2) to serve as a magical and religious practitioner, conducting sacrifices, divining, performing marriages, and the like. Here, then, is an example of what Dumézil has labeled the first function: the relationship or correspondence between Mitra and Varuna, together with their celestial "assistants" (a set of lesser deities who share certain aspects of the sovereignty, e.g., Bhaga, Aryaman), and the priestly caste or class (as it appears to have been in the earliest period). In summarizing the nature of the first function, Dumézil (1952*b*, p. 7) claims that it is concerned with "l'administration à la fois mystérieuse et régulière du monde."

At the second supernatural level, one finds a set of young, virile, warlike gods (i.e., the *Maruts*), dominated by the imposing figure of Indra, who is the personification of the warrior ideal. It is Indra who fights monsters (e.g., Vṛtra), leads armies, and, unlike Mitra and Varuna, generally gains his ends through the exercise of physical strength. Indra, thus, is a collective representation of the *Kṣatriya* caste, whose prime function is to protect the society from the threat or actuality of armed invasion. This relationship, then, between the warrior caste or class and its personifications constitutes the second function and is defined (Dumézil, 1952*b*, p. 7) as "le jeu de la vigueur physique, de la force, principalement mais non uniquement guerrière."

8

Finally, at the lowest level, there appear a number of deities whose principal function is to maintain and promote plant and animal fertility, to assure bountiful harvests, and generally to preside over matters of human physical well-being and comfort. Chief among these are the Aśvins, or "Divine Twins." Also included here (and elsewhere, as we shall see) is a female figure, the goddess, Sarasvatī. This lowest divine stratum, whose occupants are seen as collectively representing the food-producing class, constitutes the third function, defined by Dumézil (1952b, p. 7) as "la fécondité, avec beaucoup de conséquences et de résonances, telles que la santé, la longue vie, la tranquillité, la volupté, le 'nombre.' "

This, in brief, is the picture Dumézil draws of ancient Indian myth and society: three functionally integrated strata of men and gods, dominated by the conception of a joint or dual sovereignty shared by a pair of gods representing, respectively, juridical and magico-religious processes. Together, these strata, or functions, form an integrated social and supernatural whole.

If the foregoing system were limited to Vedic India, it would be difficult to generalize it as I-E; but, as noted earlier, Dumézil has attempted to demonstrate the presence of these same three functions, as well as the concept of joint sovereignty, in the myths and social structures of most of the ancient I-E-speaking communities. Outside India, his best evidence so far comes from the rest of the Indo-Iranian-speaking region, as well as from those regions historically associated with Italic-, Germanic-, and Celtic-speaking peoples.

By far the oldest datable example of tripartition among the Indo-Iranians—or any other group of I-E speakers, for that matter —can be found in the famous treaty of the fourteenth century B.C., preserved in the archives at Boghazköy, between the Mitannian king, Matiwaza, and his Hittite conquerers. Matiwaza, who belonged to an Indo-Iranian (or perhaps already Indic; see Thieme, 1960) military aristocracy that had imposed itself several centuries earlier upon the predominantly Hurrian population of this north Syrian state, invoked his gods as witnesses to the treaty; among them appear, unmistakably, and in the following order, the names Mitra-Varuna, Indara (i.e., Indra), and Nāsatyas (i.e., the Aśvins). That these gods represented the same social and supernatural functions and conception of sovereignty as their later Vedic

9

counterparts seems certain, Dumézil feels, pointing out (1945, pp. 8–11) that, although relatively little is known about the social organization of fourteenth-century B.C. Mitanni, the fact that its I-E-speaking ruling class is referred to as *marya* or *maru* (cf. Indra and his *Maruts*) would seem to indicate the presence at least of the I-E warrior stratum; that the other two strata were also present seems quite probable, he asserts, given the series of gods listed in the treaty.

Another, albeit much later, Indo-Iranian example can be found in Herodotus' account (4.5–6) of the Scythian origin myth, wherein three objects of burning gold—a cup, an ax, and a plow with yoke —fall from the sky and are recovered by the youngest son of Targitaos, the primeval being. Dumézil recognizes in this myth a clear expression of social and mythological tripartition. The three objects symbolize, respectively, the first, second, and third functions, and from their recoverer, Kolaxaïs, springs the dominant Scythian class or tribe. From Kolaxaïs' two elder brothers, who successively failed in their attempts to recover the burning implements, issue the Scythian warrior and food-producing classes. Thus, among this westernmost group of Indo-Iranians, the three I-E functions are collectively represented by three brothers, the youngest of whom is sovereign. Although the joint or dual aspects of the first function are lacking here, Dumézil feels that the rest of the evidence is clear enough to support his thesis, especially the symbolic associations of the celestial objects. The cup, for example, associated as it is with the preparation and consumption by priests of sacred beverages—an I-E pattern that has long been recognized (cf. Dumézil, 1924a—of which mead, *madhu*, *soma*, and *haoma* are examples, serves as a symbolic expression of the first function in a number of ancient I-E traditions, as well as in modern European folklore.

As far as Iran itself is concerned, it is in the theological reforms of Zoroaster during the seventh and sixth centuries B.C. that Dumézil sees the clearest expression of the I-E system. In attempting to substitute an ethical and metaphysical dualism for the ancient Iranian polytheism, a polytheism that appears to have been broadly similar to that of Vedic India, Zoroaster conceived of a series of more or less abstract beings as part of the retinue of the Good Principle (Ahura Mazdah). These beings, labeled *Ameša Spentas* ('Immortal Beneficences'), remarkably parallel the Indic gods previously discussed: Aša ('Order') and Vohu Manah ('Good

Thought'), respectively, correspond to Varuna and Mitra and thus may be viewed as representatives of the first function; Xšathra ('Physical Force') parallels Indra and represents the second function; the pair Haurvatāt ('Health') and Ameretāt ('Immortality') parallel the Aśvins and relate to the third function, as does the female figure Armāiti ('Pious Thought'), a Zoroastrian version of the archaic Iranian goddess Anāhitā and a counterpart of the previously mentioned Sarasvatī.

Before leaving the Indo-Iranian area, it should be pointed out that not all the evidence is as clear-cut as the few examples given above would seem to indicate. For example, the ancient Iranian god Mithra, whose cult survived the Zoroastrian reforms and flourished in Iran and elsewhere until the spread of Islam and Christianity put an end to it, presents some rather difficult problems when viewed from a Dumézilian perspective. Despite the obvious onomastic similarities to Mitra, and despite the prominence of the Mithraic cult, the god exhibits both first- and second-function characteristics. Indeed, in the later *Avesta* (cf. especially *Yt.* 9, the so-called Mithra *Yašt*) and in graphic art, Mithra is usually represented as a young and virile warrior, a trait rarely if ever associated with Mitra.

Concerning the West, Dumézil claims to have uncovered some excellent examples of social and supernatural tripartition in early Rome. Here, in my opinion, he has made a most important contribution to scholarship, whatever may prove to be the fate of his overall system.

At first glance, Rome appears to have possessed a culture characterized by an abundance of ritual and a paucity of myth. There is Virgil; there is Ovid; there are numerous identifications between Roman and Greek divinities; but on the surface, at least, there seems to be little in the way of native Roman myth. However, after an exhaustive examination of the admittedly legendary early history of the city, as found in the first books of Livy and elsewhere, Dumézil has concluded that Rome's myths had indeed become historicized. In a brilliant series of works devoted to the subject (1941–1948), he finds in the three earliest kings of Rome, Romulus, Numa, and the warlike Tullus Hostilius, the characteristic gods of the joint sovereignty (Romulus equaling Varuna, and Numa, Mitra) and the god of the second function (Tullus Hostilius equaling Indra). The third function is less clearly evident, although Dumézil

11

feels it was represented by the Sabines, who were traditionally viewed as devotees of luxury, "la tranquillité," and "la volupté." In the legendary Sabine War, Dumézil sees an expression of an I-E mythic theme not yet mentioned: a struggle between representatives of the first two functions and those of the third, wherein the latter are defeated and thus brought into the social system. Granting his interpretation here, the foregoing would serve to explain the lowly position of the cultivator in I-E society; he was the last to be admitted to it, as far as myth is concerned. This assumed war between the functions is further discussed in connection with its appearance in ancient Scandinavian myth.

On another level, that of the Roman pantheon, Dumézil also sees an expression of the tripartite system. In the so-called pre-Capitoline or archaic triad, consisting of Jupiter, Mars, and Quirinus, he finds, respectively, the magico-religious half of the first function, the second function, and part of the third function. The picture is completed by several obscure and little-known early Roman gods: Dius Fidius, who is often coupled with Jupiter, represents the Mitra half of the sovereignty, and Ops (related to the root of the English word "opulent"), who is often paired with Quirinus.

Among the Germanic-speaking peoples, especially the Scandinavians, Dumézil once again claims to have uncovered some examples of mythological and social tripartition. In his *Les dieux des Germains* (1959a) and elsewhere, Dumézil attempts to demonstrate that the Norse gods, Othinn and Tȳr, respectively, represent the magico-religious and juridical aspects of the sovereignty, and that Thōrr, the warrior, corresponds to Mars and Indra and is a second-function figure. The twin gods, Freyr and Njorðr, are seen to be third-function figures, corresponding to Quirinus and Ops, as well as to the Aśvins. In addition, Dumézil has indicated the presence of a third-function female figure here, the goddess Freyja, whom he links with Sarasvatī and Anāhitā. Finally, the previously mentioned theme of a war between representatives of the first two functions and those of the third is expressed, he asserts, in the mythical conflict between the *Aesir*, the dominant group of gods, to which Othinn, Tȳr, and Thōrr belong, and the *Vanir*, to which Freyr, Njorðr, and Freyja belong. Like the Sabines, the *Vanir*, representing the third function, are defeated and thus brought into the system.

12

As I see it, the myths pertaining to this conflict and its outcome may well have served to justify the lowly position of the I-E cultivator, this time in Scandinavia: his gods, here the *Vanir*, who are essentially terrestrial in character and thus especially important to those who till the earth, were the last to be included in the pantheon. That this theme, expressed clearly and independently in Roman and Norse myth, reflects some historic event or events, such as a war or a series of wars between an agricultural and a nonagricultural people, wherein the latter were victorious, is, of course, highly conjectural. Yet such a victory on the part of a warlike, nomadic (or seminomadic), hunting and gathering people over one possessed of a more sedentary, Neolithic type of economy could easily have resulted in the formation of a new and larger society, as well as a new speech community—perhaps that of the Proto-Indo-Europeans.[7]

I should emphasize immediately that Dumézil himself does not offer this conjecture; it is my own, based upon the evidence he presents. Admittedly, it may be somewhat overly euhemeristic, although it should be borne in mind that in other areas and in other times comparable events have indeed formed the basis of myths, and that their memory has thereby been preserved long after they ceased to be "history" in the usual sense of the term (cf. Bascom, 1957).

Dumézil and his students have uncovered among the Celts a number of tripartitions that seem to relate to the three assumed I-E functions: for example, the traditions surrounding the three *Machas* of Ulster, one of whom was a prophetess, the wife of Nemed the Sacred; the second, a female warrior who fought her way to the throne; and the third, the beautiful wife of a farmer, to whom she brought additional riches and presented twins (Dumézil, 1954*a*). Yet, no overall division of either the Irish, Brythonic, or Gallic pantheons has yet been made with any degree of certainty. This, of course, is in large part the result of imperfect knowledge of these pantheons, especially that of ancient Gaul. As far as the latter is concerned, more often than not scholars are forced to rely upon the

---

[7] Cf. the theories of Trubetzkoy (1939), who abandoned altogether the idea of a single I-E protolanguage in favor of the notion that from the beginning I-E has been a group of related languages which, in the third millennium B.C., served as a bridge between the Caucasic and Semitic speech communities to the south and the Finno-Ugric and Altaic communities to the north and east.

interpretatio romana, which, it would appear, was often quite arbitrary and based upon political expediency (cf. Le Roux, 1961*a*). For reasons too detailed to enumerate here, Dumézil claims that the three Gallic techniques of human sacrifice, as reported by Lucan and others, represent a tripartite formula, and that each technique can be seen as ensuring the social and supernatural effectiveness of one of the three I-E functions. Thus, drowning in a keg related to the first function, burning related to the second, and hanging ensured the effectiveness of the third.

Elsewhere among the early I-E-speaking communities the evidence is at best much less abundant and in all cases less certain. Among the Greeks, for example, despite the fact that their mythology is perhaps the best known of all the world's mythologies, only a few hints of the tripartite system have as yet been detected.[8] As far as the pantheon is concerned, the Dioscuri, or "Heavenly Twins," do indeed seem to correspond to the Aśvins, an observation made long before Dumézil's time (cf. Müller, 1872), and can, in Dumézil's opinion, be reckoned as representing the third function. The other two levels, however, are not clearly defined; for example, Zeus, like Mithra, exhibits traits characteristic of both the first and second functions. The chief of the Olympians achieves his ends through a combination of magical spells (cf. Varuna) and physical force (cf. Indra), and at the same time upholds universal order and the sanctity of oaths and contracts (cf. Mitra).

Perhaps the best single Greek example of mythological tripartition so far uncovered concerns the well-known judgment of Paris, wherein the Trojan prince must choose between the regal Hera, the warlike Athena, and the voluptuous Aphrodite. So as to influence him in his choice, each goddess, here seen as a representative of one of the three functions, offers Paris a gift: Hera offers world sovereignty (first function), Athena promises military prowess (second function), and Aphrodite tenders the gift of earthly pleasure (third function). Paris chooses the latter goddess and thus,

---

[8] The difficulty here, apparently, results from the fact that the Greeks, like the Hittites, were profoundly influenced by the non-I-E-speaking civilizations of the eastern Mediterranean, and that this is reflected throughout their myths and epics. Dumézil has as yet avoided any interpretation of Hittite religion, although Palmer (1955), working independently, has attempted to demonstrate the presence of a tripartite, feudal social structure in the Hittite texts found at Boghazköy. The correctness of this demonstration remains to be confirmed.

14

by alienating Hera and Athena (i.e., the first two functions), ensures Troy's ultimate downfall (Dumézil, 1953a).

Other Greek examples are drawn from the celebrated dialogue between Croesus and Solon, as reported by Herodotus (1.30–33, 86–92), and from Plato's *Republic*. Croesus asks the Athenian lawgiver to name the happiest man he had ever met, confident that he himself will be named (cf. Dumézil, 1953a); however, Solon names Tellos of Athens, a rich man and a vaunted warrior, who died gloriously in battle. Croesus then asks who is next. This time Solon names two young and athletic Argive brothers, Cleobis and Biton, who died serving Hera in her temple. Finally, Croesus asks about himself, and Solon merely points out that he is rich, being unable to say whether his death will be happy or not; and, as Dumézil reminds us, Croesus was not rich at the time of his death and died neither gloriously (eventually he became a vassal of Cyrus) nor piously. Dumézil sees the three I-E functions doubly represented here, though in each instance they are not expressed in the usual order. In terms of the figures themselves (including Croesus), they represent, respectively, the third, second, and first functions; however, the manner of death reflects, respectively, the second, first, and third functions. As far as Plato is concerned, Dumézil sees the I-E system reflected in the Greek philosopher's tripartite concept of the ideal state. Later on (pp. 72–73) I discuss in some detail this most interesting example of what appears to be the persistence of the I-E ideological heritage in Greek social thought.

In addition to the gods of the three functions, Dumézil asserts that in most of the I-E pantheons there are certain deities who must be viewed as essentially outside any one level of the tripartite structure, gods (and goddesses) whose function is to support or integrate this structure by summing together in their persons traits characteristic of all three levels. Included here are a number of gods who, like the Roman Janus and Vesta and the Vedic Vāyu and Agni, are primarily associated with beginnings and endings. In ancient India, for example, Dumézil points out that Vāyu was usually invoked at the beginning of a ritual, prior to the invocation of Mitra and Varuna, and that Agni was invoked subsequent to the invocation of the Aśvins (or Nāsatya). These, then, are what he terms "dieux premiers" and "dieux derniers": beings who, in canonical lists of divinities or in ritual invocations, are mentioned

Introduction

prior to and/or subsequent to the gods of the three functions. Thus, "dieux premiers" generally serve to introduce such lists (e.g., Vāyu) while "dieux derniers" serve to terminate them (e.g., Agni). Still others in this same general category (e.g., Janus, the Norse Heimdallr) would seem to be both introducers and terminators. Among I-E female figures, Anāhitā, Sarasvatī, and Freyja are usually classed by Dumézil as both "déesses dernières" and third-function figures; however, the Greek Athena would appear to relate more or less equally to all three functions (cf. Vian, 1952), although in some contexts Dumézil (1953a) also views her as a representative of the second function. Perhaps the clearest example of a female figure who cuts across the system is furnished by the trio of Irish *Machas* discussed earlier, who appear to be but aspects of a single goddess. In any event, Dumézil sees these multifunctional gods and goddesses, wherever they occur, as logically and functionally related to the overall tripartite structure of the pantheon. They form, as he puts it, "l'épine du système" (Dumézil, 1947a, p. 1352).

Although it has been subjected to surprisingly little criticism from Dumézil's adversaries, who are usually more than willing to disassemble any theory that he has constructed, this notion of an "épine" supporting the tripartite system is, in my opinion, one of the weaker links in his chain of ideas. The extent to which gods such as Janus and Vāyu belong merely to a residual category of deities not otherwise classifiable in terms of the three assumed functions is examined later on (pp. 81–83).

Turning to matters of social organization, Dumézil hastens to point out that, save for India, mythological tripartition far outlasted the social tripartition upon which it originally seems to have been based; only in India was the archaic I-E social system preserved. Nevertheless, fragments of this social system can be found, he feels, in most, if not all, of the early I-E-speaking communities just discussed. I have already mentioned the *marya* or *maru* of Mitanni as indicative of the presence of the warrior stratum and have noted the situation presented by the Scyths, wherein three hierarchically ranked strata (or tribes) were conceived to have been founded by the sons of Targitaos. Among the ancient Iranians and Celts, Dumézil points to the presence of a clearly defined, *Brāhmana*-like priest class, respectively, the *Magi* (or *Magavans*) and the Druids; and in the *Avesta* he finds evidence of three other archaic Iranian

16

social groups, composed of warriors, cultivators, and artisans, although the extent to which the latter group either represented the indigenous, pre-I-E population of Iran (cf. the *Śūdras*) or was an aspect of the third function is unclear.

At Rome, Dumézil cites the persistence of a priestly group (if not class), the *Flāmines*; indeed, in an early work (1935) he attempts to relate philologically the words *flāmen* and *Brahman*. This idea has not been generally accepted, but the cultural comparisons he makes between these two sacral groups, especially in regard to common sets of taboos and patterns of ritual cleanliness, certainly suggest a possible relationship; for example, neither the *Flāmen dialis* nor a *Brāhmana* could undress completely, look at a horse, or engage in physical combat. Also, he points out that the three original Roman "tribes," the *Ramnes* (reputedly founded by Romulus), the *Luceres*, and the *Titienses*, perhaps represent a division, respectively, into priests, warriors, and cultivators.

The Germanic-speaking communities generally present a negative picture when it comes to social tripartition. Even the priestly segment seems to be absent (however, see pp. 132–133). Yet the presence of a *Männerbund*, or *Marut*-like group of young warriors surrounding the king or chief, is significant; indeed, such a group also seems to have been present among the Celts, if the tales concerning Finn and the *fianna* are any indication of early Irish (and by extension, Celtic) social life. Moreover, both the Germans and the Celts seems to have been characterized by a cultivator class set apart from that of the warriors, though the distinction here, especially among the Germanic speakers, is by no means as clear as that between *Kṣatriya* and *Vaiśya*.

In Greece, the fourfold set of early Ionian "tribes" or *bioi*, which included (1) priests and magistrates, (2) warriors, (3) laborers, and (4) artisans, may possibly reflect the I-E social functions. If, as Dumézil holds, the last two groups can be lumped together, there appears a tripartite social structure not unlike that described elsewhere among the early I-E-speaking communities (cf. Dumézil, 1941*a*, 1953*a*).

Finally, as mentioned earlier, Dumézil claims that this characteristic and uniquely I-E tendency to view phenomena as divided into three hierarchically ranked strata became a deeply ingrained habit of thought; it became, in short, an ideology. As a result, replications of tripartite formulas, including tripartitions within

17

tripartitions, are frequently encountered by Dumézil and his colleagues. For example, it is noted that threefold divisions of the universe, wherein the upper atmosphere is assigned to the first function, the lower atmosphere to the second, and the earth itself to the third, can be found throughout the later Indic literature. In addition, exhortations, like that found in the famous inscription of Darius at Behistun, to preserve the sanctity of contracts, to defend the society against foreign invasion, and to guard against famine and plague, and tripartite divisions of catastrophies into those affecting, respectively, the sovereignty, the military, and the food supply, are found repeatedly within I-E writings, from the Irish *Lebor Gabala* ("Book of Conquests") to the *Śatapatha Brāhmana*.

Some years ago the eminent Swedish mythologist, Stig Wikander, perhaps Dumézil's most brilliant disciple, discovered that a tripartite division of heroes and semidivine beings can often be found in I-E epic and saga as well as myth. For example, in the great Indian epic, the *Mahābhārata*, he has demonstrated that the five central figures, the *Pāṇḍavas*, all derive from one or another of the earlier Vedic gods: for example, Yudhiṣṭhira, the leader of the five, derives from Varuna and is thus a first-function figure; Arjuna, the great epic warrior, derives from Indra and is a second-function figure.

Wikander, among others, has also pointed out that later Norse literature, notably Snorri's *Edda*, the *Heimskringla*, and the "histories" of Saxo Grammaticus, reflects a euhemerized version of the Norse pantheon previously outlined. This literature, of course, belongs to a post-Christian era, and Othinn was viewed merely as a culture hero who, escaping from the ruins of Troy, led a band of Trojan refugees (i.e., the rest of the *Aesir*) across Europe and ultimately into Scandinavia. The parallels to the *Aeneid* are obvious and suggest that the newly Christian Norse, like the Romans before them, were eager to establish ties with the ancient and prestigious civilizations of the eastern Mediterranean. Yet even here, despite the presence of Christian symbolism and euhemerization, the tripartite ideology persisted.

More recently, Lucien Gerschel (1953), another of Dumézil's students, has demonstrated that the Romans indeed applied this inherited I-E habit of thought to an interpretation of their defeat of Carthage, an event that can, of course, be documented historically. The Carthaginians were assigned to the third function; thus Rome's final triumph was viewed (after the fact) as never having been in doubt, for it was Rome's destiny, so the augurs argued, to occupy a sovereign position vis-à-vis all its rivals.

The foregoing is the essence of Professor Dumézil's system as it stands today, and a sample of some of the evidence he and his colleagues adduce to support it.[9] In Part II, I trace the steps that have led to the development of this system, beginning with the gradual abandonment of a Frazerian (or neo-Frazerian) orientation in favor of what Dumézil terms "la méthode sociologique" (1924–1937) and culminating in the discovery of the I-E penchant for social, supernatural, and ideological tripartition, and a joint sovereignty. First, however, in order to obtain an adequate perspective and to render our discussion and evaluation of Dumézil's theories more meaningful, it is necessary to review briefly the several distinct sources from which he has drawn in the development of these theories.

---

[9] An earlier version of this overview of Professor Dumézil's tripartite system is contained in Littleton (1964).

PART I
The Background

1

The Nature and Location of Proto-Indo-European Culture

The scholarly tradition to which Dumézil, as an Indo-Europeanist, belongs is not yet two centuries old. It began early in the nineteenth century[1] with the demonstration by Jones (1796; see Jespersen, 1921, pp. 33–34), Schlegel (1808; Eng. ed., 1859), Rask (1818), Grimm (1822), Bopp[2] (1833–1849; Fr. ed., 1866–1874), and others that the ancient liturgical languages of India and Iran (Sanskrit and Avestan) were distant linguistic cousins of Latin, Greek, and Gothic, and that this kinship is expressible in a set of systematic correspondences. It matured in the efforts of such scholars as Rapp (1841), Schleicher (1871), and Curtius (1873) to reconstruct the protolanguage or *Ursprache* from which these several ancient languages were descended, a language that has come to be known as Proto-Indo-European.

---

[1] Shortly before 1600, Filippo Sassetti pointed out the similarities between *Sanscruta* ('Sanskrit') and his native Italian (cf. Thieme 1957a, p. 185); even earlier, in 1583, Thomas Stephens, a Jesuit missionary, observed: "Many are the languages in these places [Goa and its environs]. Their pronunciation is not disagreeable and their structure is allied to Greek and Latin" (quoted in *ibid.*, p. 185 n. 4).

[2] It was Bopp who first suggested the term "Indo-European," as preferable to "Indo-Germanic" or "Aryan," including as it does the European and Indic branches of the family rather than a single European subfamily and/or the Indic branch alone. Bopp's suggestion has been followed by most French, British, and American linguists (save those who still follow Sturtevant [1947] in using the now generally discredited term "Indo-Hittite"), but his fellow Germans have usually followed a more nationalistic trend in employing *Indogermanisch*.

23

The Background

Although challenged from time to time by those who would substitute diffusion for common inheritance (cf. Schmidt, 1872; Trubetzkoy, 1939), the fundamental assumption underlying the reconstruction of Proto-I-E has stood the test of time. Indeed, the assumption that for each set of corresponding forms a single proto-form can be reconstructed must rank as one of the major triumphs of nineteenth-century scholarship. Without it there would be no science of historical linguistics (cf. Bloomfield, 1933, p. 310), nor would the sort of comparative mythology practiced by Dumézil be possible.

I do not mean to infer that the picture of Proto-I-E developed by Schleicher and his colleagues has remained unchanged; far from it. In the course of the past fifty-odd years, a great many of the specific reconstructions attempted in the nineteenth century have had to be discarded as the methods of historical linguistics became more precise and new data came to light. For example, the discovery that Hittite was an I-E language, the realization that the so-called palatal law, annunciated by Thomsen (1875; 2d ed., 1903) and Verner (1879; 2d ed., 1902), cannot account for the differences between the eastern and western branches of the I-E family (cf. Hockett, 1958), and the development of the concepts of phoneme and morpheme (cf. Bloomfield, 1933) have contributed to what amounts to a revolution in our conception of the specific character of Proto-I-E. No small contributor to this progress was the late Antoine Meillet, under whom Dumézil studied at the École des Hautes Études.

This tradition, rooted in the comparative philology of Grimm, Bopp, and others, and modified by Meillet, Bloomfield, and others, has ramified in many directions. Almost from the beginning scholarly attention began to be focused upon problems relating to the place of origin, material culture, social organization, and, of course, mythology and religion of those who spoke the parent I-E language —those who are labeled the Proto-Indo-Europeans—and of their earliest descendants in Europe, India, the Near East, and elsewhere. Although Dumézil is concerned primarily with the mythological, ideological, and social stratificational aspects of the Proto-I-E-speaking community and has had little if anything to say about the matter of I-E origins and material culture, it nevertheless seems necessary to comment very briefly upon some of the fundamental assumptions that have been made in this regard. They form the

24

basic culture-historical framework upon which Dumézil's specific theories must necessarily be hung.

Perhaps no single set of archeological and culture-historical questions has given rise to as many conflicting theories and hypotheses as that concerning the nature and location of Proto-I-E culture. The carriers of this culture have been variously characterized as simple hunters and gatherers, sedentary Neolithic cultivators, and warlike, bronze-using (or even iron-using) pastoral nomads. At one time or another, Scandinavia, North Germany, Hungary, Poland, the lower Danube Valley, the Balkans, South Russia, Anatolia, Central Asia, and even Mesopotamia have been suggested—sometimes solely on the basis of nationalistic feeling (cf. Piggott, 1950, pp. 247–248)—as the I-E *Urheimat*. Drought, a population explosion, external pressure, and sheer wanderlust have all been advanced as reasons for the I-E diaspora.

It would be neither germane nor feasible to summarize here even the most important and influential theories that have been advanced regarding the location of Proto-I-E culture: for example, those of Otto Schräder (1890), who first argued for a Central Asian origin; those of Gustav Kossinna (1914), who championed a homeland within the borders of Germany; and those of Feist (1913, 1924), Meillet (1922), Childe (1926, 1929, 1947), Poisson (1934), Gimbutas (1952, 1961), Hencken (1955), and Bosch-Gimpera (1961). Rather, I shall confine my discussion to a brief and admittedly incomplete survey of what seems to me to be the best evidence, both internal (i.e., linguistic and mythological) and external (i.e., archeological), so far adduced.

THE NATURE OF PROTO-INDO-EUROPEAN CULTURE:
INTERNAL EVIDENCE

Economically and technologically, the Proto-Indo-Europeans appear to have been in a transitional phase between the Neolithic and Bronze ages. At the time the migrations began (*ca.* 2500 B.C., a date supported both by lexicostatistical analysis [Swadesh, 1953, 1955; Trager and Smith, 1950, 1953] and by archeological evidence), it can be inferred that at least one metal was known, though it was probably rare and not locally produced. No Proto-I-E form for "metallurgy" can be reconstructed, and the form for "cop-

25

per" (*roudhos) seems to be derived ultimately from the Sumerian urud(u); 'metal' (cf. Childe, 1926, 1947). Weapons formed an important part of the Proto-I-E artifact inventory, and strong evidence is available to support Proto-I-E use of the club or mace, the sling, the bow, the spear or pike, the knife-dagger, and the ax (Childe, 1926, p. 85). The light, spoked-wheel battle chariot seems almost certain to have been present,[3] though no certain reconstruction here is as yet possible (cf. Meillet, 1922, p. 361; Piggott, 1950, pp. 276–280; Hencken, 1955, p. 44).

Agriculture coupled with stockbreeding seems to have been the basic source of sustenance, and hunting appears to have been of minor importance. That some form of the plow was known can be inferred from the root *ar(ā)-, attested in all but the Anatolian and Indo-Iranian branches of the family (Puhvel, 1964, pp. 189–190). The domestic animals present appear to have been the horse (*eḱwo- or *eḱwa-), which was probably more often driven than ridden (cf. Thieme, 1953, p. 600), sheep (*owis), pig (*sūs), goat (*aiǵ-), and cow or cattle (peḱu[s]). The variant terms for cattle (e.g., Sanskrit vaśā, Latin vacca; Sanskrit dhēnu-, Old Irish dīnu), the terms for ox (*gʷou-) and steer (*[s]tauros), as well as the many references to cattle and activities associated with them in I-E mythic and epical literature, have led many scholars to infer that cattle raising was the principal economic activity (e.g., Linton, 1955; Piggott, 1950). This may very well have been true, for cognate forms for grain and its products are much less widespread. According to Childe (1926, p. 84), "the state of things observed among many of the cow-keeping tribes of the Sudan and other parts of Africa approximates most closely to the primitive Aryan economy."

The question of the degree to which the Proto-Indo-Europeans were nomadic has long been debated, and it would be impossible to summarize the debate here (cf. Palmer, 1955). Although the best internal evidence leads to the conclusion that they were not true nomads, in the sense of the Bedouin or the Central Asian pastoralists, and that they at least knew semipermanent dwellings (the presence of both wattle-and-daub huts [Feist, 1924] and pit houses [Childe, 1926] has been inferred), Linton's speculation (1955, p. 261) that "on any excuse they [the Proto-Indo-Europeans] would

---

[3] For a more thorough discussion of problems relating to the I-E chariot, see Fox (1947); see also Piggott (1950, pp. 280-281).

pile their goods in ponderous ox carts, burn their huts, and set out on long treks into unknown territory" seems to be close to the truth.

Beyond the realm of material culture, the evidence becomes much less clear. From what can be reconstructed of it, the overall social structure seems not unlike Bacon's (1958) expandable and retractable *obok*-type, which she associates with Central Asian pastoralism; it also seems to resemble the minimal-maximal lineage structure that Evans-Pritchard (1940) and others have so often delineated in various African societies. That some form of kingship (perhaps paramount chieftaincy) existed can be inferred from the form *$reĝ$, though the social unit over which a *$reĝ$ presided is unclear. Palmer (1955) presents an argument for the presence of a god-king of the Mesopotamian type; however, as I have already observed, Dumézil is convinced that the Indo-Europeans were unique in their concept of a *secular* kingship.

As to Proto-I-E social structure, by far the most important current theory is Dumézil's thesis that it was tripartite. This theory has been materially strengthened by the independent findings of Piggott (1950, p. 259) and Palmer (1955). Yet it should be noted here that others have suggested alternative patterns. Linton (1955, p. 263), for example, argues for a weakly developed, twofold structure including as a noble class all family heads, with the rest of the society forming an undifferentiated commoner class. He also claims that "specialists in dealing with the supernatural emerged, but their status was low," and that priests did not form a distinct class. However, I feel that Dumézil, Piggott, and Palmer, who, unlike Linton, are working with primary sources, present the best case.

In matters of religion and ritual, it should again be pointed out that Dumézil's theory, together with a number of alternative hypotheses suggested by his critics, is discussed in detail in succeeding chapters. Nevertheless, one item should be be mentioned here, as it bears specifically upon the problem of origins. This is the matter of burial practices. According to Piggott (1950, p. 284), "there is reason to believe that in the early Aryan phase inhumation and cremation were alternative rites existing side by side, though the latter was soon to become dominant." He cites a reference (*Rig Veda* 10. 18) indicating that the above-mentioned inhumation almost always involved a single grave covered by a mound or tumulus. As we shall shortly see, this practice of mound burial is crucial as far as the location of the I-E *Urheimat* is concerned.

The Background

Finally, before turning to a consideration of the external evidence, some of the salient climatological, geographical, floral, and faunal features of the Proto-I-E habitat as revealed by linguistic analysis should be noted. The climate must have been severe, with hot, rainy summers and cold, snowy winters. No certain form for "sea" can be reconstructed, indicating possibly that the bulk of the community lived too far inland to have had much contact with either the Baltic, the Black, or the Caspian Sea. Rivers seem to have been the chief obstacles to movement. Fox, lynx, bear, beaver, and rabbit all seem to have abounded. Fir, beech,[4] and birch trees appear to have been present (cf. Thieme, 1953), although the largest portion of the terrain would appear to have been of the open, grassy steppe variety. Some years ago Childe (1926, p. 90) summed up rather succinctly what must have been the nature of the habitat in question, calling it "a continental region traversed by rivers, sufficiently wooded to afford shelter to bears and beavers but open enough to nourish hares and swift horses and to permit of the unimpeded progress of vehicles."

THE LOCATION OF THE PROTO-INDO-EUROPEAN COMMUNITY: EXTERNAL EVIDENCE

Of the many regions proposed as possible I-E homelands, only two can be considered seriously in terms of the environmental evidence just discussed: (1) eastern Europe, from the Baltic to the Black Sea, and (2) the Kazakh-Kirghiz steppes. Of these, only the latter meets all the requirements imposed by the internal evidence, for, unlike the Neolithic cultures associated with the South Russian and North Pontic steppes, wherein collective graves were the rule (e.g., the Mariupol culture), the culture indigenous to the Kazakh-Kirghiz steppes practiced individual inhumation under mounds or tumuli from the earliest period for which there is any clear evidence (*ca.*

---

[4] As the beech tree does not at present grow east of an imaginary line running from Königsberg to the Crimea and then extending to the Caucasus (Childe, 1926, p. 89), earlier scholars (e.g., Bender, 1922) asserted that the I-E homeland must have been located west of this line. Although paleobotanists are unable to determine exactly the eastern limits of the beech in the third millenium B.C. and few contemporary scholars place much emphasis upon the so-called *Buchengrenze*, 'beech tree boundary,' there are indeed a host of good reasons for locating almost all of the I-E homeland east of this boundary.

3000 B.C.; Gimbutas, 1961, p. 193). Moreover, it is clear that most of the artifacts, domestic animals, house types, and other features now seen as characteristic of the late Neolithic and early Bronze ages in this trans-Volga steppe region (cf. Gimbutas, 1961, 1963) are similar to those that philologists assume must have been characteristic of the Proto-I-E community.

About 2500 B.C.[5] this culture, termed by Gimbutas (1961) the "Kurgan culture" (from Russian *kurgan*, 'mound'), began to expand westward across the Volga into the North Pontic region, and from this period can be dated the earliest phases of the *kurgan* sites at Maikop, Tsarskaia, and elsewhere in South Russia and the Kuban (cf. Piggott, 1950, p. 249). At the same time (i.e., the latter half of the third millennium B.C.), other Kurgan people were pushing south into the Caucasus. Shortly before 2000 B.C., they had reached eastern Anatolia, and their descendants eventually emerged into the light of history as Hittites, Luvians, and so on.

The western expansion of the Kurgan culture continued along the north shore of the Black Sea, some of its carriers following the Danube Valley into Central Europe, and others moving into the Balkans and eventually to Greece. Still other elements of the culture pushed north and west into Germany and Scandinavia. From the descendants of these several groups of Kurgan people ultimately emerged the Celts, Italians, Greeks, Illyrians, Germans, and so forth.

In the middle Bronze Age (after 1800 B.C.), a branch of the Kurgan culture, commonly referred to as the Andronovo culture (cf. Mongait, 1959; Gimbutas, 1963), which appears to have remained in the homeland area began to push south into the vicinity

---

[5] As this book goes to press, it has come to my attention that this date may be several centuries too recent. In a paper presented at the Third Indo-European Conference, Philadelphia, April, 1966, Homer L. Thomas suggested that some I-E speakers may have reached the lower Rhine area as early as 2600 B.C. His suggestion is based on a radiocarbon date of 2602 ± 55 B.C. published by the Natuurkundig Laboratorium der Rijks-Universiteit, Groningen, for charcoal from a tumulus grave belonging to the Corded Ware culture. This culture, widely distributed in Central and East Europe, has clear associations with the Neolithic and early Bronze Age cultures of the Kazakh-Kirghiz steppes and has long been linked with the first I-E speakers to reach Europe. If this new date is correct, it would mean that the initial I-E expansion began perhaps as early as 2800 B.C. Thomas cites other recent evidence, notably from Iran and Anatolia, which would also suggest the earlier date.

of the Aral Sea and up the Syr and Amu rivers.[6] Some of its carriers, almost certainly the ancestors of the authors of the *Rig Veda*, eventually reached North India (*ca.* 1450 B.C.) where they destroyed the indigenous Indus Valley civilization. That another segment of this Proto-Indo-Iranian community (cf. Gimbutas, 1963, p. 835) headed southwest from the Aral region and ultimately found its way into northwestern Iran and northern Mesopotamia seems probable, although the exact routes takes by various Indic- and Iranian-speaking groups, especially those Indic speakers[7] who established themselves in Mesopotamia and Syria (the rulers of Mitanni, the Kassites, etc.), remain uncertain and are a matter of much scholarly debate (cf. Gimbutas, 1964; Heine-Geldern, 1964). Still later (*ca.* 1200–800 B.C.) another Indo-Iranian-speaking community, the Scyths, expanded westward (cf. the expansion of the so-called Timber Grave culture [Gimbutas, 1963, pp. 835–836]).

Although the archeological evidence is unclear, it is possible on linguistic grounds to assume that the ancestors of the Balts and the Slavs settled in their most ancient known habitats at a time coincident with the beginnings of the Indo-Iranian expansion.

That the expansion of the Kurgan culture and its presumably I-E-speaking carriers profoundly affected the subsequent course of human history goes without saying. In Europe all but a few traces of the indigenous pre-I-E cultures were wiped out, and in India an entire civilization, comparable in antiquity and achievement to those of Mesopotamia and the Nile Valley, was all but overwhelmed. Yet in any assessment of the overall effects of these migrations, it must be borne in mind that the Indo-Europeans were latecomers. These invaders from the Kazakh-Kirghiz steppes arrived on the stage of history long after the basic patterns of civilization, including literacy and urbanism, had crystallized. Their culture, though unique in many important respects, was in large measure ultimately derived from economic and technological patterns that were several thousand years old in the Near East when their ancestors had barely emerged from the Upper Paleolithic. The presence of Sumerian

---

[6] This southern extension of the Andronovo culture is referred to as the Tazabag'jab culture (Gimbutas, 1963, p. 835).

[7] Thieme (1960) has pointed out that the names of the gods invoked as witnesses by the Mitannian king Matiwaza in his treaty with the Hittites (1350 B.C.) were specifically Indic rather than Indo-Iranian in form (see also in Gimbutas, 1964).

loanwords in Proto-I-E, to say nothing of Mesopotamian trade goods or copies thereof in the sites associated with the speakers of this language, serves to underscore this fact. In short, I cannot help but agree with Piggott's (1950, p. 245) observation: "We can recognize the Indo-European group of languages as a relatively junior member of the Old World linguistic family, evolving at a time when such languages as Sumerian and those in the Semitic and Hamitic groups were of respectable antiquity."

2

Comparative Mythology, Frazerian Anthropology, and Durkheimian Sociology

The foregoing linguistic, archeological, and culture-historical material forms a necessary basis for the following brief consideration of some of the major approaches to comparative I-E mythology which preceded that of Dumézil, as well as the anthropological and sociological theories developed, respectively, by Frazer and the French sociological school under Durkheim, Mauss, and others, upon which Dumézil has drawn so heavily in the formulation of his system.

COMPARATIVE MYTHOLOGY

Comparative mythology refers to the systematic comparison of myths and mythic themes drawn from a wide variety of cultures and involves attempts to abstract common underlying themes, to relate these themes to a common symbolic representation (e.g., the forces of nature, fertility, or, for Dumézil, social organization), and/or to reconstruct one or more protomythologies.[1] Studies of this sort can claim at best a history of less than 200 years, for they were generated by the same awareness of Oriental culture in the late seventeenth and eighteenth centuries[2] which led to the development of comparative philology.

---

[1] Here it is necessary to distinguish between the kind of approach just mentioned and the so-called allegorical approach, which dates from classical times (cf. Chase, 1949, p. 2).

[2] Indeed, many eighteenth-century scholars had occasion to comment upon the myths, rituals, and religious beliefs discovered in India and Persia.

As the nineteenth century dawned and passed into its early decades, interest in myth was given added impetus by the growth of
romanticism and philosophical idealism, especially in Germany.
Most of the German idealists, aware of the new evidence from the
Orient and elsewhere, were very much concerned with myth. Hegel,
for example, in *The Philosophy of World History* (1832; Eng. ed.,
1900), "longed for a 'polytheism in art' and imagination, a plastic
and mythological philosophy" (Chase, 1949, p. 39; cf. Aiken,
1956). Among artists, poets, and critics, myth came to be viewed
as "the key to national artistic and religious survival" (Chase, 1949,
p. 39). The effects of this romantic concern with myth were not
lost upon those who were shaping the science of language, and most
of the early philologists had something to say about I-E myth.
Schleicher was convinced that an I-E *Urmythologie* could be reconstructed. Grimm's research (1883) into the nature of Germanic
folklore, which he viewed as the detritus of ancient Germanic
myth, still serves as a basic, albeit outdated, reference point in
Germanic studies. Friedrich Creuzer (1819) and Otfried Müller
(1854), though not comparativists in the strict sense of the term,
applied the newly developed principles of philology to analyses of
Greek myth which still have much to recommend them (cf. Chase,
1949, p. 43).

As the methods of comparative philology improved, so did those
of comparative mythology; and with the perfection of the comparative method in the 1840's (cf. Jespersen, 1921) came new insights
into the complex relationships among the several I-E mythic traditions.

MÜLLER AND THE NATURISTS

By all odds the most significant single figure in nineteenth-century
comparative mythology was Friedrich Max Müller. A student of
Bopp and later of the great French Sanskrit scholar, Burnouf,
Müller, who settled in England at the age of twenty-six, was trained
as a philologist, and his methods and theories were essentially

---

Fontenelle, for example, in his *Discourse on the Origin of Fables* (1724; cited
by Eliade, 1961), even anticipated to an extent the rationalist theories that
were to develop in the next century; and Dupuis (1794; cited by Eliade, 1961)
anticipated Müller, Kuhn, and others with the suggestion that the "histories
of the gods, and even the life of Christ, are only allegories of the motions of
the stars" (Eliade, 1961, p. 229).

linguistic. Conceiving of a "mythopoeic age" in which the speakers of Proto-I-E had not yet developed the means to express abstractions, and in which metaphors were thus essential to communication, he asserted that the conceptions later to develop into gods were initially mere figures of speech. To him, the primary source of these figures or metaphors was the sun: "I look upon the sunrise and sunset, on the daily return of day and night, on the battle between light and darkness, on the whole solar drama in all its details . . . as the principal subject of early mythology" (Müller, 1869, p. 537). In time, as abstract concepts such as "dawn" and "sunset" became common among the speakers of the several ancient I-E daughter languages, the meanings of these solar metaphors were lost; this loss Müller terms the "disease of language." This disease may be further described as "a kind of insanity to which men were vulnerable because their insufficient language was incommensurable with the emotional demands placed upon it" (Chase, 1949, p. 46).

Müller's solar mythology rapidly gained adherents, both at home and abroad.[3] Perhaps the most important of these—at least as far as the evolution of Dumézilian mythology is concerned—was the English classicist, George W. Cox (1887), who, despite his excessive Pan-Aryanism, added a new and important dimension to comparative mythology through his emphasis upon structural as well as etymological equations, an emphasis that, stripped of its naturalistic bias, persists in the work of Dumézil and his colleagues. Concerning the extent to which the total configuration of a tale could yield clues as to its origin and distribution, Cox "was actually moving onto the sounder ground of type and motif analysis" (Dorson, 1955, p. 29).

Müller, of course, was not the only nineteenth-century philologist to arrive at the conclusion that natural phenomena are the stuff of myths. In 1859, Adalbert Kuhn published his famous *Die Herabkunft des Feuers und des Göttertranks*, wherein thunderstorms and their attendant bolts of lightning, rather than the sun, were conceived to be the basic ingredients of myth. Kuhn, thus, was the father of the meteorological school of naturism; however, Müller's approach was by far the most widely held.

---

[3] Two Americans also contributed to the literature of solar mythology. John Fisk (1888) attempted to reconcile the meteorological and solar varieties of naturism, and Daniel Brinton (1896) sought to demonstrate parallels between North American Indian and I-E mythical personages (cf. Dorson, 1955, p. 35).

Solar mythology—and indeed, naturism in general—did not persist long into the twentieth century. In a very real sense, its demise can be credited to the efforts of one man, the brilliant and iconoclastic Scotsman, Andrew Lang, whose running debate with Müller in the late 1880's and 1890's must be ranked among the most significant scholarly controversies of modern times (cf. Dorson, 1955). Though Lang's objections to Müller's mythology (e.g., Lang, 1897) were largely founded upon an anthropology that did not survive far into the twentieth century, naturism remains untenable in the eyes of most contemporary students of myth. Some years ago Chase (1949, p. 48) summed up quite succinctly the principal criticisms that can be levied against Müller, Cox, and Kuhn: (1) their thinking was implicitly based upon the fallacious idea of "degradation" which, although the chosen people in this instance were the Aryans rather than the Jews, was modeled on traditional Christian historiography; (2) too much emphasis was placed upon language and linguistic processes, even by Cox, and too little upon the differential effects of this social, cultural, and physical setting wherein myths originated; and (3) there was too much concern with origins and not enough with the historical development of myths and mythmaking.

SPECIALISTS AND NEOCOMPARATIVISTS, 1900–1924

As the nineteenth century waned, the comparative method began to fall into disrepute. In the hands of the naturists it had been pushed far beyond its reasonable limits, and an increasing number of scholars—classicists, folklorists, anthropologists, and even philologists—came to focus their attention more and more exclusively upon specific mythic traditions, seeking to explain these traditions by means of intensive internal analysis rather than by means of equations that might be found between them. Most of these "specialists," as we may label them, relied (and still rely) heavily upon the methods of textual criticism, phrasing their analyses in terms of translations, new etymologies, and the like. Save for the purposes of linguistic reconstruction, the idea of a common I-E religious and ideological heritage was rarely encountered in the first two decades of the twentieth century (cf. Dumézil, 1958a, p. 90). Nevertheless, despite their failure to "see the forest for the trees"—perhaps as a result of too much forest and too few trees in previous decades—

35

the specialists, Latinists, Celticists (especially Vendryes, who perhaps should be ranked as a comparativist), Iranianists, and, above all, Indologists (especially Bergaigne), have contributed (and still contribute) much that is useful to Dumézil and his colleagues.

In spite of this emphasis upon regionalism, a number of authors continued to speak of "Indo-European religion," albeit cautiously and without much elaboration. Among these was Antoine Meillet, who, though not primarily a mythologist, nevertheless encouraged his students—one of whom was Dumézil—to think in broad comparative terms when confronting I-E materials. Even Meillet, however, tended to focus much of his attention upon Vedic materials (cf. his 1907 article on Mitra, mentioned earlier, which loomed so large later on in Dumézil's thinking) and did not attempt with I-E myth the kind of broad synthesis that characterizes his *Introduction à l'étude comparative des langues indo-européennes* (1922) and other linguistic works.

In the early 1920's, a reaction set in. Becoming more and more aware of the artificiality of the hypotheses that sought to explain "la genèse et les premiers développements des religions qu'ils étudiaient" (Dumézil, 1958a, p. 90), a few scholars began once more to adopt a broad comparative framework in their approach to the several I-E mythic traditions. Perhaps the earliest of these was Albert Carnoy (1921), who speaks in no uncertain terms about a "religion indo-européenne." Shortly thereafter, although differing widely in inspiration and orientation, a number of Germans, including Walter Otto, Herman Güntert, Friedrich Cornelius, and Franz Rolf Schroeder, came to the same general conclusion: that it is impossible to understand any single ancient I-E religious system without reference to a common set of deities, rituals, and myths, and that it is indeed possible to conceive of such a common I-E religious system without reference to the discarded theories of Müller and Kuhn. In France the leading exponent of this new (or better, perhaps, renewed) approach to I-E religious matters was Georges Dumézil, and although his ideas crystallized only after a dozen or so years of experimentation, from 1924 on the history of this "neo-comparativism," as it may be termed, is part and parcel of the evolution of Dumézil's thinking, which forms the subject matter of Part II.

Mythology, Anthropology, and Sociology

While the controversy over solar mythology and the efficacy of the comparative method was raging, two wholly different approaches to myth and ritual (*all* myth and ritual), which were to have a profound influence upon Dumézil, were taking shape. These were the well-known theories of Sir James Frazer, and of Émile Durkheim, Marcel Mauss, and others. It was first to Frazer and then, after several cul-de-sacs, to Durkheim (more properly to Durkheimian principles) that Dumézil turned as he sought to find a theoretical foundation upon which to build a new comparative I-E mythology.

FRAZER

Drawing heavily upon Tylor (1871), Robertson Smith (1889), and Mannhardt (1877), and using the sacred grove at Nemi as a starting point, Frazer (1922) developed his famous thesis that gods or images thereof are everywhere periodically sacrificed in order to keep them from decaying and, by extension, to keep the world and its inhabitants from suffering a similar fate. Thus myths inevitably reflect this magical relationship between natural and supernatural phenomena, he asserts, for the initial or "mythopoeic" age in the development of supernaturalism was a magical one, and the most fundamental myths are those that express the periodic rejuvenation of the world and the spirits that animate it.

In essence, this thesis is the logical extension of that advanced by Mannhardt: the spirits of the *Wald* and the *Feld* must be magically manipulated so as to ensure the continued prosperity of those who believe in them, and myths arise as symbolic expressions of such manipulations (cf. Spence, 1921, p. 53; Reinach, 1941, pp. 91–92). Frazer's "Age of Magic" is, in the last analysis, coterminous with the period postulated by Mannhardt as producing the basic substratum of religious belief and practice, and the doctrine of survivals is of prime importance to both.

Although Frazer developed a number of other related theories about the nature of supernatural phenomena (e.g., his ideas about totemism [1910] which so profoundly influenced Freud [cf. Littleton, 1962]), it would not be germane to consider them here. It was the theory of the "dying god," as expressed in the *Golden Bough*,

37

which specifically influenced Dumézil's early efforts (see chap. 3).

Certainly most, if not all, of Frazer's specific ideas about myth and religion, predicated as they are upon an uncritical acceptance of unilineal evolutionism, must today be discarded, and it is to Dumézil's credit that he saw fit to shrug off the Frazerian influence as early as he did. Yet the author of the *Golden Bough* is not without his defenders, even among those who were poles apart from him on almost all theoretical and methodological matters. Malinowski (1960, p. 190), for example, commends Frazer for his insistence that "religious and magical belief has always functioned as a principle of order, of integration, and of organization at primitive and higher levels of human organization." His influence lingers on in the thinking of Raglan (1937), Gaster (1950), Hyman (1955), and other contemporary advocates of the so-called ritualist school of mythology (cf. Harrison, 1903, 1912; Murray, 1907; Cornford, 1912), and it is certainly not absent in the works of some of Dumézil's chief critics, especially the late H. J. Rose (1947, 1955).

DURKHEIM AND MAUSS

The essence of the theoretical position relative to myth and ritual developed by Durkheim and Mauss can be found in the former's well-known definition of religion as "a unified system of beliefs and practices relative to sacred things, that is to say, things set apart and forbidden—beliefs and practices which unite into one single moral community called a Church, all those who adhere to them" (Durkheim, 1961, p. 62). In Durkheim's eyes the central problem facing the student of religious phenomena is to account for the origin of "sacred things"—or better, perhaps, to uncover the realities that are represented or symbolized by such sacred things.

Rejecting both naturism and animism as efficient explanations of why certain things are "set apart and forbidden," and drawing heavily upon the ideas of Robertson Smith (1889) and Fustel de Coulanges (1864; Eng. ed., 1958),[4] Durkheim focused his attention upon the moral order that inevitably accompanies collective or social life. This moral order, he asserted, is by far the most im-

---

[4] To say nothing of such scholars as Boutroux, St. Simon, Spencer, and of course, Comte, whose spiritual heir Durkheim was in many, but by no means all, respects (cf. Gehlke, 1915; Merton, 1933; Alpert, 1939; Parsons, 1951).

portant reality confronting the human species, far outweighing the impact of natural forces or the effects of dreams and hallucinations, and as such is the ultimate source of the sacred. As Timasheff (1955, p. 113) puts it, to Durkheim the "source and object of religion are the collective life; the sacred is at bottom society personified" (cf. Alpert, 1939).

If the stuff of the sacred is to be found in the facts of social life and in the moral order that accompanies them, then the context of myths and the rites associated with them are "sacred things" reflecting these social and cultural realities (cf. Durkheim, 1961, p. 421); and most, if not all, gods, spirits, totems, and the like are representations either of society as a whole or of various important segments within it. What is more, these socially derived representations inevitably form categories of understanding in terms of which the individual experiences and interprets the world around him. It is upon these two fundamental assumptions—that divine beings are necessarily "collective representations" of important social and cultural realities, and that such representations necessarily give rise to categories of understanding—that Dumézil's conception of the nature of I-E mythology is founded.

Of all those associated with Durkheim in the early years of the twentieth century, perhaps the most important was Marcel Mauss, who contributed much to the development of the concept of collective representation and who was, himself, an authority on various facets of primitive religion (cf. Mauss, 1954). Mauss is especially important to this discussion, for it was he who, as mentor and for many years a senior colleague of Dumézil in the École Pratique des Hautes Études, was principally responsible for the latter's adoption of *la méthode sociologique*. Indeed, Mauss's (and, by extension, Durkheim's) influence is evident from the beginning of Dumézil's career and can be seen in his concern, even in his earliest works, with the social context and effects of ritual and in his awareness of ethnology. In the late 1930's and 1940's, as Dumézil came to conceive of I-E religion in terms of a set of collective representations or functions, this influence became even more apparent.

Mauss, of course, was not the only link between Dumézil and Durkheimian sociology.[5] It should be emphasized that Meillet, who

---

[5] In our conversations and correspondence Professor Dumézil has often emphasized the extent of his debt to Granet (see Dumézil, 1951*a*, p. 222).

perhaps had more influence upon Dumézil in his formative period than any other single individual, was a close colleague of Durkheim and his fellow sociologists and is often cited in *The Elementary Forms of the Religious Life.* Indeed, Meillet's (1907) previously mentioned conception of Mitra as Contract personified is cited by Durkheim (1961, p. 97) as proof of the fallibility of Müller's thesis. Nor should the possible influence of Dumézil's Durkheimian colleague, Claude Lévi-Strauss, be overlooked. Yet until his death in 1950, Mauss remained the chief link between sociology (and social anthropology) and neocomparativism. It was through him, as a teacher and as a fellow "historian of religion," that Dumézil became an heir to the great sociological tradition founded by Durkheim. If he had not received this legacy, this study would not be in order.

PART II

The Evolution of the System

3

The Formative Phase: 1924-1938

Now that the linguistic, mythological, and sociological sources of Dumézil's neocomparativism have been taken into account and the archeological and culture-historical evidence bearing on the nature and location of the Proto-I-E community has been surveyed, it is possible to trace the evolution of his tripartite thesis. This chapter is concerned principally with the formative phase of this evolution, the period from 1924 to 1938. It was a period of experimentation, during which Dumézil's mounting enthusiasm for I-E matters led him down many blind alleys and caused him to develop a number of theories regarding the nature of I-E myth and ritual which, in later years, he was forced to discard. Yet in spite of these blind alleys and untenable theories, the period in question also saw the beginnings and gradual growth of his awareness of the inevitable, functional relationship between social and supernatural phenomena, an awareness that was to culminate in his discovery of tripartition as the keystone of a common I-E ideology. The logical place to begin tracing the evolution of Dumézil's tripartite thesis is his doctoral dissertation, *Le festin d'immortalité*, published in 1924.

THE "AMBROSIA CYCLE"

Dumézil's initial venture into comparative mythology (1924a) was, in its day, a radical departure from orthodoxy. Save for a handful of scholars, the idea that the ancient I-E-speaking peoples shared a common religious heritage was still viewed with much suspicion

43

—after all, Max Müller had been in his grave less than three decades—and the subtitle of Dumézil's thesis, *Étude de mythologie
comparée indo-européenne*, was hardly calculated to lessen this
suspicion. Yet even more radical was the thesis Dumézil proposed:
that there is a common set of I-E myths concerning the origin of
immortality, its personification as a sacred drink (e.g., beer, *amṛta*,
ambrosia), and its loss through trickery. His evidence ranges from
Greek and Vedic myth to medieval Christian legends of the Holy
Grail and modern Ossetic[1] folklore.

Like many primitive peoples,[2] Dumézil asserts, the Proto-Indo-
Europeans accounted for the origin of death (i.e., the loss of immortality) through the actions of a trickster figure. Prometheus,
who ran afoul of Zeus in his devious attempts to aid mankind, is
an excellent example of such a figure, as is the figure of the "fausse
déesse" who appears in both Germanic and Indic myth. In all instances, this figure attempts to steal the secret of everlasting life
from the gods and is foiled in the attempt (cf. the quest for the
Grail—in Dumézil's opinion, a Christian adaptation of an ancient
I-E trait—in which the sacred drink could be contained), and thus
only the gods remain immortal. Because ambrosia is perhaps the
best-known example of the deified drink, Dumézil refers to this
cycle of myths and rituals as the "ambrosia cycle."

The "festin d'immortalité" is both a divine and a mortal phenomenon, Dumézil claims. The mortal (or ritual) version can be seen
in the preparation and consumption of beverages—almost always
alcoholic ones—such as *soma*, *madhu*, and mead. From Ireland
to India, such rituals formed an integral part of I-E religious ritual
and—here, perhaps, Dumézil took a leaf from Robertson Smith—
survive to some extent in the Christian Eucharist.

The influence of Frazer is strong here. It can be detected in the
extent to which ritual drunkenness is viewed as serving to restore
magically the vigor of the gods. As the human devotees consume
their beer or other alcoholic beverage and thereby experience the
godlike feeling that often accompanies intoxication, so are the gods
nourished and invigorated; symbolically, they, too, partake of the
death-defying beverage, and thus their immortality is ensured, at
least for the time being. Indeed, it is Frazer's "Law of Sympathy"

---

[1] The Ossetes are an outlying Indo-Iranian-speaking people of the northern
Caucasus.

[2] E.g., the Tribrianders (cf. Malinowski, 1955*a*) and the Luiseño (cf.
White, 1957).

44

in action. Moreover, as the drink itself (e.g., *Amṛta*) is conceived to be a god, its consumption is an act of sacrifice (cf. the rituals surrounding the Vedic deified drink *soma*) which, in the best Frazerian tradition, serves to maintain the vigor of the god in question.

In the last part of his dissertation (pp. 240 f.), Dumézil includes an interesting, if not wholly germane, discussion of the Kwakiutl potlatch (taken from Boas) and the degree to which it differs from the I-E "festin." Although the forms of the two ritual feasts are somewhat similar, Dumézil concludes that the purposes are quite different. The potlatch, he asserts, with its attendant rivalry and conspicuous consumption, is not concerned with the maintenance of divine immortality. The idea of a deified drink and the ritual of its consumption are thus seen as uniquely I-E, having no parallels either in contemporary primitive religions[3] or in those of the ancient non-I-E civilizations.

Perhaps as a result equally of the novelty of its thesis and the obscurity of its author, the dissertation was not reviewed in journals such as the *Journal Asiatique*, the *Revue de l'Histoire des Religions*, or the *Zeitschrift der Deutschen Morgenländischen Gesellschaft*, periodicals that ordinarily would have paid some heed to a work of this sort. So far I have been able to find only a single review, a short but favorable one by Meillet (1925), who praised his former student's insight and imagination and his skill in dealing with widely divergent materials.

Although Dumézil has long since repudiated the "ambrosia cycle," it continued to dominate his thinking for several years after *Le festin*. Shortly after the appearance of his dissertation, another strongly Frazerian, or perhaps even Mannhardtian, work appeared, *Le crime des Lemniennes* (1924b), which followed certain doubtful lines of inquiry laid down in *Le festin*. Overly concerned with the "dying god" motif, this monograph probably bears less on Dumézil's later work than any other of his formative phase publications; it is the low point of a "période d'explorations maladroites, nécessaires sans doute, mais directement infructueuses" (Dumézil, 1952b, p. 39). A number of shorter works concerned with the ambrosia cycle and associated phenomena also were produced during this period. In 1925, for example, Dumézil published an article

---

[3] But cf., for example, the position of *pulque* in Aztec religion and that of *chibcha* beer in Inca religion. Also, the ritual consumption of peyote among American Indians parallels, in many aspects, the assumed I-E *festin*.

entitled "Les bylines de Michajlo Potyk et les légendes indo-euro-péennes de l'ambroisie" in which he examined the Russian *bylinas*, or folk ballads, of Michajlo Potyk and found in them humanized representatives of this cycle. Outlining the pattern as found in other literature, he excerpts and reviews the pertinent Russian texts, including the closely related tale of Michalko Ofonaskin, discusses the relation of earlier to later texts, and attempts to isolate the I-E core from the folkloristic elements[4] that surround it. In doing so, he finds in the name of the central female character of the *bylinas* a linguistic link to the name of a Slavonic patroness of spring. More-over, he points out the relationship between these Russian texts and other Slavic materials, such as the Bulgarian legend of Michel of Potuka.

Even more interesting in this connection is a paper published in 1926 in which Dumézil concerns himself with the extent to which an Armenian rite of spring contains elements related to the am-brosia cycle. This rite, which involves the use of water, is centered on two magic flowers, Haurot and Maurot. The prototypes of these flowers—the Zoroastrian *Ameša Spentas*, Haurvatāt ('health') and Ameretāt ('Immortality')—are the genii of water and plants, re-spectively, and are traced through Mazdean texts and marginal secondary reflections (e.g., the Islamic *Harut-Marut*, the Jewish Purim feast and Esther story, the Manichaean cosmogony) in search of ambrosial elements. The date of the Armenian borrowing is left open but is held, on purely linguistic grounds, to be post-Parthian at the earliest (cf. De Menasce, 1947). The interesting point here, as far as the evolution of the system is concerned, is not the ambrosial aspect, which represents one of the blind alleys mentioned above, but rather Dumézil's involvement with Haurva-tāt and Ameretāt; today he asserts that this Iranian pair are mythi-cal cognates of the Aśvins, the Dioscuri, and the like, and are clearly third-function figures.

CENTAURS AND INDO-EUROPEAN RITES OF SPRING

Although Dumézil devoted two books and several articles to the ambrosia cycle and its associated figures, this was not the only area

---

[4] I.e., traits, themes, motifs, etc., which are too widespread and occur in too many variations to be linked necessarily with a single tradition or set of traditions, such as the "swan maiden" motif. Cf. Thompson (1946) and Lessa (1961), who stresses this point.

of I-E myth and ritual which commanded his attention in the years following the publication of his dissertation. In 1929, while teaching in Istanbul, he turned his attention to an I-E myth-ritual complex relating to the celebration of the beginning of spring. The result was *Le problème des Centaures* (1929), his second major publication.

Proceeding from a discussion of modern European carnivals and the ritual behavior associated with them, Dumézil surveys evidence from a number of widely separated I-E areas. His conclusion is that the Iranian *Gandarevas*, the Indic *Gandharvas*, the Roman *Faunus* and *Februus* (cf. the Lupercalia), and the Greek *Kentauroi*, among others, all relate to a common I-E class of young, virile, partly theriomorphic, partly anthropomorphic divinities who govern human and animal fertility, and who are particularly important in ensuring the success (i.e., the fertility) of marriages. Dumézil cites the Roman Lupercalia as a prime example of such a myth-ritual complex. The Luperci, who appear naked, ritually represent this class of inherited I-E deities. Another example is the Iranian *No-Roz* or new year celebration.

From *Gandharva, Gandareva*, the Lithuanian *Gondu, Kentauroi*, and others, Dumézil reconstructs *$G^w h^e / o(n)dh$-r-u-o* as a possible Proto-I-E form designating this class of supernatural beings. Although by no means universally accepted, this reconstruction does conform generally to the phonetic laws governing Proto-I-E[5] and indeed lends weight to Dumézil's mythological argument. Here, as elsewhere, however, there is always the possibility that the Proto-I-E form denoted a phenomenon quite different from those denoted by the several derivative forms (*Kentauroi, Gondu*, etc.) in terms of which it is reconstructed, and that the similarities observed between the various rituals and their attendant myths are the result of a later interpretation in one area which subsequently spread widely across the I-E domain. If this is what happened, it would hardly be correct to speak of the Centaur theme as Proto-I-E. It is also possible that the whole complex of myths, rituals, and labels was invented in one area. In this event, the reconstructed form in question would simply reflect phonetic modification of the original term as it passed from one I-E language to another.

---

[5] I am indebted to Professor Jaan Puhvel, of the University of California, Los Angeles, an expert in comparative I-E linguistics, for this observation, though Professor Puhvel, like most of his colleagues, has some reservations and cannot fully accept the form in question as a part of Proto-I-E (cf. Thieme, 1953).

Evolution of the System

As has often been pointed out (cf. Bloomfield, 1933; Hymes, 1960; Hockett, 1958), intrafamilial borrowing is one of the chief complicating factors in linguistic reconstruction; it is certainly no less of a factor when one attempts to prove a genetic relationship between a set of similar myths and rituals. In emphasizing the complicating effects of internal borrowing, I do not mean to infer that it is impossible to establish a genetic relationship between the myths and rituals of those who speak related languages. On the contrary, I share Dumézil's fundamental assumptions that basic social and religious ideas *tend* to be tied closely to the language of those who possess them, and that if the speakers of a language become separated from one another, such ideas *tend* to undergo the same sort of differential development that ultimately yields a set of related yet distinct daughter languages. Yet I must emphasize the word "tend," for ideas, even the most sacred ones, seem to be somewhat more amenable to diffusion than phonemes or grammatical features. Before one assumes that a given set of parallel myths, rituals, or social structural features is the result of differential development of a common protomyth, ritual, or structural feature, one should take all possible care to rule out internal borrowing.

OSSETIC MYTH

Since the beginning of his career, Dumézil has been much interested in the outlying Indo-Iranian-speaking communities of the northern Caucasus, especially the Ossetes, and has devoted a long series of articles and monographs to their mythology, folklore, and language.[6] Indeed, Ossetic data are often used to support his larger theories, though here Dumézil qualifies as a specialist and much of his work in this connection is concerned with local problems of interpretation and textual criticism. One of the earliest and most important of his publications dealing with Caucasian myth appeared in 1930. Entitled *Légendes sur les Nartes* (1930a), the bulk of the monograph consists of translations of Ossetic and other north Caucasian tales concerning the *Nartes*, a legendary band of heroes not unlike those found elsewhere among I-E speakers (e.g., the Irish *fianna*, the Vedic *Maruts*, and the companions of Jason in Greek myth). The texts are preceded by an introduction dealing

---

[6] Dumézil's studies of the Ossetic language and its relationship to other Indo-Iranian languages rank among the best in this field.

mainly with the geographical distribution of the tales with their state of preservation and means of transmission, and with a summary of previous scholarship in this area.

At the end of the volume there are "cinq notes mythologiques" which deserve mention here as being indicative of the kind of scholarship Dumézil is capable of bringing to bear on specific mythological traditions and the kind of comparative framework in which these scholarly endeavors are inevitably cast. In the first of these "mythological notes," Dumézil presents an extensive list of parallels between the customs of the Ossetes and of their legendary heroes on the one hand, and those of the Scythians and Sauromati, as recorded by Herodotus and Ammianus Marcellinus, on the other. In the second note, he traces the Ossetic legendary characters, Uryzmag and Satana, mainly to literary and romantic, rather than to mythic, sources; cites correspondences between the latter and Satanik, a legendary princess of the Alans reported by Moses of Khorene; and notes a resemblance between the Ossetic pair and the mythical parents of Targitaos. In the third and fourth, he examines the figures of Batradz and Sozryko in their aspects of storm-hero and solar-hero, respectively, and cites parallels from other Indo-Iranian areas and from Scandinavia. In the fifth note, Dumézil opposes the position of Miller and Kovalevsky, which supports a specifically Persian source for the correspondences between the customs, beliefs, and legends of the Ossetes and those of the Iranians, and demonstrates parallels that extend into India, suggesting a basic I-E heritage that has, however, been influenced somewhat by late Iranian materials, especially Firdausi's *Shāhnā- meh*. Last but not least, he finds the influence of the Russian *bylinas* on Ossetic legends to be minimal.

Although Dumézil's focus has ranged widely within the area of ancient I-E studies, the Ossetes, with their ongoing oral tradition, have remained his special province, and he continues to devote much attention to them while actively pursuing his interest in Caucasian linguistics, mythology, and folklore.

THE FIRST HINT OF TRIPARTITION

In addition to *Légendes sur les Nartes*, Dumézil published in 1930 what, in retrospect, is a most significant article, "La préhistoire indo-iranienne des castes" (1930*b*), for in it appeared the first

49

hint of his later concern with tripartition. Citing references in the *Avesta* to three basic social classes (*athrāvan-*, *rathaēstar-*, and *vastriyō.fšuyant-*, which he renders, respectively, as 'priests,' 'warriors,' and 'cultivators') and a fourth subclass (*hūitiš-*, which he renders as 'artisans'), Dumézil concludes that ancient Iran, together with the rest of the early Indo-Iranian community, was characterized by a tripartite (or perhaps quadripartite)[7] social organization, a conclusion buttressed with evidence drawn from later Pahlavi and Persian texts (especially Firdausi), as well as from materials on the Scyths and the Ossetes. He finds that the first two classes (priests and warriors) were clearly defined throughout this community, from Vedic India to Scythia, though the third (cultivators) and especially the fourth (artisans) are inconsistent and irregular. Moreover, save for India, these class distinctions were more theoretical and traditional than practical and current. Because of this last consideration, and as a result of the basically Hindu (rather than Vedic) nature of the historic Indian caste system, he suggests that the latter is probably not directly descended from an ancient Indo-Iranian tripartite scheme. (Here, of course, he has long since changed his opinion; despite its convolutions and involutions, the modern Indian caste system, he now feels [cf. 1958*a*, p. 32], is indeed ultimately derived, not merely from an Indo-Iranian prototype, but from an I-E one [cf. Benveniste, 1932, 1938]). Finally, Dumézil points out that the Iranian and later Indic texts exhibit a secondary correspondence in that the division of functions is ascribed to a human rather than a divine agent; he attributes this to later popular tradition, a grafting of Indo-Iranian migratory legend onto divine myth.

Closely associated with Dumézil in this early attempt to delineate a common Indo-Iranian social organization was the brilliant Iranianist, E. Benveniste. In 1932, following Dumézil's lead,[8] Benveniste also turned his attention to the problem of ancient Iranian social organization. The result was an article, "Les classes sociales

---

[7] Initially, Dumézil seems to have conceived of the artisan group as a distinct, if not well-defined, stratum in Proto-Indo-Iranian society; later on, of course, he, like Benveniste, was to reject this idea in favor of a tripartite system (cf. Benveniste, 1938).

[8] Benveniste cannot be classed as a disciple, for his initial conclusions (1932) regarding the nature of Indo-Iranian society were arrived at independently of Dumézil; he simply covered the same ground and reached the same conclusions.

dans la tradition avestique," which, as it largely confirms Dumézil's conclusions, has played a most important part in the evolution of Dumézilian mythology and is frequently cited in Dumézil's later works.

After stressing that the Indic castes and the Iranian "classes" are two very independent developments of a nucleus of Indo-Iranian heritage, Benveniste examines the textual sources that relate to the division of social classes in ancient Iran and reaches the same conclusions as Dumézil in regard to the meaning of the Avestan terms *athrāvan-*, *rathaēstar-*, *vastriyō.fšuyant-*, and *hūitiš-*. What is more, he points out that this division into priests, warriors, cultivators, and artisans may be ascribed to the "mythic moment" when Yima[9] created his subterranean kingdom at the command of Ahura Mazdah. Zoroaster's reaction to this system was not to maintain it, Benveniste asserts, but to level it into a united community of the faithful; and the Gathic[10] terms *xaētū-*, *verezēna-*, and *airyaman-* are not, as has often been held, new designations for the old Avestan social classes, but refer rather to the Avestan kinship group distinctions, which include *nmāna-* or *demāna-* ('extended family'), *vis-* ('clan'), *zantu-* ('tribe,' 'district'), and *dahyu-* ('tribal confederation' or 'province').[11] Benveniste also emphasizes that the reappearance of the Avestan class terms in the Sassanid era (i.e., in the Pahlavi texts) does not indicate that they were understood in their original sense. On the contrary, demonstrable errors show that the terms in question were badly understood and artificially resurrected. Finally, he suggests that Jamshid's division of men into four professional classes, as related by Firdausi in the *Shāhnāmeh*, reflects the Yima story (Jamshid is a euhemerized version of Yima) rather than the Sassanid theological revival.

Benveniste's basic contribution was the confirmation and amplification of Dumézil's initial efforts to comprehend ancient Iranian social organization; and the latter has more than once recognized the importance of this contribution (cf. Dumézil, 1958a, p. 8), despite the fact that he and Benveniste have not always been in

---

[9] In the *Avesta*, literally the "first man." Yima is equivalent both linguistically and mythologically to the Vedic Yama.

[10] I.e., from the *Gāthās*, a set of hymns reputedly composed by Zoroaster himself and written in an old, obscure, eastern Iranian dialect. The *Gāthās* form the core of the *Avesta* and are the basis of much (but by no means all) of later Zoroastrian theology.

[11] Cf. Herzfeld, 1947.

perfect agreement. In this connection, I should perhaps mention a second article by the French Iranianist published in 1938, one that has also had its effects upon the course of Dumézilian mythology, "Traditions indo-iraniennes sur les classes sociales." Here, Benveniste begins by citing the Scythian origin myth. Disagreeing with Dumézil's assumption (1930*b*, p. 123) that the sons of Targitaos represent, respectively, the three social strata of Scythian society, he sees them simply as the mythic ancestors of the several Scythian ethnic or tribal divisions. More important, however, Benveniste does indeed see the golden objects fallen from the sky as symbolic of the tripartite division of Scythian society and as evidence for an ancient tripartite division of Indo-Iranian society. To support this conclusion, one that he had first reached six years earlier, he cites a number of Avestan passages; for example, *Yašt* 29, wherein the Spirit of the Cow demands as a protector a *priest* who will have the power of a *warrior* so as to protect the *agriculturist*, and *Yašt* 13.67–71, in which the *Fravartis*[12] are seen, according to Benveniste (1938, p. 540), to (1) assure the fertility of the soil, (2) repel enemy attacks, and (3) fight against demons and the enemies of religion (i.e., to act as priests). To such Avestan evidence he adds some Indic evidence, mostly in the form of hymns to Agni: for example, *Rig Veda* 7.71.1–15, in which Agni is implored to grant protection to priests, warriors, and cultivators. Especially interesting here is Benveniste's rendering (1938, p. 548; following L. Renou) of *Rig Veda* 7.71.11: "Agni dans les prières, Agni dans les combats, Agni pour la prosperité du champ."

All the foregoing led Benveniste to affirm his—and Dumézil's—earlier conclusion that before it fragmented into Iranian, Scythian, and Indian segments, the common speech community that is labeled "Indo-Iranian" was characterized by a tripartite social organization. The fourth group, which Dumézil had found occurring irregularly and inconsistently, was by this time seen as a later ramification of the cultivator class.

By 1938, then, the basic outline of Indo-Iranian social and, to some extent, religious tripartition had been fairly well established. It remained for Dumézil to fill in this outline, to apply the Durkheimian concept of collective representation, and to extend the

---

[12] In the *Avesta*, personal spirits who guide the destinies of individual mortals; the lowest level of supernatural beings forming part of the "host" of Ahura Mazdah.

tripartite hypothesis to I-E society as a whole; but before he could do so, there were still a number of blind (or partially blind) alleys to be investigated.

THE "BINDER-GOD" THEORY: *Ouranos-Varuna* (1934)

In *Ouranos-Varuna: Étude de mythologie comparée indo-euro-péene*, a brief work published in 1934, Dumézil continued his pre-tripartite comparative studies of I-E myth. Here an attempt is made to prove that the Greek Ouranos and the Indic Varuna both stem from a common I-E prototype. Dumézil's evidence is based primarily upon an etymology (today suspect, even in Dumézil's opinion) which would derive the Greek and Indic names from I-E *Uorueno-*, in turn derived from an I-E root *uer-*, 'to bind' (Dumézil, 1934, p. 49). Thus, both Ouranos and Varuna are here seen as "dieux lieurs," as gods who are capable of physically restraining or binding, by one means or another, all those who oppose their interests. Ouranos "binds" his offspring by consigning them to Tartaros; Varuna "binds" his fellow creatures (including his son, Bhṛgu [*ibid.*, pp. 54–55]) by means of magical spells. To Dumézil, both gods appear to be prototypical "dieux-rois," or 'god-kings,' from whom all other divine beings are descended. He also points out that in the *Atharva Veda* and elsewhere (*not*, however, in the *Rig Veda*) Varuna's impotence, as well as the cure sought for it, is frequently mentioned, and that this forms an important element in the *rājasūya*, or Hindu royal consecration ritual. The foregoing can be compared, the author claims, with the emasculation of Ouranos by Kronos as recounted by Hesiod, Apollodoros, and others (cf. Littleton, 1966). Pointing out that the *rājasūya* is almost the only ritual in which, in later times, Varuna plays an important part, Dumézil concludes that the reason Ouranos is, in classical times, a "dieu sans culte" is directly related to the early decline in Greece of the I-E concept of kingship, a concept that survived much longer in India.

Here, indeed, the influence of Frazer and Mannhardt is much less evident, though still detectable in the extent to which Dumézil is concerned with the magical importance of the potency and impotence of god-kings. Moreover, the etymological and mythological links by which Ouranos and Varuna are "bound" together are weak ones, as Dumézil has often admitted in his later works (cf. especially 1940a, 1948a). Yet in *Ouranos-Varuna*, despite the fact that so much of its central thesis has had to be rejected, Dumézil took a long step forward in the development of his thinking about I-E matters, for it was here that he first began to play seriously with the notion of sovereignty. Ouranos and especially Varuna are seen as personifications of the I-E concept of sovereignty, a sovereignty based, not on the physical prowess of the warrior, but on the awesome capacity to command the forces of the universe and to maintain, through magical means, the sanctity of oaths, contracts, and other mechanisms that strengthen and perpetuate the moral order. Later he was to recognize the dual or joint nature of this concept of sovereignty, that is, its division into magical and judicial aspects. But the basic outlines of this concept, a most important contribution to I-E studies, were drawn in *Ouranos-Varuna*; and, although this book has been rightly subjected to a great deal of criticism as far as specifics are concerned (cf. Rose, 1947; Gonda, 1960b), it must nevertheless be ranked among the most significant efforts of Dumézil's formative phase.

THE INDO-EUROPEAN PRIEST CLASS:
Flāmen-Brahman (1935)

Although Dumézil's comparative framework and range of interests broadened considerably after 1934, he became increasingly dubious about the extent to which ancient Greek mythic data could shed light upon I-E matters. "La Grèce," he remarked some years ago (1958a, p. 91), "—par rançon sans doute du 'miracle grec,' et aussi parce que les plus anciennes civilisations de la Mer Égée ont trop fortement marqué les invahisseurs venus du Nord[13]—contribue

---

[13] I should point out here that Palmer (1960) has made a strong case for two major I-E invasions of Greece. The first, occurring between 1800 and 1600 B.C., included Luvians (first cousins of the Hittites) pushing west from Asia Minor; the second, beginning about 1500 B.C., included the Mycenaean Greeks, authors of the tablets written in Linear B script, who, in turn, were overwhelmed in the twelfth century B.C. by their cousins, the Dorians. If Palmer is correct, Greece received successively two quite different versions of the I-E heritage. The first, brought in by the Luvians, was probably already adulterated by exposure to Mesopotamian civilization; the second, brought in by various Greek-speaking groups, seems to have been profoundly affected by the one that preceded it. This blending of various I-E traditions, over and above the effects of neighboring non-I-E civilizations, may well account for the absence in classical Greece of a clear-cut I-E tradition like the one Dumézil finds at Rome, among the Germans, etc.

54

peu à l'étude comparative: mêmes les traits les plus considérables de l'héritage y ont été profondement modifiés." In any event, in the years following *Ouranos-Varuna*, Dumézil's focus shifted farther to the west, to Ireland, Scandinavia, and especially to ancient Rome. The first work to reflect this new area of interest was *Flāmen-Brahman* (1935), the precursor of a long and distinguished series of works (1941–1948) establishing the I-E nature of early Roman "history."

In *Flāmen-Brahman*, Dumézil attempts to prove that the Indic *Brahman* (or *Brāhmana*), the Iranian *Baresman*, and the Roman *Flāmen* are cognates and that they bear witness to a common I-E category or class of sacred personages whose primary (or better, perhaps, primeval) function was to serve as sacrificial victims. Here, of course, the influence of Frazer is strongly evident; Dumézil sees the **Bhlagh(s)-men*, or I-E prototype of the sort of priest in question, as a "substitute victim" for the **reĝ-* (Lat. *reg-*, Skt. *rājan-*, etc.), and in order that such a substitute be acceptable to the gods, he must be equal to or greater than the actual ruler. Thus, he points out (cf. the "histoire de *Çunahçepa*," Dumézil, 1935, pp. 21–23), the primary role of the *Brahman* is not that of priest, but rather that of "l'homme sacré" par excellence; only later, in post-Vedic times, when the caste system had crystallized, did the priestly duties take on great importance. The same thing may be said, he asserts, of the *Flāmen* in monarchal and early republican Rome. In both Latin and Indic cases, the prosperity of the king was directly dependent upon the prosperity and vigor of the sacred *Flāmen* or *Brahman*. Over and above these broad similarities, Dumézil finds many detailed similarities in the roles defined in historic times as proper, respectively, to the *Brahman* and the *Flāmen*. Both were surrounded by many identical taboos: for example, neither could be executed, no matter how grave the crime; neither could ever undress completely; neither could have anything to do with horses.

Dumézil's thesis concerning the relationship between the Roman and Indic sacerdotal classes has by no means met with universal approval (cf. Keith, 1937; Dandeker, 1942; Gonda, 1950). Especially suspect is his reconstruction of **Bhlagh(s)-men*.[14] Nevertheless, in *Flāmen-Brahman*, Dumézil took a step further toward clarifying his thinking relative to what, in his later works, he refers to as the "first function." Stripped of its Frazerian overtones, this recog-

---

[14] Professor Puhvel informs me that such a reconstruction is within the limits of possibility, if not probability.

nition of the existence of a priestly group equal to or greater than the secular rulers is fundamental to his tripartite interpretation of I-E myth and society. That the Roman *Flāmen*, the Iranian *Baresman*, and the Indic *Brahman*—to say nothing of the Celtic Druid—all bear witness to the presence of such a group in Proto-I-E times is still firmly held by Dumézil and his colleagues (cf. Dumézil, 1950*a*, 1951*c*, 1958*a*).

SUMMARY

Dumézil's formative phase included the development of his mythology from its inception to the point where it begins to take on its contemporary character, beginning with his early involvement with the "ambrosia cycle" (1924–1926) and with Ossetic myth (1930) and proceeding through the widening of his range of interests in the late 1920's and early 1930's to the first tentative steps that he and Benveniste took in recognizing the tripartite structure of Indo-Iranian society. He attempted to show a relationship between Ouranos and Varuna in 1934 and one between *Flāmen* and *Brahman* in 1935, and later became disenchanted with Greece as a source of mythic data for comparative I-E studies. During this period he oscillated between Frazerian (the "ambrosia cycle," *Flāmen-Brahman*) and sociological (Indo-Iranian tripartition) interpretations of his subject matter. This was the phase in which Dumézil, after much experimentation and exploration, laid the foundations for his comparative mythology. No attempt has been made to discuss all of Dumézil's formative phase publications;[15] nor shall I attempt such a task in the phases yet to be surveyed. My next task is to survey the developmental phase, which begins in 1938 and ends approximately in 1949.

---

[15] In 1936, for example, Dumézil published a most interesting article in the *Recherches Philosophiques* entitled "Temps et mythes" (1936), which details the several ways time is treated in myths. Especially interesting is his discussion (pp. 243-246) of what he terms "le Grand Temps," i.e., that time period, set apart from all others, in which divine and heroic events occur. It may be compared, he suggests, with "le temps ordinaire," or the time in which history per se unfolds, which only begins after "le Grand Temps" has run its course. The implication here is that this dichotomy is well-nigh universal—the article is not specifically concerned with I-E matters; in his discussion of time, Dumézil cites works by Mauss, Levy-Bruhl, Granet, and Hubert.

4

The Developmental Phase: 1938-1949

For two years after the appearance of *Flāmen-Brahman* (1935), Dumézil published little of any great importance; but these two years, silent as they were, saw a major change in his thinking. It was a period of lecturing (he had by this time long since returned from Turkey and had joined the faculty of the École des Hautes Études, once again coming into close personal association with Mauss), synthesizing, and, above all, reevaluating what he had done before and the theoretical postulates upon which his work had been based. It was during this period that he abandoned permanently the Frazerian-Mannhardtian approach in favor of "la méthode sociologique" as advocated by Mauss, Granet, Hubert, and others (cf. Dumézil, 1951*b*). Dumézil himself (1958*a*, p. 91) attributes much of the change in direction and focus of his research in these years to a growing awareness of the extent to which "le vocabulaire religieux des Indo-Iraniens d'une part, ceux des Celtes et des Italiotes d'autre part, présentent un grand nombre de concordances précises, et qui leur sont propres," and underscores his indebtedness to Vendryes (1921) for having first made this most important observation. In any event, the net result was a programmatic article, "La préhistoire des flāmines majeurs" (1938*a*), published in the *Revue de l'Histoire des Religions*; with it begins the developmental phase in the evolution of Dumézilian mythology.

ROMAN TRIPARTITION

Ostensibly a continuation of his 1935 monograph, "La préhistoire des flāmines majeurs" is in actuality the first of a number of pro-

57

grammatic articles and published lectures (cf. 1951*a*) in which, from time to time, Dumézil has summed up the state of his thinking about various I-E matters and has laid out a program for further research. He begins by noting the analogy between the Indic *brāh-mana-kṣatriya-vaiśya*, the Celtic *druides–equites–bo airig*, and the Roman *flāmen diālis–flāmen martiālis–flāmen quīrinālis*. At first glance, the latter trio would seem to be merely a sacerdotal one when compared with the Celtic and Indic divisions of society; but upon closer inspection, he asserts, it can be seen that the Roman triad of gods (i.e., Jupiter, Mars, and Quirinus), with its associated *flāmines* or priests, actually is composed of the three elements that, taken together, constitute the totality of Roman society: the *flāmen diālis* (the *sacerdōs* par excellence) is concerned with Jupiter, the god of magico-religious sovereignty, and with the *rēx*; the *flāmen martiālis* is concerned with Mars *bellātor* and the *milites*, or soldiers; the *flāmen quīrinālis* is concerned with Quirinus (as a result of syncretism, understood in later times as the *tranquillus* aspect of Mars and basically associated with things agrarian) and with the agricultural *quirites*.

There are, of course, a number of major differences here, especially between the Indic and Roman systems; these he characterizes as follows: (1) the Indic triad represents three rigidly defined classes of society, while the Roman (as we know it) refers only to three social functions, to three modes of activity; (2) the Indic system is adapted to a royal, almost feudal, society, whereas the Roman serves a state composed of citizens; and (3) the Indic *brahman* could exercise his duties over the whole range of the pantheon, while the Roman *flāmen* was confined to the service of a single god. Yet, in spite of these differences, the fundamental similarity among these Celtic,[1] Indic, and Roman triads cannot be overlooked. A further point of comparison between the Indic and Roman systems is noted: the Indic triad mirrors the Indic tripartite cosmogony of earth, atmosphere, and heavens; the Roman *ius fetiale*, which in one place invokes the triad and in another invokes three groups of gods, *caelestes*, *terrestres*, and *inferni*, corresponding respectively to Jupiter, Mars, and Quirinus, similarly reflects this tripartition. The article ends by noting that, in the

---

[1] Like the Indic *Brahman*, the Celtic Druid seems to have been able to exercise his functions over the whole range of the pantheon (cf. Le Roux, 1961*a*).

Umbrian sacred triad (Juu-, Mart-, Vofion(o)-), the name Vofion(o)- (or Vofionus) replaces that of Quirinus. This name, Dumézil suggests, may be an allusion to the Latin *devotio*, a ritualistic contract between man and the gods of the underworld (third function).[2]

Thus, by 1938, Dumézil came to assert that early Rome, like ancient India and Iran (cf. 1930*b*), knew a tripartite division of social functions (and by extension, of social strata that served these functions), and that this tripartition was reflected in the structure of the college of *flāmines*. It is on this Roman–Indo-Iranian equivalence,[3] an equivalence that, in Dumézil's opinion, can be explained only in terms of a common I-E heritage, that he has anchored the bulk of his subsequent theories.

The way in which Dumézil approaches the evidence of ancient Roman social and supernatural tripartition is, perhaps, even more important. Here, for the first time, he conceives of a threefold set of functions that transcend the social groups that serve them and are collectively represented by a triad of gods. Jupiter, Mars, and Quirinus are seen not simply as collective representations of certain social strata (i.e., respectively, those occupied by priests, warriors, and cultivators), but also—and at a more profound level of interpretation—as embodiments of the functions served by these strata (i.e., respectively, maintenance of a harmonious relationship between the social and supernatural worlds and the exercise of moral sovereignty, physical protection of society, and provision of nourishment and maintenance of physical well-being). Much more work with Roman and other materials remained to be done before the full ideological meaning of these structures was realized, before it was recognized that they served to shape the I-E "conscience collective," to use Durkheim's phrase; but here, indeed, can be seen the beginnings of this recognition. Here, also, can be seen the beginnings of Dumézil's concern with the extent to which the early I-E-speaking communities of Italy, Scandinavia, Ireland, Iran, and India shared a common, tripartite ideology, a common set of

---

[2] I.e., the herder-cultivator function, whose representative deities are generally terrestrial or subterranean and concerned primarily with the maintenance of human physical well-being.

[3] The equivalence between *Flāmen* and *Brahman*, although never entirely rejected, was soon overshadowed, in Dumézil's opinion, by a whole host of comparable Roman and Indic tripartite formulas as he delved more deeply into early Roman history.

categories in terms of which the members of these communities conceived of themselves, the world around them, and their gods.

In addition to "La préhistoire des flamines majeurs," Dumézil published several other articles and reviews in 1938. One, entitled "Jeunesse, éternité, aube: Linguistique comparée et mythologie comparée indo-européennes" (1938*b*), was concerned with the mythological inferences that could be drawn from Benveniste's (1937) proof that words like the Latin *aevum* and *iuvenis* are derived from the same I-E root with a range of meanings including 'vital force,' 'youth,' 'life(-span),' 'age,' and 'eternity.' The Latin goddess Iuventas, 'Youth,' and the Irish Oengus or Mac Óc, 'Young Son' (*óc*<**yuwn̄ko-*), were both dispensers of "vital force," but Iuventas was also the guarantor of the eternity of Rome. With Terminus, she refused to be evicted from the Capitol when Tarquinius Superbus built a shrine there to the Capitoline Triad; this obstinacy was considered a good omen.[4] In addition, Dumézil compares the role of *iuvenes* in the Roman Lupercalia with the name Āyu-[5] in the Indic *Gandharva* traditions (cf. Dumézil, 1929). Armenian *ayg-*, 'dawn,' 'daybreak,' is also connected with this assumed I-E root in the meanings 'youth' and 'vigor' (i.e., when the day is young). In another 1938 article (1938*c*), published in the *Bulletin de la Société de Linguistique*, he derived Armenian *Ikin-*, 'youthful,' 'undisciplined' (regarding the latter meaning, cf. the centaur theme discussed earlier [Dumézil, 1929]) from the other root form, the cognate of "young," like the Latin *iuvenis*.[6]

Thus, despite Dumézil's growing preoccupation with the delineation of an overall, common I-E ideological heritage, he nevertheless found time to attack secondary problems in I-E myth and linguistics, such as those surrounding the relationship among *iuvenis*, Mac Óc, *ayg-*, and the like, and the extent to which there was a common I-E personification of Youth, Vital Force, Eternity, and so on, with the same vigor that characterized his approach to the larger problems relating to I-E social and supernatural tripartition.

---

[4] I.e., the 'ακμή, 'prime,' of Rome would suffer no change (cf. Dionysius of Halicarnassus [3.69]; also Florus 40.7: "siquidem firma omnia et *aeterna* pollicebantur" [italics mine].

[5] A son of Pururavas.

[6] Cf. Unbegaun's (1958) demonstration that Slavonic *věkŭ* (= Lith. *viēkas*, 'vital force') developed to 'life' > 'age' > 'long period' > 'eternity,' much like the Greek αἰών.

THE THREE-HEADED MONSTER

Another example of the way in which Dumézil deviates from his primary course to concern himself with secondary problems—an example that also serves to exemplify his skill as a folklorist[7]—can be found in an article, written in 1939, entitled "Deux traits du monstre tricéphale indo-iranien" (1939*a*). As I see it, the central objective of this article is to demonstrate the usefulnes of the comparative method, even when the investigator cannot derive a "common denominator" for the traditions and texts under consideration. Here Dumézil, through an examination of the Indic and Iranian retellings of the story of the slaying of a three-headed monster with accompanying descriptions of his nature (demonstrably products of a common heritage), displays the process whereby narrative materials are reshaped to conform to the values and attitudes held by the various cultures in which they appear. Aside from the physical appearance of the monster and the linguistic accord of the names of the slayers (Indic Trita, Iranian Thraetauna[8]), he points out several other correspondences between the extant stories and traditions of the two cultures in question: the monster is characterized by the trait of duplicity; the stories describe the inauguration of the practice of killing animals for food (for ordinary nourishment in Iran; for sacrificial purposes in India); a part of the body (in Iran the two additional heads; in India the brain and the marrow) is created by the action of whistling (Iran) or spitting (India) on the part of a supernatural being; the stories involve a particular characterization of the brain (in Iran it becomes the horrible nourishment of a monster; in India an impure nourishment forbidden to men).

Equally important are the basic divergences: in India the Tricephalus (or Tvaṣṭar) wishes to prevent the killing and eating of animals; in Iran he wants to incite this practice. Dumézil's point here is that the subject matter of the narrative has been realigned to suit the differing values and attitudes characteristic of the two religious systems. The Indic story is unconcerned with any moral point, but centers on magical action and sacrificial practice, whereas the Iran-

---

[7] I.e., quite apart from Dumézil's skill as an Indo-Europeanist, his ability to recognize a given theme or motif, to trace its various manifestations in time and space, and to understand its relationship to other themes and motifs (cf. Gerschel's [1957] discussion of this aspect of Dumézil's scholarship).

[8] Who becomes Feridun in the *Shāhnāmeh*.

ian version, a product of the Zoroastrian moral reform, hinges upon a moralistic precept and is a lesson in conduct. To illustrate this process further—a process well known to anthropologically oriented students of folklore[9]—Dumézil briefly surveys the progress in ancient Iran, Iranianized Armenia, and Islamic Iran of the story that, in India, told of the theft and regaining of the drink of immortality, *amṛta* (cf. Dumézil, 1924a).

GERMANIC TRIPARTITION AND THE CONCEPT OF JOINT SOVEREIGNTY, 1939–1940

It is perhaps ironic that it was in 1939, the year Hitler's legions began their grisly march, that Dumézil first focused his attention upon the Germanic branch of the I-E-speaking world. Yet, irony or no, the recognition of a common ideological bond between the ancient Germans and their linguistic cousins to the south and east was to play an important part in the development of his thesis. Given the relative abundance of Germanic texts (when compared with the number of Slavic or even Celtic texts) and the relative isolation of the Germanic community in early times, this recognition added a third cardinal point in Dumézil's comparative scheme, the other two such points being, of course, the Italic and Indo-Iranian regions.

In *Mythes et dieux des Germains: Essai d'interprétation comparative* (1939b), the first of a number of works devoted to the subject, Dumézil finds that there exists in Germanic mythology, despite the glorification of warlike deeds, and novelties in cosmogony and eschatology, a trifunctional pattern in Othinn, Thõrr, and Njorðr (which he equates with Caesar's interpretation of Sun, Vulcanus, and Moon). Othinn, the magico-religious sovereign, has the magic of runes,[10] the ability to paralyze his foes, the role of chief of the warriors without himself being a physical fighter, and the position of god of the chiefs as well as that of chief of the gods. Othinn's often violently inspired magic is complemented by the legislative-ordering capacities of a second figure, equal in rank,

---

[9] Cf. Lessa's (1961, pp. 172-174) discussion of the ways in which the Oedipus story has been shaped and reshaped as it has diffused eastward into Oceania.

[10] Still holding to the position developed in *Ouranos-Varuna* (1934), Dumézil connects *runes* etymologically with Ouranos and Varuna, deriving it ultimately from the same I-E root meaning "to bind."

termed variously Tȳr, Ullr, Mithothyn, or *Tiwaz. Accounts of the dethronement and subsequent restoration of Othinn recall, Dumézil suggests, the dynastic conflicts of Ouranos and his successors (cf. Wikander, 1952a). Further correspondences are seen between the Germanic bands of wild warriors (Othinn's band in *Valhöll*, the *Harii*, the *Berserkir*, etc.) and the Indo-Iranian *Gandharvas*, Greek *Kentauroi*, and the like; and between Germanic and Indo-Iranian tales of the killing of a great bear, boar, or giant (e.g., Othinn's victory over Hrungnir, or his slaying and dismemberment of Ymir, which parallel the slaying of Puruṣa, the exploits of Vṛtrahan ['Slayer of Vṛtra'], etc.). Dumézil also points out the similarities between Thōrr and Indra as thunder wielders, between Germanic and Indic accounts of the obtaining of the vessel to hold the intoxicating drink (here Dumézil retracts his earlier naturalistic interpretation of his story [cf. 1924a]), and between Njorðr and Freyr and other pairs of third-function figures. Also discussed at some length is the concept of sovereignty qua concept, especially the extent to which, among I-E speakers, it is believed to exist in the dynastic blood rather than in the individual carrier. Finally, Dumézil suggests that there may be a relationship between the purported early Germanic practice of "liquidation of the elders" and tribal migrations, and notes the functional aspects of the importance of riches in Germanic lore.

Dumézil's *Mythes et dieux des Germains* is more than merely an attempt to include the ancient Germans and Scandinavians in his then rapidly crystallizing scheme for the interpretation of I-E myth; for in it the scheme itself is refined (especially the concept of function) and the ground prepared for the next major step in its development. The latter came in 1940 in the first edition of Dumézil's *Mitra-Varuna: Essai sur deux représentations indo-européennes de la Souveraineté* (1940a) and involved, as the title suggests, the I-E concept and collective representations of sovereignty.

Although the full ramifications of this most important element of early I-E ideology were not finally realized until 1948, it was in this 1940 monograph that Dumézil first focused his attention upon the characteristic I-E tendency, hinted at earlier in *Mythes et dieux des Germains* and elsewhere, to conceive of a joint or dual sovereignty. Using Mitra and Varuna as models, he points out that in early Indic literature a distinction is invariably made between the roles of these two deities: the former, as the personification of Contract (cf. Meillet, 1907), is defined as acting in a rational and legal manner, settling contractual disputes and generally behaving in a fashion immediately beneficial to mankind; the latter, on the contrary, still defined here as a "binder" (cf. Dumézil, 1934), is apt to behave irrationally and not always in a manner beneficial to his devotees, achieving his ends through the exercise of his consummate magical powers. Capriciously "binding" gods and mortals alike with his *māyā*, or spells, he generally presents himself as an awesome and rather terrible being. Mitra is thus primarily concerned with the maintenance of the moral and legal order of things, while Varuna is principally concerned with the magical manipulation of the forces of the cosmos (forces that are, indeed, part of his makeup) and with the maintenance of proper magico-religious beliefs and practices among men. Both gods are sovereign, each in his own sphere, and together they exercise a joint sovereignty over all other beings and creatures, mortal and divine.

This distinction between the Varuna aspect and the Mitra aspect of sovereignty in ancient India is paralleled throughout the I-E world, Dumézil asserts, and can be seen in the distinction between Othinn and Tӯr, Jupiter and Dius Fidius, and others. In 1940, of course, Dumézil had not yet recognized the extent to which the I-E heritage had carried over into Zoroastrianism (cf. Dumézil, 1945) and was only beginning to realize the extent to which early Roman "history" reflected I-E themes. It remained for the second edition of *Mitra-Varuna* (1948*b*) to take these new discoveries into account and to complete the picture of the I-E concept of sovereignty which was only sketched eight years before.

Yet the idea of a duality contained within an overall tripartition, first suggested in 1940, remains fundamental to Dumézil's interpretation of I-E ideology. Indeed, it is part of what makes this ideology, in his opinion, uniquely I-E. Save for those areas of the Old World which were conquered, or at least influenced by migrating I-E bands, Dumézil asserts that nowhere else in the non-I-E-speaking world can one find a similar ideology, a similar set of collective representations, or a similar social organization. On this last point, of course, he has been the object of much criticism, from the late 1930's to the present; and I shall take account of these criticisms later on (chap. 7), but some critical comments seems to be in order here. Perhaps they might best be phrased as questions, to

64

be kept in mind as the subsequent course of the evolution of Dumézil's system is traced and the increasing complexity of his theories and interpretations is observed.

First, and probably most important, to what extent are the data (Roman, Celtic, Zoroastrian, etc.) brought to bear, both by Dumézil and by the growing number of scholars who, since the early 1940's, have followed his lead, selected simply because they happen to fit the preconceived model? This basic question must be asked concerning the research efforts of *all* anthropologists, sociologists, psychoanalysts, and the like, who are seeking to validate a theory, and it is certainly germane in Dumézil's case. The latter, of course, has stoutly maintained (cf. 1960*a*) that neither he nor his colleagues are selective in their research. To bolster this assertion, they emphasize that even today there remain many lacunae, many problems (e.g., Greece), and that as scientists they are simply uncovering a structure already present in the mass of myths, folktales, religious lexicons, rituals, and social patterns which, in one form or another, can be documented among the several I-E-speaking communities of Europe and Asia.

Granting the foregoing, at least for the moment, a second, related question arises: To what extent have these valid I-E data (i.e., "valid" in that they are not "selected" data) been *interpreted* in such a way that they fit the model? For unlike the "hard" data of physics, chemistry, or even biology, mythological data, perhaps even to a greater extent than those of the other social sciences, consist, in the last analysis, of ideas and symbols and as such are subject to an extremely wide range of possible interpretation. And any mythologist, no matter how empirical his methods, is necessarily forced to interpret the meanings of these ideas and symbols; if he did not do so, he would be unable to arrive at any synthesis or structure. But there are limits here, limits imposed by the manifest forms of the data themselves; and the question posed above asks whether Dumézil and his colleagues have, in their eagerness to validate their theory, sometimes pushed their interpretations beyond the limits of credibility. For example, there is obviously a distinction between Mitra and Varuna; Dumézil was not the first to point this out.[11] But is he exceeding the reasonable limits of interpretation, given the manifest forms of the data relative to the two gods in question, when

---

[11] Cf., for example, Meillet (1907), who was the first to conceive of Mitra as Contract personified.

he emphasizes the rational and nonmagical aspects of Mitra and the irrational and magical aspects of Varuna? In this particular instance the answer appears to be no; but it is a question that must be kept in mind continually when confronting similar assertions made by him about Italic, Germanic, and Celtic first-function divinities.

A third question concerns the extent to which, as Brough (1959) and others have suggested, this I-E ideology is not unique, but merely the "natural order of things," and, if sought for, can be extracted from almost any body of narratives, including the Old Testament. Again, Dumézil (e.g., 1958*a*, 1960*a*) has insisted that the I-E pattern is indeed unique and that he has demonstrated this uniqueness fairly, empirically, and beyond contradiction.

Among the articles and reviews by Dumézil appearing in 1940, one of the most interesting ("La tradition druidique et l'écriture: Le Vivant et le Mort," 1940*b*) deals with the possibility that the well-known Druidic aversion to writing stemmed from the notion that the vivifying spirit of the spoken word, the spirit that renders sacred words powerful in themselves (cf. Malinowski, 1955*a*, pp. 73–74), would die if these words were committed to letters and thus "fossilized." Pointing out a similar aversion attributed (by Plutarch) to Pythagoras, Numa, and Lycurgus, Dumézil cites an Irish tale[12] that describes how Cormac's retainer, Dubdrenn, deceitfully robs Socht of his wonderful sword (once the sword of Cuchulainn) by falsifying the inscribed name, and goes on to denounce writing: "It was then that the Dead prevailed in testimony over the Living, as primacy was awarded to the written word." Such a priestly attitude toward writing may well be I-E, Dumézil suggests, pointing out that in India written literature truly begins with *Kṣatriya* domination and with the epics. Moreover, he holds that the Druidic doctrine of metempsychosis, or transmigration of souls, is possibly I-E; and the stress laid on the oral transmission of the sacred word reflects, in his thinking, an analogous attitude, each successive generation rejuvenating and reincarnating the same text.

Jupiter, Mars, Quirinus

In 1941, picking up where he had left off in "La préhistoire des flâmines majeurs" (1938*a*), Dumézil once again turned his full atten-

---

[12] Cf. *Irische Texte* 3.1:185-229.

tion to ancient Rome. The result was *Jupiter, Mars, Quirinus: Essai sur la conception indo-européenne de la société et sur les origines de Rome* (1941*a*), the first volume of a distinguished series bearing the same title (abbreviated *JMQ*) in which he was to examine not only the history, society, and religion of early Rome, but also the theology of Zoroaster—to say nothing of the parallels presented in Indic, Germanic, and Celtic literature—and to find in each a clear-cut example of the survival of the common I-E heritage. What is more, in *JMQ*, and in the parallel series, *Les mythes romains*, begun in 1942, he was to refine his theoretical framework, discarding the last vestiges of Frazerian and other nonsociological (i.e., non-Durkheimian) methods of interpretation.

The first volume of *JMQ* begins with a survey of the evidence pertaining to Indo-Iranian tripartition. The materials adduced by Dumézil (1930*b*) and Benveniste (1932, 1938) are reviewed and amplified: The Avestan and post-Avestan evidence for a threefold class stratification is presented, together with a number of non-Avestan tripartite formulas (e.g., the three admonitions of Darius as preserved at Behistun); the Vedic and Brahmanic evidence (Dumézil finds much germane material in the *Brāhmanas*, especially the *Śatapatha Brāhmana*) for ancient Indic social and supernatural tripartition, including that relative to the joint sovereignty of Mitra and Varuna, and to the double or twin figures (i.e., the Aśvins) who represent the third function, is laid out in detail; and the tripartite formula contained in the oldest surviving Indo-Iranian document, the previously mentioned Hittite-Mitanni treaty of the fourteenth century B.C., is duly noted, as is the tripartite character of the Scythian origin myth.

Having thus demonstrated the nature of Indo-Iranian tripartition, Dumézil goes on to suggest that this unique fashion of ordering social and supernatural relationships was not limited to the eastern end of the I-E world, but was indeed part of the common I-E heritage, a heritage especially apparent in the picture left to us of early Roman history, society, and religion by such historians as Titus Livy, Plutarch, and Quintus Curtius.[13] Drawing upon his earlier Roman studies (e.g., 1935, 1938*a*) and upon his discussion (1940*a*) of the concept of sovereignty, Dumézil expands his already well-founded thesis that the archaic or pre-Capitoline triad of Roman gods, Jupiter, Mars, and Quirinus, together with the shadowy

---

[13] To say nothing of the poet Propertius.

67

figure of Dius Fidius and the equally obscure, though less shadowy, figure of Ops, are representations of the three I-E functions and thus are comparable to the three major categories of gods which present themselves in the *Vedas* and *Brāhmanas*. Jupiter and Dius Fidius, respectively, correspond to Mitra and Varuna, dividing between them the same two aspects of sovereignty; Mars corresponds to Indra; and Quirinus and Ops together correspond to the Aśvins. It was to the service of these three Roman gods that the most sacred, if not most popular, Roman priestly group, the *flāmines*, was dedicated, just as in India the *Brahmans* were dedicated to their counterparts.

Of course, as Roman society became more sophisticated and cosmopolitan, the relative importance of this triad qua triad declined markedly, and with its decline the importance and prestige of its associated priests declined also. It was ultimately replaced in popular esteem by the so-called Capitoline Triad of Jupiter Capitolinus, Juno, and Minerva,[14] in which only Jupiter, in a much altered and, in later times, Hellenized form, persisted. As a separate entity, Mars continued to be the object of a special and important cult; Quirinus, however, seems to have faded rapidly from popularity and, by the beginning of historical times, was already viewed as archaic and obscure. Ops and especially Dius Fidius shared a similar fate.

Yet despite the changes wrought by time and the acquisition of an empire, Jupiter, Mars, and Quirinus, together with Dius Fidius and Ops, remained the canonical gods of Rome, Dumézil asserts. These three deities, as a triad (Dius Fidius and Ops must be seen here essentially as aspects, respectively, of Jupiter and Quirinus), collectively represented the three fundamental, functionally integrated segments of Roman society, the priests, the military, and the food producers. Not that the latter were rigidly stratified into classes or castes; far from it. From the earliest period about which we have adequate information, the class system, while fairly rigid, cut across these segments; military commanders and administrators were usually recruited from the same socioeconomic stratum, and the backbone of the army was composed, in theory at least, of the free peasantry. But the functions, administrative and sacerdotal, military, and agricultural, remained distinct; and it is as the summation of these functions, which is tantamount to saying the summation of

---

[14] Probably of Etruscan origin, although later equated with Athena, who has some tripartite attributes.

Roman society, that these three deities were canonical. Jupiter, as the god who presides over the cosmic order of things, is the representation of the priestly function, and, in the aspect of Dius Fidius, presides over the maintenance of the moral order and is the representation of the administrator or magistrate; together, as joint sovereigns, they represent the first function. Mars, as the god who presides over the exercise of physical prowess and the force of arms, is the representation of the *milites*, or soldiery. Quirinus[15] and Ops, presiding over the day-to-day activities of the population as a whole (considered in its civilian context rather than in the context of *milites*), especially its physical well-being and nourishment, are representations of the *quirites*. (Dumézil suggests that the fact that the *quirites* could be mobilized at a moment's notice into *milites* later gave rise to the notion that Quirinus was merely an aspect of Mars.)

The term *quirites*, manifestly related to the name Quirinus, is also closely connected with the *curia*, "les hommes rassemblés dans leurs cadres sociaux, la masse sociale organisée"; Quirinus, indeed, was the patron of the *curia* and, by extension, of its component, *quirites Romani*. Here, then, we encounter another aspect of the third function: the mass of the population performing its daily tasks, as opposed to those segments of it primarily concerned, at any one time, with religion or warfare. In India, of course, this division of labor became the basis of the caste system; but there, as at Rome, the essential feature is the collective representation of the three functions served, rather than those who serve them.

This triad of gods, however, is by no means the only example of Roman tripartition. As noted elsewhere, perhaps Dumézil's most important single contribution to scholarship—aside from the merits of his overall thesis—is the demonstration that much if not most of the legendary history of monarchal Rome is historicized I-E myth.[16] For example, in the persons of Romulus, Numa, and Tullus Hostilius, the first three kings of Rome, he sees clear-cut representations of the first two functions. Romulus, king and augur, eponymous founder of the city, is the Varuna figure in this regal

---

[15] Sometimes, though erroneously in Dumézil's opinion, viewed by both ancient and modern scholars as the "agrarian Mars" (cf. Dumézil, 1944, pp. 38-71).

[16] Although it appears that Dumézil was beginning to think along these lines as early as 1935 it was in *JMQ*, Vol. I, that he first systematically attempted to demonstrate the mythical aspects of Roman origins and to tie them in with other I-E mythologies.

triad. Like Varuna, Romulus is concerned with the establishment and maintenance of religious beliefs and practices; from him descends, in a sort of "Romuline succession," the supernatural power of the priests and augurs. Moreover, the founder of the city is consistently viewed as the protégé of Jupiter (thus linking these two ideological levels) and is, in a very real sense, a human (or heroic) personification of the chief deity. Numa, the second king, reflects the Mitra aspect of sovereignty. More a protégé of Dius Fidius than of Jupiter, "Good King" Numa is essentially a lawgiver concerned with the establishment and maintenance of the moral and jural relationships between members of the society. Like Mitra, with whom he may be compared, Numa is also a sovereign, the prototype of the magistrate and administrator, a figure more concerned with contractual values than with magico-religious ones. Together, then (despite the troublesome fact that one succeeded the other), Romulus and Numa represent the first function. And like most first-function figures, divine or semidivine, neither is renowned for physical prowess, neither gains his ends principally through force of arms. It is to the third king, Tullus Hostilius, that this latter trait is attributed, for it was Tullus who decisively defeated the Sabines and thus began Rome's career of expansion. A protégé primarily (but not wholly, for, as *rēx*, Tullus was indeed a sovereign) of Mars, Tullus Hostilius is the Indra figure here, a representation of the second or warrior function.

The third function is represented by the Sabines, close cousins of the Romans, who, under Titus Tatius, were present at the founding of the city, and who were renowned not for their magico-religious or administrative capabilities, not for their military prowess, but rather for their devotion to luxury and physical well-being—to say nothing of the fertility of their women. Once incorporated into Roman society, the Sabines became the prototypes par excellence of the *quirites*; indeed, Dumézil cites later references, perhaps a shade sarcastic, to Quirinus as the "Sabine Mars." The Sabine War itself appears to be a manifestation of a common I-E theme, and is paralleled in Scandinavian myth by the war between the *Aesir* (first and second functions) and the *Vanir* (third function), in which, as at Rome, the third-function representatives are defeated and absorbed into the community (here supernatural), rendering it complete.

Another example of this replication of tripartite themes in early

Roman "history" may be seen in the account of the founding of the three original Roman "tribes." The most important, the *Ramnes*, reputedly founded by Romulus, was charged with the maintenance of religious and administrative authority. The second, the *Luceres*, stemmed from Lucumon, Romulus' Etruscan military ally, and was charged with the defense of the city; and the third, the *Titienses*, stemming from the Sabine, Titus Tatius, was charged with the maintenance of physical well-being.

In addition to this novel interpretation of early Roman history—characteristically, Dumézil credits Piganiol (e.g., 1939) with first having noted the mythical basis of the Sabine War, and claims that he is simply carrying Piganiol a step further by pointing out the extent to which this newly discovered font of Roman myth reflects I-E themes—the first volume of *JMQ* includes a survey of the Germanic evidence for tripartition, some Celtic parallels, and even some interesting, but by no means certain, examples drawn from ancient Greek social organization and philosophy. On the Germanic side, drawing largely (but not wholly) upon his 1939 monograph, Dumézil points out the parallels between the Roman triad, Jupiter, Mars, Quirinus, and the Germanic triad, Othinn, Thōrr, and Njorðr, noting that Tȳr and Freyr occupy positions that correspond, respectively, to Dius Fidius and Ops. I have already mentioned the parallel between the war fought between the two classes of Scandinavian gods (*Aesir* versus *Vanir*) and that between the Romans and the Sabines.

Celtic myth is less clear in this respect, but Dumézil is able to indicate a number of possible examples of tripartition; for example, he adduces (1941*a*, pp. 241–245) the four talismans of the Irish *Tuatha dé Danann* ('People [or 'Tribes'] of the Goddess Danu'), including the "Cauldron of Dagda," which never failed to provide nourishment; the "Spear of Lug" and "Sword of Nuada," which rendered their owners invincible in battle; and, finally, the "Stone of Fal," which served as the seat of sovereignty (cf. Powell, 1948). These objects are symbolic of the three I-E functions, the cauldron symbolizing the third function, the two weapons symbolizing the second function, and a coronation stone representing the first. Another, less clear Celtic example can be seen, Dumézil asserts (1941*a*, pp. 115–116), in the Irish tales concerning Queen Medb, whose husband must be as brave in war (second function) and as wealthy (third function) as she; the first function, however, is less

71

easy to discern here. Perhaps it is represented by the Queen herself, who, after all, is a sovereign. In assessing this latter example, it would be well to keep in mind the questions posed earlier, especially the one pertaining to the degree to which the evidence has been "overinterpreted."

The Greek examples are drawn from the fourfold set of ancient Ionian "tribes" or *bioi* (literally, 'types of life') as described by Plutarch, Strabo, and others, and from Plato's *Republic*. Although neither their names nor their functions are clear, these *bioi* seem to have included (1) priests and magistrates, (2) warriors or "guardians," (3) laborers, and (4) artisans. Lumping the last two categories together (as with Iran) results in a class structure not unlike that of Vedic India, Avestan Iran, or monarchal Rome, a class structure that, if assumptions regarding its makeup are correct, would seem to reflect the three I-E functions. As Dumézil sees it (1941*a*, p. 257), these three functions were also reflected in Plato's concept of the ideal state or republic. Constituted as it is by three functionally interrelated, hierarchically ordered classes— philosophers, soldiers, and laborers (both agricultural and mechanical)—Plato's ideal state does indeed appear "au strict sense, une reminiscence indo-européenne" (*ibid.*, p. 259). And in the fourth book of the *Republic*, Dumézil asserts, there is evidence that Plato also conceived of the ideal citizen, the Just Man, in terms of these functions, thus indicating the depth to which the I-E ideology had penetrated his thinking. The Just Man, Plato suggests, should be a microcosm of the just or ideal state itself: he should possess the wisdom of a philosopher, the bravery of a soldier, and the wealth-producing skills of an artisan or cultivator. In short, Dumézil concludes that Plato's concept of both the ideal state and the ideal citizen was firmly rooted in the I-E tradition to which he, as a member of an I-E-speaking community, was heir.

Later, several additional Greek examples of tripartition were to come to light, especially in regard to the trio, Hera, Athena, and Aphrodite, and the wisdom of the lawgiver, Solon (cf. Dumézil, 1953*a*); but, in general, Greece has not proved to be a fruitful place of research for either Dumézil or his colleagues. Yet if Dumézil is correct in seeing in Plato's *Republic* a reflection of the I-E ideological heritage, it would seem to mean one of two things: (1) that, despite the absence of tripartite themes in all but a few fragments of Greek myth and epic, to say nothing of her pre-Platonic philosophic literature, this heritage—discernible perhaps in the early social organization of Ionia—somehow managed to linger on silently at least until the fourth century B.C., or (2) that Plato borrowed this concept from another (i.e., non-Greek) I-E source, possibly Iran. There is, of course, a third possibility not compatible with Dumézil's theory here: that Plato arrived at this particular concept of social and moral tripartition wholly independently; but, given the rarity of wholly new ideas, even in Plato, I am inclined toward the second alternative suggested above. Indeed, it is one that was suggested some years ago by Dumézil's eminent Iranianist colleague, Duchesne-Guillemin, in his most interesting and challenging book, *The Western Response to Zoroaster* (1958).

The second volume of *JMQ*, entitled *Naissance de Rome* (1944), continues and expands various aspects of Dumézil's interpretation of early Roman history. Appearing three years after *Jupiter, Mars, Quirinus*, it was able to take into account and meet the objections that had been raised by a number of Latinists (notably those of the so-called primitivist school) to the theories proposed there and in the first two volumes of his *Les mythes romains* (to be discussed shortly). Much of the book is concerned with the etymologies and nature of the three Roman tribes, and with the Sabine War (especially chaps. ii and iii). Citing Propertius' elegiac (IV, 1) account of the founding of the city, Dumézil reiterates the position taken earlier: that the Sabines, contrary to some interpretations, *were* indeed present at the founding of Rome and that the name of the Sabine chief, Titus Tatius, is incorporated in the name of the tribe charged with providing nourishment and "richesses," the *Titienses*; that the Etruscan warrior, Lucumon, or Lygmon, as Propertius renders it, lent his name to the militarily oriented tribe, the *Luceres*; and that the name of the priestly and magisterial tribe, the *Ramnes*, founded by Romulus, actually took its name from the latter's brother Remus, who, in Dumézil's opinion, is so closely associated with Romulus as to render the two almost indistinguishable from a functional point of view. As far as the Sabine War is concerned, Dumézil once again points out that it, like its Norse counterpart, reflects a basic I-E theme and that it serves as a "charter," to use Malinowski's famous term, for the incorporation of the third function and those who serve it into the community. The Sabines were from the beginning, he asserts, an integral part of the Roman community; and the idea of their separate existence is purely mythological and is rooted in the I-E heritage carried into central Italy in Proto-Italic times.

Thus, the "naissance de Rome," whether as recounted by Polybius, Livy, Quintus Curtius, or Propertius, is surely couched in myth, I-E myth in Dumézil's opinion. It was only later, as the Roman national character began to take shape, that this myth came to be conceived of as history.

In the third volume of the series, *Naissance d'archanges* (1945), Dumézil shifted his attention once again to the east, to Iran, where he tackled one of the most difficult problems in the history of religions—let alone comparative mythology—the role of the *Ameša Spentas*, or "archangels," in early Zoroastrianism. As is well known, Zoroaster instituted a sweeping reform of ancient Iranian polytheism. For such inherited Indo-Iranian deities as Mithra and Anāhitā, he substituted a dualism composed of the Spirit of Light and Truth, Ahura Mazdah, the 'Wise Lord' (later Ormazd), and the spirit of Darkness and the Lie, Angra Mainyu (or Ahriman, as he was called in later texts). Associated with the Wise Lord was a set of beings termed the "Immortal Beneficences," or *Ameša Spentas*, who were personifications of various virtues or aspects of Ahura Mazdah. The problem here lies in the difficulty and obscurity of the *Gāthās*,[17] or hymns, in which all of this was initially detailed, reputedly by Zoroaster himself. Although almost all scholars concerned, from Hyde, Anquetil-Duperron, and Darmesteter to Jackson, Nyberg, and Herzfeld, have underscored the importance of the *Ameša Spentas* in Zoroastrian theology—some, indeed (cf. Cumont, 1956; Duchesne-Guillemin, 1958), have attempted to demonstrate that the late Judaic concept of archangel was a direct outgrowth of the impact of Iranian religion upon that of the Jews in the sixth century B.C., a thesis that has been bolstered by the recent discoveries in the Jordan Valley[18]—there has been little if

---

[17] To this day, some scholars consider these hymns virtually uninterpretable (cf. Zaehner, 1961) and have concentrated their attention upon the *Yašts* and other more intelligible, albeit later, Avestan texts; part of the difficulty here stems from the obscure early eastern Iranian dialect in which the *Gāthās* were composed.

[18] Cf., for example, Dupont-Somner (1954), Davies (1956), Potter (1962), and others who have emphasized the extent to which Zoroastrian ideas are present in the so-called Dead Sea Scrolls (i.e., the texts found at Qumran and elsewhere in the Jordan Valley).

any agreement as to the basis of these concepts, let alone the role they played in Zoroastrian religion.

After a thorough reexamination of the evidence, and drawing upon his and Benveniste's conclusions regarding the tripartite nature of ancient Iranian social organization, Dumézil came to the conclusion that the answer to the problem posed by the *Ameša Spentas* is basically a simple one: they are reflections of the inherited I-E ideology. The earlier collective representations of this ideology had been replaced by new ones compatible with the monotheistic concept promulgated by the Iranian prophet. In hierarchical order, the two most important *Ameša Spentas* are Aša, 'Order,' and Vohu Manah, 'Good Thought.' Together, as agents of Ahura Mazdah, these two beings share the administration of the natural and social universe (cf. *Yasna* 44.3–4) and, in this capacity, represent the two basic I-E concepts of sovereignty. Aša, patron of fire, whose name corresponds to the Vedic *ṛta* ('cosmic order'), thus corresponds to Varuna, and is indeed the Zoroastrian replacement for the ancient Iranian representation of the magico-religious half of the first function. Like Varuna, Jupiter, and Othinn, Aša is concerned with the maintenance of the religious order, and his domain includes the far reaches of the cosmos. Vohu Manah, patron of the cow (i.e., the being who protects this sacred animal from indiscriminate slaughter), corresponds to Mitra and represents the Zoroastrian version of the juridical and contractual aspect of the first function. Like his Vedic counterpart, Vohu Manah is much closer to the world of men and presides over the moral relationships between members of the society. Aša, thus, as the Varuna figure, is more concerned with the cosmos as a whole and with the maintenance of man's magico-religious attitudes toward it; Vohu Manah, as the Mitra figure, is more concerned with "ce monde-ci," with the maintenance of "good thoughts" among his human devotees.

Next in importance is Xšathra, 'Power,' patron of metal, especially the metal contained in implements of war. The name Xšathra corresponds, of course, to the Vedic *kṣatra-* ('dominion'; cf. *kṣatriya-*), and the entity called by it is the Zoroastrian version of the second function or Indra figure. Like Indra, Thōrr, and Mars, Xšathra (cf. mod. Ir. *shah*) is the representation of the military function and those who serve it; he is the personification of physical force and prowess, the strong right arm of Ahura Mazdah.

At the lowest level appear three figures, Armāiti ('Pious Thought'), Haurvatāt ('Health'), and Ameretāt ('Immortality').

75

Evolution of the System

Together these represent the third function as it is expressed in Zoroaster's theology. The last two, Haurvatāt and Ameretāt, correspond to the Vedic Aśvins, Quirinus and Ops, and Njorðr and Freyr; patrons respectively of waters and plants, they preside over the "health" and "immortality" (here conceived as the maintenance of physical well-being not only in this world but also in the next) of the society, over the day-to-day activities of the population. Armāiti, an androgynous figure (but more female than male), conceived as the patron(-ess) of the earth, appears to be the Zoroastrian version of the ancient and popular third-function Iranian goddess, Anāhitā, with whom may be compared the Indic Sarasvatī and the Norse *Vanir* goddess, Freya. Here, yet another aspect of the third function is encountered: in addition to the twin or paired figures, there is usually (but not in all instances) an associated female figure. Like third-function figures throughout the I-E domain, these Zoroastrian conceptions represent the society as a whole considered in its nonsacerdotal, nonmilitary aspect, which means, in the last analysis, in its agricultural or food-producing aspect.

Yet, like so many of the examples considered previously, the Zoroastrian version of the third function is the least clearly (and at the same time most broadly) defined. All too often, it would seem, the third function, whether as represented by the Aśvins, the *Vanir*, the Sabines, or Haurvatāt and Ameretāt, serves as something of a residual category, including such widely separated phenomena as agriculture, "number," wealth, health, fertility, luxury, the earth, and immortality. Dumézil, of course, makes a good case for the logical relationship among these phenomena; and he finds the same general set in each of his principal I-E communities, collectively represented by parallel sets of deities. In general, I find myself positively disposed to his tripartite interpretation of I-E myth, which necessarily includes the third function; nevertheless, I do feel that the latter is one of the weakest links in his theoretical chain, a link that, unfortunately, he has yet to strengthen appreciably.

In Dumézil's opinion, if Plato was profoundly affected by his I-E heritage in the formulation of his political philosophy, then Zoroaster was even more indebted to this heritage in the formulation of his theology, more so than has heretofore been suspected. But some problems remain. Despite the Iranian religious reformer's apparent desire to eliminate the ancient gods of his people, some of them were too deeply embedded in the Iranian consciousness to suffer such a fate for very long, if at all. This was especially true of Mithra, whose cult seems to have flourished continually, not only in Iran itself, but throughout the Roman world until the rise of Christianity and Islam finally put an end to it.[19] Mithra, cognate of the Vedic Mitra, and seemingly the precursor and model for Vohu Manah, is indeed conspicuous by his absence in the *Yasnas*; but in the later *Avesta*, in the *Yašts* (cf. especially *Yt.* 9, the so-called Mithra *Yašt*), this god makes a spectacular return to official favor. He assumes a position second only to Ahura Mazdah himself in the struggle against the forces of Darkness (cf. Zaehner, 1961). But the problem here is that this resurrected Mithra does not fit the model of a first-function deity, let alone one concerned with the Mitra aspect of sovereignty. On the contrary, the picture of Mithra presented in the *Avesta*, in graphic art, and in popular tradition is that of a virile young warrior, an animal slayer, the very personification of physical prowess and vigor. In short, he manifests most of the traits associated by Dumézil and his colleagues with second-function figures. It is, of course, possible that a transformation occurred sometime after the composition of the *Gāthās* but before that of the Mithra *Yašt*; but the evidence, meager as it is, seems to indicate that Mithra possessed second-function characteristics long before the appearance of Zoroaster and his temporary disfavor. If this is true, it is quite possible, even probable, that Mithra, despite his onomastic correspondence to Mitra, was *not* the model upon which the concept of Vohu Manah was based. Just who this model might have been is a moot question. It should also be noted, perhaps, that Anāhitā, too, seems to have survived the Zoroastrian reforms; but here there is no contradiction. Both Anāhitā and Armāiti seem to have represented the same set of phenomena and to have been endowed with the same general traits.

The fourth volume of *JMQ*, entitled *Explication de textes indiens et latins* (1948a), further expands Dumézil's thesis, especially as it concerns Rome and the Indo-Iranian area. For example, certain ramifications, both social and supernatural, of the number 33 are

---

[19] Cf. Cumont's (1956; first published in 1908) classic study of the Mithraic cult, both inside and outside Iran; see also Zaehner (1961).

discussed at some length (pp. 156–170). In the *Rig Veda*, Dumézil points out, the whole of Aryan society is mirrored in a divine society composed of three groups of ten gods each plus three additional gods. With these thirty-three Vedic entities may be compared the thirty-three *ratu* ('protective spirits') of the *Avesta* and the thirty-three "figurants" of the Roman *comitia curiata*. Again in the latter example are seen three groups of ten, each of which represents one of the three original Roman "tribes" (i.e., *Ramnes, Luceres,* and *Titienses*), and the *comitia* is completed by three augurs. Thus, another I-E theme emerges: the organization of gods, councils, and the like into three groups of ten plus three additional figures. The three groups, of course, represent the three basic functions and the additional three recapitulate them. This is another example of the I-E penchant for elaborating and multiplying tripartite formulas and is further proof that tripartition, expressed in a wide variety of ways, was indeed deeply embedded in the ideology that accompanied the spread of the I-E languages.

More importantly, however, Volume IV of *JMQ* reflects a number of important ideas developed, not only by Dumézil in his previous works (including the three volumes of *Les mythes romains*), but also by the increasing number of students and disciples who, after 1945, rallied to the Dumézilian cause and have contributed much to the later elaboration and refinement of the tripartite theory (see chap. 5). These include Lucien Gerschel and especially the brilliant Stig Wikander, whose demonstration (1947) that the heroes of the *Mahābhārata* are transposed Vedic gods was translated into French and incorporated in Volume IV of *JMQ*.

Les mythes romains

The first volume of Dumézil's series *Les mythes romains* (*MR*) appeared in 1942. Entitled *Horace et les Curiaces*, it is concerned with a tripartite interpretation of the celebrated combat between the Horatii and the Curiatii, as reported by Livy (1.24) and Dionysius of Halicarnassus (3.15). In the reign of the warlike Tullus Hostilius, it was agreed that a dispute between Rome and Alba would be settled by a combat between champions. Each side chose its most renowned warriors; and, as it turned out, each was represented by a set of triplets, Rome by the three Horatii and Alba by the three Curiatii. After a prolonged and furious battle, all the Curiatii were killed and only one of the Horatii remained alive;

but one was enough and Rome emerged victorious. Upon returning to the city in triumph, the surviving Horatius was met by his sister, who had been betrothed to one of the Curiatii. Seeing the victor wearing a garment she had made for her Alban loved one, she bemoaned his death, and Horatius slew his sister on the spot for her lack of patriotism. Later, after being tried and convicted of murder, he appealed to the people and was acquitted; but he had to undergo a ritual purification to remove the taint of homicide, of having killed his *soror*, a blasphemous act no matter how "just" the motive.

To Dumézil, there are several important I-E themes here. First of all, of course, there is the notion of triplicity. The three Albans and the three Romans represented the totality of their two societies. Thus, the three Alban representatives all had to be slain before Rome could exercise sovereignty over her Latin neighbor. But even more important, Dumézil asserts, is the frenzy that gripped Horatius and enabled him to slay three terrible adversaries (after his brothers were killed, Horatius himself had to kill all three Curiatii) and later prompted him to murder his sister in the name of patriotism. This *furor*, as the Romans termed it, may be compared with the Celtic notion of *ferg*, the Germanic concept of *wut*, and the Greek idea of *ménos*; all these terms refer to the exalted state—the heightened prowess and the blind fury—which comes over the warrior and enables him to perform otherwise impossible feats. This "exaltation frénétique" is indeed seen as proper to representatives of all three functions and appears as the divine inspiration and ecstatic state exhibited by priests when performing the most sacred ceremonies and as the exhilaration felt by the cultivator in agricultural festivals, but its military (i.e., second-function) manifestation is by far the most striking. Here, indeed, one can evoke a vision of the primeval I-E warrior bands, erupting out of the steppes and attacking their opponents with an "exaltation frénétique" that caused even the well-organized and numerically superior forces of Mesopotamia and the Indus Valley to flee in panic. Some hint of this exalted state, undoubtedly much exaggerated, has perhaps been preserved in the Vedic accounts of the reckless bravery of Indra and his *Maruts*.[20] That this warlike frenzy is uniquely I-E, however, is open to some question. Indeed, a host of non-I-E parallels

---

[20] Cf. *Rig Veda* 1.53, in which Indra "with sixty thousand nine and ninety followers . . . hast overthrown the twice ten kings of men" and "goest on from fight to fight intrepidly" (quoted by Piggott, 1950, p. 261).

79

come to mind: for example, the ferocity of the Cheyenne "dog soldiers," the blind fury of the Turkish Janissaries, and the Japanese *banzai* charges during World War II. Yet it does seem clear that most of the early I-E societies manifested this trait, one that must be taken into account along with the battle chariot and the horse in any attempt to explain their widespread military successes.

Later on, as Rome developed into a major power, the idea of *furor* was played down, for it interfered with the discipline necessary to the successful functioning of the legions; single combat was superseded by a disciplined attack by massed infantry. Among the Germans and Celts, however, the emphasis upon single combat did not diminish and this aspect of their I-E inheritance remained important. Indeed, Dumézil sees many parallels between the episode of the Horatii and the traditions relating to the great Irish hero, Cuchulainn, who, like Horatius, displays a superhuman ferocity in battle, especially against the forces of Queen Medb (cf. the *Tain Bó Cualnge*).

In the ritual purification undergone by Horatius—he was commanded to veil his head and pass under a beam—Dumézil sees a "récit explicatif et justificatif d'un rituel d'initiation guerrière," a ritual that, though absent in historic Roman times, nevertheless seems to have been present in the earliest days of the city and to be I-E in origin. The basic function of the ritual seems to have been to divest the warrior of his *furor* after he has exhibited it in battle.

Perhaps it should be noted here that in 1956 Dumézil was able to add another important parallel to the Horatii story: the Vedic accounts of Trita Āptya's slaying of the three-headed monster who menaced the security and dominion of Varuna and the other gods. After killing the creature, Trita, like his Roman heroic counterpart, had to undergo a ritual purification; for, as a divine being, the monster was Trita's kinsman, and hence the slaying, despite the fact that it benefited the divine community as a whole, had to be expiated.

The second volume of *Les mythes romains*, entitled *Servius et la Fortune: Essai sur la fonction sociale de louange et de blâme et sur les éléments indo-européens du cens romain* (1943a), is concerned primarily with the career of Servius Tullius, sixth king of Rome. Born of a miraculous union between a slave woman of the previous king and a divine male organ of reproduction which suddenly appeared one day in a palace hearth fire, Servius was no ordinary child. As a young man he came to enjoy the special help and protection of the goddess, Fortuna, and eventually succeeded to the throne in place of the legitimate heir. His crowning achievement was the establishment of the *census*, or classification of the Roman people according to their social, political, and military roles. Basically identified with the people as a whole, and with a goddess who was concerned with "toute promotion humaine," he became a popular figure; as Bloch (1946, p. 36) puts it in a commentary on Dumézil's work, "Servius ne devient le premier *Censor* que parce que le premier il a été *census* par la louange universelle."

To Dumézil, Servius is an approximation of the ideal I-E king: he is generous and is rewarded with the almost universal praise of his subjects; he presides (in a Mitra-like fashion) over the societal allocation of roles and manages to maintain an identification with the society as a whole. In maintaining this identification, he is greatly aided by his close association with the principle that the Romans labeled *fortuna*, and personified as a goddess. Here it can be seen that the Romans believed in a dynamic force that gives direction to all human activities, a belief that is by no means exclusively I-E. That the Roman figure in question was a mythic rather than a historic one seems clear; that he represented certain social and moral realities present in later Roman culture also seems clear. But whether Servius is indeed an I-E figure is, in my opinion, less clear. The comparative evidence adduced by Dumézil (e.g., the Celtic *Lug*) is not convincing; it should be mentioned that, in his more recent works, Dumézil has had little occasion to refer to this "Servius theme" (cf. Dumézil, 1952*b*, 1958*a*).

Of much more importance in the evolution of Dumézil's system is the third volume of *Les mythes romains*, entitled *Tarpeia: Cinq essais de philologie comparative indo-européenne* (1947*b*). Of these five essays, the first, "De Janus à Vesta," is, in my opinion, the most significant, for a new idea is introduced: that there are certain deities who are outside any one level of the tripartite system and who serve as "dieux premiers" and "dieux derniers," gods who form the "épine" or backbone of the system. In India, he points out, the double-faceted Vāyu[21] is regularly invoked at the

---

[21] I say "double-faceted" here because Vāyu does not seem to have possessed two heads as did Janus, his Roman counterpart; the double nature of the Vedic god is, however, clearly attested (see Wikander, 1947).

81

beginning of a ritual, prior to the invocation of Mitra and Varuna. Similarly, at Rome double-visaged Janus serves as the introducer, the god of "beginnings," who regularly precedes all others in ritual invocations. At the conclusion of a ritual, another set of deities, usually (but not always) associated with fire, are invoked: in India, the god Agni; at Rome, the goddess Vesta.

In Iran, as a result of the Zoroastrian reforms, the inherited Indo-Iranian double-faceted "dieu premier" was transformed into two new entities, the two *Mainyu*, or 'Spirits.' Subordinate to Ahura Mazdah, but preceding in importance the *Ameša Spentas*, Spenta Mainyu and Angra Mainyu, the embodiments, respectively, of good and evil, serve the same function as Vāyu and Janus. They are the spirit beings who are concerned with the beginnings of all things, good as well as bad; in ritual, they are regularly invoked before the *Ameša Spentas*. As far as the "dieu dernier" is concerned, the Zoroastrian situation is ambiguous. In *Tarpeia*, Dumézil points out that the ancient Iranian goddess, Anāhitā, probably served a function analogous to that served by Vesta at Rome. Indeed, her Indian counterpart, Sarasvatī, also seems to have functioned as a "déesse dernière" along with Agni; but the problem here is that both the Iranian and the Indic goddesses were, at the same time, clearly third-function figures—indeed, Vesta herself may be so considered—and the Zoroastrian version of Anāhitā, Armāiti, was heir to the same ambiguity. Thus it appears that the "dieux premiers" are more clearly attested than the "dieux derniers," for the latter, more often than not (Agni is an exception), exhibit characteristics that could cause them to be classified as third-function deities equally as well.

Yet there is also a problem when it comes to the more clear-cut Janus-Vāyu category. If these gods belong to an I-E class of beings concerned with first causes, beginnings, and the like, then what is the relationship between this class and the sovereign deities who represent the first function? At Rome, Dumézil sees traces of what may well have been a Proto-I-E rivalry between the prototypes of Janus and Jupiter (plus Dius Fidius). The latter, perhaps as the concept of kingship developed among the Proto-Indo-Europeans, gained supernatural sovereignty; but the former managed to maintain his position at the head of the canonical list of deities and to be associated with the commencement of all things. (Once begun, their management was left to the first-function figures.) At Rome, for example, it is Janus who is invoked at the start of a war, but it is Jupiter who sees that the city's sovereignty remains inviolate and who, with Mars, watches over the conduct of the war. Although Dumézil himself does not suggest it, the foregoing could conceivably mean that the "dieux premiers" derive from an older, perhaps primeval I-E stratum of gods, dating from a time prior to the crystallization of the characteristic I-E social organization—which must necessarily have occurred some time before the final breakup of the community in the second half of the third millennium B.C.—and the concomitant development of the tripartite ideology and pantheon. But if the characteristic gods of the three functions have been an integral part of I-E religion since its inception, then the possibility that the "dieux premiers" form simply a residual category of otherwise unclassifiable beings (in terms of Dumézil's scheme) becomes much more likely.

The other essays in *Tarpeia*, while important to the extent that they clarify and elaborate Dumézil's hypothesis regarding the I-E origin of early Roman "history" (e.g., the fifth essay, in which the Sabine War and the parallels it presents to the Scandinavian war between the *Aesir* and *Vanir* is discussed in much detail), are less original than the one just discussed and do not, in my opinion, materially affect the evolution of his system. The remainder of this chapter is devoted to a brief discussion of four other major works that Dumézil published in 1948–1949 and to a review of some of the more representative articles that appeared from 1941 to the end of the developmental phase (1949).

THE SECOND EDITION OF *Mitra-Varuna* AND *Loki*
(1948)

In 1948, eight years after *Mitra-Varuna* first appeared, Dumézil brought out a second edition of it (1948b). Thoroughly revised and updated, the new edition includes the vast amount of new materials, Roman and other, which he had gathered relative to the sovereign gods of the first function; in it he is able to discuss definitively some ideas that were mere suggestions or tentative hypotheses in 1940, and to reject others that did not hold up as his research progressed. In the latter category is the equation proposed earlier (1934) between Ouranos and Varuna. This equation, it will be remembered, was based primarily upon the assumption that both gods were "binders," that they achieved their ends by magically "binding" their opponents with spells, and that their names derive from a common I-E root meaning 'to bind'; it should also be remembered that this hypothesis was developed some years before the I-E concept of sovereignty was recognized. Realizing the inadequacy of both the linguistic[22] and the mythological evidence, Dumézil here firmly rejects the "binding hypothesis." Moreover, it is now apparent that the two gods in question occupy very different positions in their respective religious systems. At no point in the development of Greek religious thought does Ouranos appear to have played a role similar to that played by Varuna in Vedic religion. The latter is one of a pair of joint sovereigns, sharing dominion in perpetuity over the natural and supernatural universe; the former, on the contrary, enjoys only a brief period of solitary sovereignty—mainly because he is an autochthonous being—which is ended suddenly and absolutely by his son Kronos. Ouranos is deposed before the mortal and celestial status quo is achieved; Varuna is concerned with the maintenance of such a status quo. In short, in order for Ouranos to be equated with Varuna, it would have to be demonstrated that the former was a representative of the magico-religious aspect of sovereignty and equatable, not only with Varuna, but also with Jupiter, Othinn, Aša, and the like. This, Dumézil asserts, is clearly not demonstrable.

It is, of course, remotely possible that Ouranos is indeed an I-E figure, though in quite a different (but perhaps related) context. The well-known succession of Ouranos, Kronos, and Zeus is paralleled in Iranian epic (the *Shāhnāmeh*) by the succession of Jamshid, Zohak, and Feridun, and in the *Avesta* by the figures of Yima, Aži Dahāka, and Thraetauna (cf. Wikander, 1952b); it also parallels the Hurro-Hittite sequence of Anu, Kumarbi, and Tešub (Güterbock, 1948), and possibly the Norse sequence of Ymir, Börr, and Othinn (Littleton, 1966). In all instances, three generations of ruling gods are successively overthrown by their offspring or close kin (who, in the process, usually resort to castration or mutilation), the third generation (i.e., that of Zeus, Feridun, and Thraetauna) establishing the supernatural status quo, usually after a fight with a monster of some sort created by the recently deposed second gen-

---

[22] I.e., the form *Uorueno-.

eration (cf. the Greek Typhon, the Hittite Ullikummi). As this so-called kingship-in-heaven theme also turns up in at least two Semitic-speaking societies (Phoenician and Babylonian) as well as among the Hurrians, there has been some question as to whether it is indeed I-E. Güterbock (1948), among others, has cogently argued for a Mesopotamian origin; Wikander (1952b), one of Dumézil's most influential disciples, has been the chief spokesman for those who feel that the theme is I-E, despite its apparent absence in Indic and Celtic tradition.[23] As far as Dumézil's thesis is concerned, if the theme is I-E, it would have to be related to the evolution of the first function, the idea of sovereignty. Ouranos may thus represent the first step in this evolution; and this brings to mind a suggestion Dumézil made earlier: Is it possible that Ouranos, too, is derived from the class of "dieux premiers," and that he perhaps bears witness to an earlier stage in the development of I-E religion? Although Ouranos presents few specific parallels to Janus and Vāyu, either in myth or ritual, he is the "beginning" of things in Greek myth. Perhaps, if more were known of Vedic (cf. Brown, 1942) and Roman cosmogony, it might be possible to say that Vāyu and Janus are to Varuna and Jupiter as Ouranos is to Zeus; but this is pure speculation. As far as Dumézil is concerned, Ouranos can be fitted neither into the tripartite scheme itself nor into the "épine" that supposedly supports it.

One of the ideas suggested in the 1940 edition of *Mitra-Varuna* and developed in some detail in the second edition concerns the extent to which the two sovereign representatives of the first function suffered from characteristic disabilities: the absence of an eye and a hand, respectively. This theory of the "dieu borgne" and the "dieu manchot" is, in large part, based upon an assumed correspondence between the Norse deities, Othinn and Týr, and the two famous Roman heroes, Horatius Cocles and Mucius Scaevola. Othinn, it appears, was blind in one eye; Týr, who represents the Mitra half of the sovereignty, lacked an arm. Indeed, in the *Völuspa* and elsewhere in the *Elder Edda*, to say nothing of Snorri's *Edda*, one finds frequent references to the chief Norse god as "one-eyed," and the term is often used in the epithets of Othinn so frequently encountered in ancient Scandinavian literature. Horatius and Mucius,

---

[23] In my opinion, Wikander has failed to establish his case for an I-E origin here. Güterbock's argument is bolstered by the patent antiquity of the Mesopotamian versions, the extant forms of which may have been composed as early as 2000 B.C. See also Littleton (in press).

who in the early days of the Roman republic saved the city (i.e., preserved its sovereignty) from the Etruscan, Lars Porsenna, also shared the same disabilities. Horatius, the "Cyclops," was blind in one eye, yet managed to hold off single-handedly the entire Etruscan army; Mucius, assigned the task of killing Porsenna, failed in the attempt, was captured, and in a grand gesture of defiance thrust his right hand into an altar fire, holding it there until it was consumed (whence the name Scaevola, or 'Left-Handed') and impressing his captors to such an extent that they sought peace.

Despite the vast differences between the Roman and Germanic figures in question—indeed, the only common denominators seem to be the absence of an eye and a hand and a concern for the maintenance of sovereignty—and despite the lack of comparative evidence, especially from the Indo-Iranian area, Dumézil feels that a strong case can be made for an I-E theme here (however, see Dumézil, 1959c). The essence of his interpretation of this theme is that it emphasizes the joint nature of interdependence of the two basic aspects of sovereignty, that one cannot function properly without the aid of the other. Thus the figures who represent these two aspects are each limited to some extent and can fulfill their assigned roles in the supernatural scheme of things only by working as a team; only by so doing will they possess the physical equipment deemed normal for men and gods.

The theory of the "dieu borgne" and the "dieu manchot" has come in for much criticism, and rightly so, in my opinion, especially given the nature of the correspondence upon which it is anchored. Granting the Roman tendency toward historicizing myth, the connection between Horatius Cocles and Othinn the One-eyed nevertheless seems remote; if Jupiter and Dius Fidius, or even Romulus and Numa, exhibited these characteristics, or if there were some evidence that Varuna and Mitra or their Iranian counterparts were so afflicted, the theory would be more convincing. The Germanic example is clear enough, but the others, including the Celtic ones that Dumézil and his colleagues have cited, are less so. It is, of course, quite probable that the episode of Horatius and Mucius is mythical rather than historical, given the massive body of evidence Dumézil has gathered to prove the nonhistorical character of early Roman "history" in general; and it is conceivable that, in the making of this myth (or legend, perhaps), some inherited I-E elements were utilized. Indeed, Gerschel (1952) has pointed out quite convincingly that later Roman savants interpreted the objectively historical relationship between their city and Carthage in terms of the tripartite I-E ideology to which they were heir. But *is* the theme of the "dieu borgne" and the "dieu manchot" an I-E element? Or is it merely a coincidental parallel between two otherwise quite different phenomena? In sum, the question posed earlier as to whether the data—in this instance, the Roman data—have been overinterpreted should be posed again; and here, the answer would seem, perhaps, to be yes.

Despite shortcomings of the sort just discussed—shortcomings that inevitably seem to accompany the elaboration of a thesis such as that advanced by Dumézil—the second edition of *Mitra-Varuna*, when compared with the first, shows a much greater sophistication in "la méthode sociologique." Here, perhaps more than in any preceding work, is crystallized the characteristic and, in many ways, unique Dumézilian methodology: a synthesis of the traditional comparative method and that of social anthropology; a blend of philological, historical, and functional analysis. Moreover, the mass of I-E facts and interpretations that Dumézil had been collecting and making in the preceding decade had, by this time, led him firmly to the conclusion that tripartition, the joint sovereignty, and the like were all theological manifestations of an underlying ideology, itself derived in large measure from the nature of Proto-I-E social organization. Mitra, Varuna, and their other I-E counterparts are here clearly seen as collective representations, as genetically related ones, which, like the languages spoken by those who shared them, had undergone separate but parallel development after the breakup of the parent society. This idea, of course, has some important theoretical ramifications, not only for students of I-E matters, but also for all those concerned with the relationship between language and culture per se. The idea that ideologies and the representations thereof are subject to the same general set of processes—other things being equal—as languages, that they exhibit regularities analogous to those exhibited by linguistic forms after the breakup of a speech community, may prove to be Dumézil's most important single contribution to the social sciences, and is discussed more fully in chapter 7.

In *Loki* (1948c), Dumézil turned his attention once again (cf. Dumézil, 1939b) to Germanic myth, especially to those aspects of

87

it which relate to the great trickster figure whose name the book bears as a title. Drawing upon the *Lokasenna* and other Eddic accounts of "le pernicieux Loki," Dumézil concludes that the god in question bears a resemblance to the Iranian Angra Mainyu ('Evil Spirit'), as well as to the Ossetic trickster figure, Syrdon. Subordinate to Othinn and Týr, Loki resents his inferior position among the dwellers in Asgard much as Angra Mainyu resents the supremacy of Ahura Mazdah and the presence of Spenta Mainyu, and as Syrdon resents his subordinate position among the *Nartes*. He is the enemy of all that is good and noble; he plots against his fellow gods, attempting to exploit their jealousies, and is responsible for the death of Baldr. Dumézil analyzes Loki's treacherous role in Norse eschatology and finds again a number of interesting, if not always conclusive, parallels in ancient Iranian myth and modern Ossetic folklore; he may, perhaps, be compared with the Roman Tarpeia, who betrayed her native city in the Sabine War. Yet in many ways, despite his treacherousness and guile, Loki emerges as a sympathetic figure, one with whom the "little man"—the lowly cultivator or herdsman, perhaps—was undoubtedly able to identify in his resentment of authority and the inevitably dull status quo.

As trickster figures, Loki, Syrdon, and the like are, of course, far from unique; in more than one way, they are reminiscent of the Babylonian Enki—to say nothing of "Coyote" among numerous American Indian groups and of Maui in Polynesia— and it would be difficult to prove that they are specifically I-E in origin. Yet the sort of binary opposition in which Loki and Syrdon so often find themselves forms the basic theme of Zoroastrianism, which, as Dumézil has shown, is a product of the I-E heritage in so many ways. Moreover, dualism of a less negative kind forms a counterpoint to tripartition in many areas of I-E ideology: the "dieu premier" and the "dieu dernier," the two representatives of the first function (and their two chief lieutenants), and the two figures (e.g., the Aśvins, Quirinus and Ops) who represent the third function all reflect this seemingly I-E tendency to superimpose a dual division upon a tripartite one (or vice versa?). Thus, the opposition between Loki and Heimdallr (or even Baldr, for that matter) has a flavor that is generally I-E.

In the evolution of Dumézil's overall thesis, *Loki* is not of great importance, save perhaps as a review of the general outlines of Germanic myth and the parallels it presents to other I-E mythologies, especially that of the modern Ossetes. Yet even Dumézil's critics are forced to admit that this book is one of the best sociologically oriented studies of this difficult and enigmatic Norse figure (cf. Liljeblad, 1963, p. 144); and for this reason, perhaps, it has remained one of Dumézil's favorite works.[24]

THE SUMMATION OF DUMÉZIL'S ROMAN STUDIES AND *Le troisième souverain* (1949)

The year 1949 saw the publication of two books that, in my opinion, mark the culmination of Dumézil's developmental phase. The first, *L'héritage indo-européen à Rome: Introduction aux séries "Jupiter Mars Quirinus" et "Les mythes romains"* (1949a), is a summation of his Roman studies and, as the subtitle clearly indicates, is intended as an introduction to the two series previously discussed. Here, the early Roman kingship, the three archaic tribes, the Sabine War, the Horatii and their adversaries, the relationship between *Flāmen* and *Brahman*, the nature of the pre-Capitoline triad (both at Rome and at Iguvium), Horatius Cocles and Mucius Scaevola, and so on, all are reviewed systematically, and their parallels with Indic, Iranian, Germanic, and Celtic mythical events and persons are duly noted. Moreover, the book takes account of many of the criticisms that had appeared by 1949, especially those of primitivists such as Wagenvoort (1947) and Rose (1947), who have sought to explain early Roman religion in terms of the concepts of mana and naturism à la Frazer and Mannhardt, to say nothing of Harrison and Cornford. Dumézil here repeatedly hammers home his thesis that early Roman "history" is euhemerized I-E myth and that neither this myth nor the theology and ideology it embodies can be understood without reference to the rest of the ancient I-E-speaking world, without reference to such phenomena as the Norse war between the *Aesir* and the *Vanir*, the Indic *Brahman*, and the Iranian *Mainyu*. Early Roman religion cannot be studied in isolation, and the concepts of mana and naturism are not sufficient as explanatory devices.

As in the second edition of *Mitra-Varuna*, the notion of an I-E ideology (as opposed to a mere body of related myths) is clearly evident; and the Roman "héritage indo-européen" is treated as an

---

[24] So Professor Puhvel informs me.

ideological one, manifest in social organization, theology, and legend. It is perhaps ironic that, by 1949, Dumézil was strongly opposing the sort of Frazerian-Mannhardtian explanations he himself had preferred in the twenties; the gap between *Le festin* and *L'héritage* is indeed a wide one!

The second work that appeared in 1949, *Le troisième souverain: Essai sur le dieu indo-iranien Aryaman et sur la formation de l'histoire mythique de l'Irlande* (1949*b*), is more important for the evolution of the system, despite the fact that it has been the object of much criticism, especially from Thieme (see pp. 177–179, below). Here Dumézil delineates yet another class of I-E deities, "les dieux souverains mineurs," of whom the Vedic figures, Aryaman and Bhaga, are prototypical.

In the *Rig Veda*, it is clear that the two sovereign deities, Mitra and Varuna, do not stand alone. In the last analysis they are but the most frequently mentioned and, by all odds, the most powerful members of a family referred to as the Ādityas, or sons of the goddess Aditi ('The Free'). Prominent among the less powerful Ādityas are the figures, Aryaman and Bhaga, both of whom appear as subordinate to Mitra and as representations of certain aspects of the latter's sovereign domain. Aryaman ("Airyaman" in the *Avesta*) is the patron of the community that designates itself as that of the *Arya*, or 'people,' as opposed to that of the non-*Arya*, or barbarians, and as such is concerned with "les principales formes de rapports naturels ou contractuels entre Arya." He is the patron of hospitality and of the formal relationships that necessarily accompany it (especially the giving and receiving of gifts), and is very much concerned with marriage in its contractual aspects. In short, Aryaman is the immediate collective representation of the *Arya* themselves; he is the immediate link between this community and the Mitra (or juridical) aspect of sovereignty. Bhaga (cf. Slavonic *bog*, 'god') occupies a somewhat different position here; his principal role is to see that all men receive their proper "share" (cf. *Rig Veda* 7.41.2), that they receive their just proportion of the goods the society has to offer. As the agent of Mitra's benificence, Bhaga is concerned with the distributive aspects of his master's sovereign domain. Between them, Aryaman, as the collective representation of the *Arya* and the patron of their social relations, and Bhaga, as

90

the patron of just distribution, serve as the chief assistants of Mitra and are, therefore, first-function figures.

Although Varuna, for the most part, "restait solitaire dans ses lointains," he also has some celestial assistants, who are counterparts of those of Mitra. Dakṣa, the Varunian counterpart of Aryaman, is the representation of "l'énergie propre du sacrifice" and, as such, is concerned principally with the maintenance of correct ritual relations between the community and the divine; he is, in a very real sense, the personification of the *Brahman*.[25] Amśa, counterpart of Bhaga, is also concerned with matters of distribution, but his concern is with the distribution of the fate divinely determined (i.e., by Varuna) for each individual (cf. *Rig Veda* 10.31.3; *Atharva Veda* 21.1.5 and 11). These two Varunian beings, though probably later in conception than those associated with Mitra, complete the first function as defined in ancient India: on the one hand, the beings associated with the maintenance of juridical and moral relationships between members of the human community and who oversee the just distribution of goods and services (Mitra, plus Aryaman and Bhaga), and on the other, the beings associated with the maintenance of the supernatural scheme of things, with correct ritual relationships between the human and divine communities, and with the distribution of individual fates (Varuna, plus Dakṣa and Amśa).

Irish myth presents some interesting parallels, especially between Aryaman and Mac Óc, or 'Young son' (cf. Dumézil, 1938*b*). Like the chief associate of Mitra, Mac Óc is concerned with the protection of the community, with the maintenance of the vital force necessary for it to persist as a community; though less clearly associated with contracts, hospitality, and marriage, this Irish figure nevertheless presents many broad similarities to the Vedic "souverain mineur" and, in Dumézil's opinion, is a representative of the same class. At Rome, some even more definitive parallels to the two companions of Mitra can be seen. Earlier, I mentioned the legend that tells of the refusal of Iuventas and Terminus to be evicted from the Capitol when Tarquinus Superbus built a shrine

---

[25] In the single *Rig Veda* myth concerned with Dakṣa (10.72.3-5), he appears as the father-in-law of the gods, as the father of Aditi and thus the ancestor of Mitra, Varuna, etc.; indeed, he appears here as the prototype of the father-in-law.

there to Jupiter. The reason that these two were not evicted, Dumézil asserts, is that they represented the same two aspects of sovereignty as Aryaman and Bhaga: on the one hand, Iuventas was concerned with the maintenance of the vitality of the Roman people, with the protection of the social relationships obtaining within that society, which, by definition, would include contractual and marital ones; Terminus, on the other hand, was concerned with the equitable distribution of goods and the like among the people (cf. Ovid's *Fasti*, 2.642). Thus, respectively, the counterparts of Mitra's two associates, Aryaman and Bhaga, are seen here. Terminus, indeed, was reputedly installed on the Capitol by Numa (cf. Plutarch's *Numa* 16), who is clearly a euhemerized Roman counterpart of Mitra; Iuventas, though here defined as female, is indeed the patroness of the *iuvenes* (i.e., the majority of the population; those falling between the categories of *puer* and *senex*) and, by extension, of the youth and vitality of the society. Thus Rome, like Ireland and India, had its "souverains mineurs,"—though the Varunian figures are absent in each instance, and this absence would seem to lend weight to the theory that the latter are uniquely Indic and not I-E in origin.

There are some interesting and very specific links between the Roman and Irish figures. As mentioned earlier, *Iuventas* and (Mac) Óc seem to be derived from the same I-E stem (**yuwen-*), and both relate to the idea of "vital force"; they also share a common mythical experience in that the latter, too, refused to leave a sanctuary, in this case that of the Dagda. Although Dumézil does not suggest it, it occurs to me that this specific correspondence between Iuventas and Mac Óc may bear witness, not to an I-E pattern, but rather to one that may have developed during a phase of Celtic and Italic proximity in Central Europe after the breakup of the parent I-E community.

Among the Germanic speakers, Dumézil once again sees evidence of the "dieux souverains mineurs" in the two brothers of Othinn, Vili and Ve. Despite the obscurity of the evidence relating to them (he draws largely upon the *Ynglingasaga* and the *Lokasenna*), Dumézil (1949*b*) is confident that Vili corresponds to Aryaman as the being who "assure la continuité sociale," and that Ve corresponds to Bhaga as the one who "repartit les biens"; however, I might add that in recent years he has lost much of this confidence and now (1959*a*) considers the evidence pertaining to these two shadowy figures too meager to support such a conclusion.

Finally, what of Iran? As might by this time be expected, Dumézil is able to see a set of Zoroastrian counterparts to the Vedic "souverains mineurs." As has been seen, in post-Gathic times Mithra made a triumphant reentry into the religious system; the same may be said for Airyaman and Baga (the latter name came to designate the gods in general; cf. the inscriptions of the Achaemenian kings at Behistun and elsewhere). As for Zoroaster himself, however, these inherited Indo-Iranian deities had to be replaced by more or less abstract personifications. If Vohu Manah was Mithra's replacement, who then replaced Airyaman and Baga in the mind of the author of the *Gāthās*? Although not in the strict sense *Ameša Spentas*, there are two Gathic entities who seem to constitute a possible answer to this question: Sraoša ('Discipline') and Aši ('Retribution'). Both are repeatedly associated with Vohu Manah, especially in the later Avestan texts such as the *Vidēvdāt* and in the Pahlavi literature (e.g., the *Bundahisn*). Moreover, in later times the connection between them and Mithra is clear (cf. *Dēnkart* 7.3, 17); and that Sraoša and Airyaman are linked is obvious even as early as *Yasna* 57.15–17.

In the moralistic climate of early Zoroastrianism, the inherited functions of these two beings are altered somewhat: as the personification of discipline, Sraoša presides over the Iranian community, ensuring that human social behavior will conform to the proper moral standards; Aši, as the personification of retribution, sees that each man receives his proper "share" in the hereafter rather than in "ce monde-ci." But the essential elements remain the same: (1) concern with the human community and the social relations therein, and (2) concern with the distribution of rewards.

This, then, is the theory of the "souverains mineurs," the 'minor sovereigns.' Unfortunately, the work in which it was initially presented, *Le troisième souverain*, contains, as Dumézil himself admits (1958*a*), many errors in citation, especially of pertinent Vedic and Avestan texts—his excuse is that he was unable to proof it adequately before it went to press—and these inaccuracies have added much fuel to the fires ignited by critics such as Thieme and Gershevitch. To be sure, Dumézil has had to reject what seemed to be a clear Germanic parallel, and no counterparts of the Varunian "souverains mineurs" have, as yet, come to light outside India. Yet the theory in question has indeed become an integral part of his

93

Evolution of the System

system; it has been reviewed and expanded several times since it first appeared (notably in 1952 and 1958), and the errors that crept into the 1949 monograph have long since been corrected.

SOME ARTICLES, 1941–1949

To round out this survey of the developmental phase, it is necessary to survey very briefly some of the more significant articles published by Dumézil between 1941 and 1949. In "L'étude comparée des religions indo-européennes" (1941b), which appeared in *La Nouvelle Revue Française* (*NRF*), Dumézil sketches for a general audience the background of I-E religious and mythological studies and introduces some of his then quite recent discoveries (i.e., those relating to the function of sovereignty). The year 1941 also saw the opening round (Dumézil's "Le nom des 'Arya'") in the still ongoing debate with Thieme over the meaning of the Sanskrit word *ari*, a debate that is discussed in some detail later on (see pp. 176–177).

In 1943, three articles appeared which are worthy of mention here. The first, also appearing in *NRF*, is entitled "O fortunatos nimium . . ." (1943b); in it Dumézil ties in his trifunctional interpretation of Propertius' elegy, *De urbe Roma*, with Virgil's eulogy of rural life at the end of Book II of the *Georgics*. Dumézil sees in "Sabini . . . Remus et frater . . . fortis Etruria" (532–533) the three components of "rerum . . . pulcherrima Roma" (534), corresponding, respectively, to the *Titienses, Ramnes,* and *Luceres.* (It will be remembered that Lucumon, founder of the *Luceres,* was an Etruscan warrior.) Thus it appears that Virgil was also heir to the tripartite I-E ideology. The second article, "Les débuts de la religion romaine" (1943c), is a review of, and brief commentary upon, recent scholarly approaches to the study of Roman religious origins. Dumézil devotes most of his space here to a critique of the "intuitional" method of Altheim and the archeological approach of Piganiol (especially 1939) and to his own comparative work; he also includes a basic (and still useful) bibliography of research on Roman religion as of 1943. In the third 1943 article in question, "Légendes sur les Nartes" (1943d), published in the *Revue de l'Histoire des Religions* (*RHR*), Dumézil turns once again to what is perhaps his favorite single body of myth, that of the Ossetes and their neighbors in the northern Caucasus. He includes a collection of texts gathered after 1930, and, in closing, quotes two remarks (one by Trubetzkoy, the other by Deeters) concerning the extent to which the Caucasian festival of Merem contains elements that relate to the *Nartes* and other Caucasian figures.

In 1946 Dumézil published in the *RHR* what amounts to a catalogue of trifunctional odds and ends. Entitled " 'Tripertita' fonctionnels chez divers peuples indo-européens" (1946*a*), the article is a good illustration of the extent to which Dumézil searches for examples of tripartition and of his broad familiarity with the literature. It begins with a comment on Benveniste's (1945*b*) discussion of social symbolism in Greco-Italic cults, then cites Basanoff's (cf. 1947) discussion of white, red, and blue color symbolism in a Hittite ritual. These colors are viewed by Dumézil as symbolic of the three functions: white for the first, red for the second, and blue or green for the third. In the same context, Dumézil comments favorably upon de Vries' "Rood, Wit, Zwart" (1942). Finally, he cites two Scandinavian examples: (1) a passage from the Icelandic *Grettissaga Asmundarsonar* (72), in which the free landholders (*godi*), the warriors, and the rest of the people are distinguished, and (2) the runic stone from Sparlösa (Sweden), which contains an inscription detailing 'good harvest' (*ār*), 'victorious renown' (*sigmaerr*), and 'runic knowledge' (*runar thar raginukundu*) as three characteristics of the royal person, Alrik.

Another article published in 1946, "Les 'énarées' scythiques et la grossesse du Narte Hamyc" (1946*b*), is concerned with the comparison of Ossetic and Scythian traditions, a subject that is close to Dumézil's heart (cf. 1930*a*). Here, he compares the accounts of Herodotus (1.105, 4.67) and other Greek observers of androgyny among the Scythian nobles with the Ossetic legend of the hero, Hamyc. The latter came to the sea-god, Don Battyr, and married his daughter, who always had to be protected from the heat of the day by a turtle shell. The trickster Syrdon (cf. Loki) deprived her of her shell, and thus she had to leave Hamyc forever (i.e., the "fairy bride" motif; cf. Psyche, etc.). But, before leaving, she magically transferred to Hamyc her pregnancy, which grew as an excrescence on his back until there was born a burning homunculus, Batradz. Hamyc's pregnancy was considered a disgraceful affliction, like the Scythian "female sickness"[26] which Herodotus attributed to an offense against Aphrodite Urania (who may, in-

---

[26] I.e., θήλεα νοῦσος.

deed, correspond to the daughter of Don Battyr in the Ossetic legend). Although this Ossetic-Scythian correspondence is marginal to Dumézil's central thesis, it nevertheless may reflect a western Indo-Iranian tradition of great antiquity. Linguistically and mythologically, the modern Ossetes are clearly linked with the Scyths of Herodotus' time and earlier.

Two articles published by Dumézil in 1947 deserve to be noted. One, "La triade 'Jupiter, Mars, Janus'?" (1947c), is a brief refutation of Basanoff's attempt (1947) to substitute, on the basis of a passage in Festus, Janus for Quirinus in Dumézil's canonical Roman triad of Jupiter, Mars, and Quirinus. The other, "Mitra-Varuna, Indra, les Nāsatya, comme patrons des trois fonctions cosmiques et sociales" (1947d), is an attempt to vindicate his interpretation of the Mitanni deities. Dumézil points out that his trifunctional grouping of the duties of these divinities is not fortuitous but rather is found throughout Vedic ritual, myth, and theology, and that the significance of these instances is that of a functionally interrelated hierarchy. To illustrate this second point, Dumézil explains and presents examples of his three working methods, and herein lies the importance of the article. These methods are, he claims: (1) the study of the character of a god viewed independently in his relation to the whole of Vedic religion; (2) the study of the significance of each god in the textual references to the trinity; and (3) the comparison with similar trifunctional constructs in other religions. He then undertakes an examination of material in *Rig Veda* 10.125 and *Atharva Veda* 4.30 which suggests a general classification of deities into Ādityas, Rudras, and Vasus, backing this up with additional Vedic citations and references to Roman analogues. He explains that his work is an attempt to discover the social skeleton of the Aryan religion in its original form, before the onset of the changes that resulted in its evolution into classical and modern Hinduism. Here, of course, these methods are delineated specifically in an Indo-Iranian context; but it is reasonable to assume that he applies them throughout his work, and indeed the article in question is perhaps the best single statement by Dumézil of his working methodology (cf. also 1958a, p. 91), as opposed to his overall framework of interpretation (i.e., "la méthode sociologique").

Finally, I should mention two articles that appeared in 1948: a contribution to the *Histoire générale des religions* in which

Dumézil attempted a general survey of "Religion et mythologie préhistorique des Indo-Européens" (1948*d*), presenting his own ideas as unchallenged truth, and, in the *Revue de l'Histoire des Religions*, a piece entitled "A propos de latin 'jus' " (1948*e*), in which various I-E terms and formulas related to the Latin term are discussed from a trifunctional point of view. For example, he points out that Avestan *yaož-dā-* (cognate to the Latin *iūs*) means 'to purify ritually,' referring in the *Vidēvdāt* especially to contamination from corpses (i.e., by the demoness Nasu). Interment is a pollution of the sacred earth (as cremation is of the holy fire), and the penalties alluded to (*Vidēvdāt* 3.38–39) are trifunctional: *cithā*, 'restitution, fine'; *āperetiš*, '(corporal) punishment'; and *yaoždāthrem*, '(ritual) purification.' Another example is found, he asserts, in the Vedic formula *śam yoh*, 'hail and weal,' which seems to relate to the third function, probably because healing and fertility (the antithesis of death) are so closely connected with the Nāsatyas (or Aśvins).

SUMMARY

In 1938 Dumézil came to the realization that tripartition was not merely an Indo-Iranian phenomenon (cf. 1930*b*) but was indeed a widespread and uniquely I-E trait manifesting itself in social organization, myth, and religion. In two brilliant series of works devoted to Roman origins (1941–1949), he was able to demonstrate conclusively that early Rome, like ancient Iran and India, knew this tripartite system, and that it was present among the ancient Germans and Celts as well. At the same time, other basic I-E characteristics emerged: the joint sovereignty (1940, 1948), the notion of "dieux premiers" and "dieux derniers" and the I-E concern with "beginnings" and "endings" (1947), and the "dieux mineurs souverains" (1949). Increasingly, these I-E patterns, so closely integrated and mutually sustaining, came to be viewed as elements of an overall I-E ideology; and in the course of his analysis Dumézil was able to show that, despite their originality, neither Plato (1941) nor Zoroaster (1944, 1947) was able to escape this ideology to which they were joint heirs as speakers of I-E languages.

Thus, systematically, in the eleven years between 1938 and 1949, the years I have labeled the "developmental phase," the essential elements of Dumézil's scheme for the interpretation of I-E

97

mythical, religious, and social data came to light. By 1949, this scheme was fairly well crystallized; the edifice that is Dumézilian comparative mythology was nearly complete. But there remained some important work to be done; some important interpretations (and reinterpretations) had yet to be made, both by Dumézil himself and by the increasing number of students and colleagues who, after the end of World War II, joined him in his research. The contributions of these students and colleagues are discussed in chapter 6; those of Dumézil are the subject of chapter 5, which is concerned with the "florescent" or final phase in the evolution of Dumézilian thought (from 1949 to the present).

5

The Florescent Phase:
1949 to the Present

In a very real sense, the final or "florescent" phase in the evolution of Dumézil's system can be said to have begun on Thursday, December 1, 1949, in a lecture hall of the Sorbonne. On that date Dumézil delivered his inaugural lecture as occupant of the Chair of Indo-European Civilization in the Collège de France, a position especially created for him. This was, indeed, the culmination of a distinguished career that had taken him to Turkey, to the Caucasus, to Scandinavia, to the École des Hautes Études as a director of studies, and now, finally, to the august ranks of the Collège de France. The significance of this December day lies not merely in the ceremony that signaled a change in Dumézil's academic status and recognized his stature as perhaps the foremost comparative mythologist of his time, but rather in the lecture itself, for in it Dumézil charted a course that he and his colleagues are still following.

Entitled simply "Civilisation indo-européenne" (it was subsequently published [1951a]), this lecture strives to convince its audience that the now familiar tripartite ideology characteristic of Indo-Iranian, Roman, and Scandinavian mythology is truly I-E in origin and not the result of borrowing, chance, or "la nécessité naturelle," as Dumézil puts it. This ideology, he asserts, is indeed the core of "la civilisation indo-européenne," and its presence to a greater or lesser extent in almost all ancient I-E societies can be explained most efficiently by reference to an "héritage commun." While the general outlines of this "héritage" are well known (i.e., as of 1949)

99

—thanks to the work of Dumézil and others with Indic, Iranian, Roman, and Germanic materials—there is much that remains to be done. Here Dumézil lays out a program, to be followed by him in the lecture hall and by those scholars who wish to work with him in pushing back the frontier of I-E studies: for example, much more analytic work needs to be done with the large but amorphous body of Celtic (for the most part Irish) myth, legend, and pseudo-history; Baltic and Slavic evidence must be sought for and fitted into the scheme; various facets of the scheme itself must be refined, perhaps redefined, as old texts are subjected to more intensive examination and as new ones appear. In its programmatic aspects, this lecture is indeed comparable to the 1938 article that launched the developmental phase.

Even more interesting is Dumézil's assertion that, as a comparativist, he is primarily concerned with systems: ". . . car tout, dans les représentations humaines, ou du moins tout l'essentiel, est système, implicite ou explicite, maladroit ou vigoureux, naïf ou subtil, mais système" (1951a, p. 223). And as a student of system, he fully acknowledges his debt to the French sociological school in particular and to sociology and social anthropology in general, a debt as great as, if not greater than, that owed to the pioneers in comparative mythology. Singled out for special recognition are Mauss, Hubert, and Granet, and the Durkheimian[1] idea of "les représentations collectives." Thus, in this lecture, perhaps more so than in any of his previous publications, Dumézil emerges as something more than an Indo-Europeanist; he emerges as a social scientist, as a student of system qua system. Of course, the particular system with which he is concerned is that manifested in ancient I-E myth, ritual, epic, legend, folklore, society, and the like; but this involvement with the general theoretical applications and ramifications of his research, implicit for many years, is now explicit. Also explicit are the basic sociological assumptions that have implicitly (for the most part) guided his research since the late thirties. In short, "Civilisation indo-européenne" marks the beginning of a new era in Dumézilian mythology.

I should add immediately that this does not mean that there was a sharp break with what had been done in the past; far from it. The

---

[1] Dumézil does not mention Durkheim explicitly here; however, it should be remembered that Mauss was a major contributor to the collective representation concept (cf. Durkheim and Mauss, 1903).

system continued (and still continues) to evolve, interpretation by interpretation, text by text. What I do mean, however, is that from 1949 on the emphasis has been upon filling in the gaps, adding new evidence, and completing the picture of I-E ideology already well painted in the previous decade, rather than upon radical new theories or interpretations. (There are, of course, a few important exceptions, as I shall point out shortly.) The attention to detail, noted toward the end of the last chapter, continues, both on the part of Dumézil and on the part of his students and disciples; at the same time, new syntheses of the system as a whole, or of major aspects thereof (e.g., the second function), appear periodically. This, then, is the beginning of the florescent phase, the phase in which Dumézilian comparative mythology has come to its maturity, its "full flowering."

SOME ARTICLES, 1950–1952

The florescence of this phase is well illustrated in the increased number of articles Dumézil has published since 1949, articles that range from detailed analyses of very specific (and not always trifunctional) aspects of Roman religion and ritual to discussions of minor figures in Ossetic folklore, from attempts to compare various Roman, Celtic, and Zoroastrian concepts, to more or less popularly written syntheses of his system aimed at convincing the general public of its validity. Added to these, of course, are the many reviews of conflicting theories and rejoinders to criticism—Dumézil has never been one to shrink from an acrimonious academic debate—which, in recent years, have amounted to a fair share of his literary output. These latter, the pieces solely or in large part devoted to the refutation of his critics or rival theorists, are surveyed along with the major criticisms in the section on critics in chapter 6.

Typical of Dumézil's early florescent phase articles is one published in 1950 in the *Journal de Psychologie*, "Les Archanges de Zoroastre et les rois romains de Cicéron" (1950*a*). Here he points out an interesting parallel between the Zoroastrian concept of the former Indo-Iranian deities and Cicero's concept of the early Roman monarchy. He notes that the Zoroastrian reform placed a seemingly moralistic cast upon the nature of its deities, in contrast with the freer and more personalistic representations of cognate figures in Vedic mythology; gods that in India had reflected oppos-

101

ing tendencies in the natural and supernatural worlds became unified in their service to the all-embracing values of the monotheistic Ahura Mazdah. A similar change is seen in the Roman historical tradition, where the early kings, who had been represented as subject to human vices (Romulus' tyranny, Tullus' impiety), were leveled by Cicero into models of kingly conduct. This equivalence in outlook between the Iranian prophet and the Roman man of letters cannot be explained by recourse to the common I-E heritage, Dumézil asserts; for, given its absence in the *Vedas*, it must have developed long after the period of I-E unity. In short, Dumézil simply points out the phenomenon without attempting to explain it. It is perhaps significant, however, that moralistic concepts of the sort promulgated by Zoroaster and Cicero seem to have been absent in the earliest phases of I-E culture history and never to have penetrated deeply into the thought of those I-E speakers remote from the centers of Near Eastern civilization (i.e., the Germans and, to a lesser extent, the Celts). The explanation may lie in the fact that both Italy and Iran were, almost from the beginning of their occupation by I-E speakers, much more subject to Mesopotamian, Egyptian, and other Near Eastern influences than was Aryan India.

Another article, "Dieux cassites et dieux védiques: À propos d'un bronze du Louristan" (1950*b*), was concerned with the extent to which certain Kassite deities (Surias, Maruttas) were Indo-Iranian in name and origin. In this article, Dumézil presents archeological evidence to support existing linguistic evidence. Examining the pictorial sequence on a Kassite bronze artifact found in Luristan (*ca.* 1300 B.C.), he concludes that in it one can see the properly subdivided tripartite pantheon of Indic and I-E tradition. Thus, the Kassites, who for a time held sway in Babylonia (seventeenth century B.C.), seem to have shared in the I-E ideology so clearly evident among their contemporaries in Mitanni. The name Maruttas alone (cf. Vedic *Marut*, Mitannian *maru* or *marya*) would be evidence enough upon which to base a tentative hypothesis to this effect; and given the rest of the linguistic[2] and archeological data, it seems to me that Dumézil is correct here in adding the Kassites to

---

[2] Cf. Thieme (1960), who marshals an impressive amount of evidence to prove that the language spoken by the rulers of Mitanni was already Indic (as opposed to Indo-Iranian). If so, a strong case can be made for the Indic origins of the Kassite dynasty.

his list of I-E-speaking communities sharing in the common ideology.

In 1951, Dumézil once again directed an article to the popular reader. Entitled "Mythes romains" (1951*b*) and published in the *Revue de Paris*, it outlines the basic problems in the study of Roman mythology and explains its author's comparative method. Dumézil points out the functional nature of myth in general, the mingling of myth and history among the Romans, and his own use of other I-E cultures in separating and identifying the two elements here (i.e., myth and history). He illustrates the comparative approach by setting the Roman accounts of Horatius Cocles and Mucius Scaevola against the Scandinavian tales of Othinn and Tÿr.

Finally, to conclude this sampling of articles written by Dumézil between 1950 and 1952, I should mention an interesting piece, "La bataille de Sentium" (1952*a*), in which Dumézil outlines the three standard devices employed by the Romans to ensure victory in battle, and links them to the I-E ideology. These devices are (1) performing rites appropriate to Mars at the outset of a fight to imbue the soldiers with the warlike spirit of this god, and doing battle during his sacred time of the year; (2) a *votum*, the promising of any honor (usually the erection of a temple) to any god by a qualified member of the group, usually the general in charge, performed if the victory seems to be in the hands of the enemy; and (3) a *devotio*, the promising of himself and of all the bodies of the enemy to the gods of the earth and subterranean regions by the general or his selected representative, also performed if the enemy appears to be gaining the upper hand. In the *devotio*, if the general makes the appeal and lives through the battle, he is henceforth disallowed from all clerical and secular duties; if a substitute is involved, he may be relieved of this injunction by the burial of an effigy along with a sacrifical animal. The *votum* is most usually directed toward Jupiter, and very rarely to Mars, while in the *devotio* there is no choice of addressees.

Analyzing these three victory-ensuring devices, Dumézil sees the following patterns: the first device involves the surface of the earth, human effort, and Mars, and reflects the second function; the second (the *votum*) involves the heavens, a "contract," and Jupiter, and reflects the first function; the third (the *devotio*) involves the underworld, blind sacrifice, and Quirinus. Pointing out the singular

103

Evolution of the System

principle of the *votum* (first function) and the collective principle of the *devotio* (third function), Dumézil notes the opposition in India between the individual gods of the first function (Mitra, Varuna, and so on) and the set of deities characteristic of the third function (the Aśvins).

Associating **co-uiriom*, 'collectivity of men,' with **Co-uir-īnos* (>Quirīnus), Dumézil observes that, just as Jupiter is mainly the god of the patricians and Quirinus that of the plebeians, so the *votum* is the specialty of a patrician supplicant and the *devotio* the specialty of a plebeian. He quotes Livy's account of the battle of Sentium (295 B.C.), which records an invocation to valor in the name of Mars, a *devotio* by a plebeian directed toward the gods of earth (i.e., Quirinus and Ops) and underworld, and a *votum* by a patrician addressed to Jupiter. This, he asserts, is an indication that the tripartite I-E ideology was a thoroughly understood and vital reality as far as the Romans were concerned, and that it remained so well into historical times, at least as late as the third century B.C. when the first historians seem to have fixed the canonical form of the birth of their city. The article ends with the assertion that this historical era (the third century B.C.) marked the high point in the importance of Quirinus; after this time, as the inherited I-E ideology was bowdlerized, the ancient representative of the third function rapidly faded into obscurity.

THE FIRST GENERAL SYNTHESIS:
Les dieux des Indo-Européens (1952)

It is fitting, perhaps, that the first major publication of the florescent phase is a summary, a synthesis of the central ideas of Dumézil's scheme. Based on a series of lectures delivered in 1951 at the University of London, *Les dieux des Indo-Européens* (1952b) begins by reviewing the "dieux des trois fonctions" and putting into evidence Dumézil's now familiar interpretations of the major Vedic, Zoroastrian, Roman, and Scandinavian divinities. This is followed by a detailed discussion of the I-E concept of sovereignty and includes materials relative to the "souverains mineurs" which had not been published previously. For example, aspects of Dakṣa and Amśa, two Varunian "souverains mineurs" in the Indic tradition, are amplified and expanded, especially the extent to which they correspond, respectively, to Aryaman and Bhaga (see pp. 90–94;

104

Dumézil, 1952*b*, pp. 54–56). Also, the Zoroastrian counterparts of the Mitraic minor sovereigns, Sraoša and Aši, are traced in detail through the Avestan and post-Avestan literature (*ibid.*, pp. 58–68); and the extent to which the Roman figures, Iuventas and Terminus, may be compared with Aryaman and Bhaga, and Sraoša and Aši, is fully explored.

In a most interesting chapter entitled "Structure et chronologie," Dumézil very systematically develops his ideas concerning the "dieux premiers" and "dieux derniers," analyzing each god in question (i.e., Vāyu and Agni, the two Zoroastrian *Mainyus*, Janus and Vesta) in terms of their manifestations in space, time, and the affairs of human beings. For example, Janus, as far as space is concerned, is seen as the "pilier du ciel," the means by which one may pass from the earth to the sky; as the patron of all places of entry and exit, he is manifested in the doorways to houses, in the mouths and sources of rivers; like Vāyu, he is also regarded as resident in, and guardian of, the air or wind. In time, Janus is defined as "le plus ancien roi de Latium [as opposed to Rome proper]," as the bringer of civilization and religion; he is the *Cerus Manus*, the 'Good Creator.' In human affairs, the Roman double-visaged deity presides over all sorts of *initia*, of beginnings (*ibid.*, p. 92):

Il [Janus] est régulièrement invoqué en tête (*prae-factio*) de tout acte religieux. Il ouvre les *labores*, et Horace le prie d'ouvrir son poème. Il signale le début de la guerre comme le retour à la paix. En parodie de l'usage humain, c'est à Janus que Jupiter, dans l'assemblée des dieux de Apokolokynthose, demande le premier son avis. L'as, point de départ de la série librale, est marqué de la tête de Janus.

In a note appended to the chapter from which this material is quoted (pp. 104–105), Dumézil analyzes the Norse figure, Heimdallr, who here is conceived as a "dieu premier," in the same fashion. In space, Heimdallr is installed "à l'extrémité du ciel"; in time, "il est né (*Hyndl.*, 35) et sa fonction a été fixée (*Lokasenna*, 48) *i ardaga*, dans les temps les plus anciens"; and in the affairs of men, he is the first to speak in the *thing*, or 'assembly' of the gods; in Norse eschatology, "il ouvre la fin du monde."

In the last chapter of *Les dieux des Indo-Européens*, "Caractères des dieux romains," Dumézil recapitulates much of what he had said in previous works about the nature of early Roman religion and about the futility of the "primitivist" approach (i.e., that of Rose, Wagenvoort, *et al.*) in its attempts to interpret it. The funda-

105

mental assumptions of this approach, that Roman religion was unique and that it can best be interpreted in terms of generalized "primitive" notions (e.g., animatism, animism), are negated, he asserts, both by the nature of the I-E comparative evidence and by the extent to which the ideology expressed in early Roman myths continued to shape the Roman world view in the historic period (cf. Gerschel, 1952). As Dumézil (1952b, p. 142) phrases it, "loin d'être archaïques, [the basic elements of the tripartite ideology] se précisent et se développent sous nos yeux au cours de l'histoire et contribuent puissamment à la fortune de Rome."

THE "DIEUX JUMEAUX": FROM NJORÐR TO HADINGUS AND A REINTERPRETATION OF ROMULUS

In 1953, inspired in large measure by Wikander's (1947, 1950) demonstration that the Vedic Ādityas had been transposed into the heroes of the *Mahābhārata*, Dumézil turned his attention to what, in his opinion, is an analogous transposition between Norse myth and epic; the result was *La saga de Hadingus* (1953b). After a thorough examination of the Hadingus saga as reported by the thirteenth-century Danish chronicler, Saxo Grammaticus (1.5–3),[3] Dumézil concludes that its central character is none other than the third-function Norse deity, Njorðr, transposed into a hero. Citing various earlier studies of the relationship between Hadingus and Njorðr (e.g., Müller, 1886; Detter, 1899), Dumézil points out that these two figures have much in common. Both are married twice (the first time incestuously) and have, in effect, two careers (Njorðr, as chief of the *Vanir*, is married to his sister Freya, but after the *Vanir* are defeated and absorbed by the Aesir, he marries the *Aesir* goddess Skaði; Hadingus is married first to Hathgrepa, the woman who had nourished him as a child, and second to Regnilda, a Danish princess); both are concerned with the sea (Njorðr is concerned with the protection of mariners; Hadingus' second career begins after a miraculous sea voyage to Denmark); both have sons and heirs whose names are philologically comparable (Freyr, closely associated with his mother Freya, is the son of Njorðr; Frodi, "la contemporain et la doublet danois de Freyr," is the offspring of Hadingus). All these elements, taken

---

[3] Cf. Wikander (1960a, 1960b).

together, firmly link the divine figure, Njorðr, with the heroic and pseudohistorical Hadingus in much the same fashion as the divine Mitra is linked to the heroic Yudhiṣṭhira, or Indra is linked to Arjuna.

The two phases in the life of Hadingus, typified, respectively, by his marriages to Hathgrepa and Regnilda, exemplify what is a most interesting, and by no means uniquely Germanic, process in the formulation of mythical and/or epical conceptions. In the first phase of his life, the Norse hero in question is clearly a transposition of Njorðr and is firmly associated with the third function; his wife, comparable in many ways to Freya, is the one who provided him nourishment as a child (Hadingus is an orphan), and he lives openly and voluptuously with her in a manner recalling the "inceste légitime" which, in Dumézil's opinion, was characteristic of the *Vanir* (especially Njorðr) before their subjugation by Othinn and his fellows. In the second phase of his life, however, Hathgrepa is dead and Hadingus lives in a "normal" relationship with Regnilda; here, he is clearly a protégé of Othinn rather than of the *Vanir*. Hadingus thus moves from a "préodinique" to an "odinique" position, from a style of life associated with the third function to one associated with the first function.

Hadingus' "préodinique" association with Hathgrepa parallels that between Njorðr and Freya (or Freyr, if the son of this incestuous match is substituted for the mother, as often occurs in Norse literature), and the Hadingus-Hathgrepa pair clearly belongs to the broad class of I-E third-function twin deities or heroes termed "les dieux jumeaux," by Dumézil. In the latter part of his book (1953*b*, pp. 114–130, 151–154), Dumézil compares the *Haddingjar*, pairs of Norse heroes onomastically and thematically related to Saxo's Hadingus, to various I-E "dieux jumeaux": for example, the Vedic Nāsatyas or Aśvins, Haurvatāt and Ameretāt, the Greek Dioscuri, and, perhaps most important of all, in my opinion, Romulus and Remus.

It appears that one of the twin founders of Rome, Romulus, underwent a transformation not unlike that exemplified by the two careers or life phases of Hadingus. Like the Norse hero, Romulus seems to have passed through two very different phases; and, though it breaks the chronological sequence I have sought to maintain in surveying Dumézil's ideas, I should comment here on a detailed discussion, built upon foundations laid in *La saga de Hadingus*, which appeared in a more recent work (*L'idéologie tripartie des Indo-Européens* [1958a]).

In their youth, Dumézil asserts (1958a, pp. 86–88), before the founding of the city, Romulus and his brother Remus clearly parallel the other I-E "jumeaux" figures; they are concerned with nourishment, the care of flocks, physical well-being, and the rest of those phenomena usually associated with the third function. But after the murder of Remus (cf. the death of Hathgrepa) and the ascension of Romulus as king, the latter, now a single figure, seems to have assumed the Varunian mantle and to have become a representative of the magico-religious aspect of sovereignty; he becomes, as it were, a heroic counterpart of Jupiter. Yet, despite the sovereign role played by Romulus as first king of Rome, there is a persistent tendency on the part of many Roman authors to identify him with Quirinus, a fact Dumézil explains by reference to his earlier third-function role as twin brother of Remus in the bucolic time before the founding of the city. Thus, Romulus, who heretofore had been viewed as a clear-cut representative of the first function and in all respects comparable to Varuna, Othinn, and Jupiter, now appears as a thoroughly ambivalent figure. To Dumézil, this ambivalence, this "upward mobility" from the third to the first function, so reminiscent of the two successive careers of Hadingus, is not detrimental to his theory; rather, it merely serves to indicate the extent to which the inherited I-E ideology permeated the thinking of those who shaped the "history" of the founding of Rome, to say nothing of those who composed the Norse sagas. As one of a set of twins concerned with rustic pursuits, Romulus must necessarily represent the third function and thus be associated with other third-function figures, such as Quirinus and Ops; but as *rēx*, as the prototype of the Roman sovereign, he must necessarily represent the first function and be associated with such divine first-function representatives as Jupiter and Iuventas. Similarly, as the husband of a "nourrice," Hadingus is necessarily associated with the third function, but as husband of a princess, he shifts to the first function and falls within the ambit of Othinn.

Although one could perhaps accuse Dumézil of stretching things a bit here, I am inclined to go along with him in his interpretation of Romulus as successively a third- (i.e., with Remus) and a first-function figure. The twin nature of the chief gods of the third function is indeed well established among the other I-E-speaking traditions upon which he has concentrated and is also apparent in the persons of Quirinus and Ops. That Romulus and Remus fit this pattern seems certain; it is also evident (though now not quite so certain) that Romulus, as king, fits the Varuna pattern. It must be remembered that the material being discussed here is not history but historicized myths expressive of a complex, tripartite theology; and theologies, whether expressed in myths or formal credos, are notable for their inconsistency. The basic tenets of the major world religions (Christianity, Islam, etc.) amply demonstrate this, and one should not assume that the various derivatives of Proto-I-E religion, Roman included, were any freer from inconsistencies in their respective theologies than those of the supposedly more sophisticated religions that (save for India) have replaced them.

THE *iuges auspicium* AND SOME INDO-IRANIAN SECOND-FUNCTION FIGURES

Turning once again to minor publications, I should mention two articles by Dumézil which appeared in 1953. One, entitled "Le *iuges auspicium* et les incongruités du taureau attelé de Mudgala" (1953*c*) and published in *La Nouvelle Clio*, is concerned with the Roman and Vedic preoccupation with the excrement of yoked animals as a divinatory device. Drawing largely upon his earlier interpretation of the inscription on the Lapis Niger[4] found in the Old Roman Forum, and upon the rules of divination as given by Cicero and Festus,[5] Dumézil concludes that it was considered inauspicious (by the augurs) if a yoked beast produced excrement, and, if this occurred, the potential disaster could be averted only by unyoking the animal. This divinatory rule, the *iuges auspicium*, is a manifestation, he asserts, of an opposition between the first function (represented here by the augurs) and the third function (here, yoked beasts and their farming masters). Turning to the *Rig Veda*, Dumézil points out the general similarity here in the hymn concerned with Mudgala (*Rig Veda* 10.102), in which Mudgala enters a race (or a battle) against the king and wins in spite of his

---

[4] I.e., IOVXMENTA, which Dumézil interprets as meaning *iuges auspicium*.

[5] E.g., Festus: "Iuge[s] auspicium est, cum junctum jumentum stercus fecit" ("A yoke is auspicious when a yoked beast makes manure"), quoted by Dumézil (1951*b*, p. 22).

old chariot and yoked bull. The text is not wholly clear, but it appears that the bull's excrement is essential to the victory. Dumézil interprets this factor as an I-E magical way of claiming possession of the soil (i.e., to have one's beasts leave their excrement upon it) and considers the *iuges auspicium* and the Mudgala incident as a victory of the third function (symbolized by the yoke; cf. the importance of the yoke as a third-function symbol in the previously discussed Scythian origin myth) over the first (the augurs) or the second (the king).

The second 1953 article, "Viṣṇu et les Maruts à travers la réforme zoroastrienne" (1953*d*), is an attempt to discover correspondences between Viṣṇu and the Iranian entity Rašnu, and between the *Maruts* and the Zoroastrian *Fravašis*. As Dumézil sees it, both Viṣṇu and Rašnu are concerned with space.[6] Viṣṇu, who surveys the world in three "paces," ultimately reaches a region to which he alone can have access, the realm beyond the visible atmosphere, which is also the home of the most fortunate souls after death. Similarly, Rašnu is intimately concerned with the progress of the soul after death, and his *Yašt* contains a lengthy enumeration of a three-part universe that mirrors Viṣṇu's three-pace survey. In both cases, of course, the three parts or paces include the earth (third function), the nearer atmosphere (second function), and the far atmosphere (first function). As far as the relationship between the *Fravašis* and the *Maruts* is concerned, Dumézil finds that their characteristics are quite similar, although the wild and bloodthirsty qualities of the divine Indic warriors are lost in the Avestan band owing to the Zoroastrian moral reform. Both are faithful armies (the *Maruts* are allied with Indra; the *Fravašis* with the monotheistic god of the *Avesta*), and both have great influence over the fall of rain and the flow of waters. Although the account of the battle between the *Fravašis* and the roar of the wind (highly reminiscent of the battles engaged in by the *Maruts*) is contained in but a vestigial reference, this, too, serves to link the two warrior bands. Thus, despite the religious reforms that separate them, the *Fravašis* and *Maruts* bear the marks of a common heritage and may be viewed in the broader context of the I-E *Männerbund* as delineated by Wikander (1938).

---

[6] I.e., Viṣṇu is to Indra what Rašnu is to Mithra: he who gives him the space necessary for his actions, and access to the zones wherein he must act.

Florescent Phase: 1949 to the Present

From 1951 to 1953, Dumézil devoted a course of lectures at the Collège de France to "éléments indo-européens dans des cultes, légendes, et notions de l'ancienne Rome." In 1954 these lectures were collected and published under the title *Rituels indo-euro-péens à Rome* (1954*b*), a work that was to excite the passions of the primitivists (Rose, Wagenvoort, *et al.*) to a greater extent than any of Dumézil's previous publications.[7] The book includes five essays, each of which is concerned with a specific point of comparison between Roman and Vedic ritual phenomena. In each instance, a case is made for a common I-E prototype. The first essay, entitled "Fordicidia," is typical of Dumézil's approach.

The Roman *Fordicidia*, which involved the sacrifice of a cow in the last stages of pregnancy, was connected with Jupiter and took place on the third day after the Ides of April. The unborn calf was extracted from its slain mother and burned by the eldest of the Vestals (cf. Ovid, *Fasti* 4.630–40). The ritual, performed to ensure a bountiful harvest, is said by Ovid to date from Numa's time. It apparently was the result of a revelation granted to the Roman king by the god Faunus: "Morte boum tibi, rex, Tellus placanda duarum, det sacris animas una iuuenca duas"[8] (Ovid, quoted by Dumézil, 1954*b*, p. 12). This rather enigmatic injunction was cleared up by the queen, who suggested the sacrifice of a pregnant beast. The next year the harvest was good—it had been bad the previous year, causing Numa to seek a vision—and the ritual became firmly established. Thus does Ovid explain the origin of this singular Roman ceremony; but, as is true of so much of Roman "history" and religion, native explanations do not tell the whole story. To see the *Fordicidia* in its true I-E context, it is necessary to examine parallel rituals practiced in Vedic India.

The Indic counterpart of the ritual in question, the sacrifice of the *aṣṭāpadī*, or 'cow with eight legs,' does not occur independently but rather forms part of several larger ritual complexes. For ex-

---

[7] Cf. Rose's review (1947) of *Jupiter, Mars, Quirinus* (1941) and *Servius et la Fortune* (1943).

[8] "Il te faut apaiser Tellus par la mort de deux vaches; mais n'en sacrifie qu'une seul et qu'elle fournisse deux vies!" (translated by Dumézil, 1954*b*, p. 12).

ample, it is regularly performed during the great *rājasūya* or royal consecration ceremony, the pregnant cow and her calf being offered to the Earth and the *Maruts* to ensure (cf. the Roman instance) the fertility of plants and beasts during the new king's reign. It may also be performed at the end of the *soma* sacrifice if the supposedly sterile cow to be offered to Mitra-Varuna is discovered to be in fact pregnant (cf. the *Śatapatha Brāhmana* IV, 5, 2). In both instances, it is the *Maruts*, together with the Earth-Sky pair, who receive the sacrifice and thus are persuaded to ensure continued plant and animal fertility (Dumézil, 1954b, p. 18).

In India, as at Rome, the sacrifice of a cow and a calf at a single stroke is clearly connected with plant and animal fertility, and is associated with popular well-being. There are, of course, some differences: in India, for example, the sacrifice is bound up with the institution of kingship; in Rome there is no such connection, not even with that shadow of former royal authority, the *rex sacrorum*. But in Dumézil's opinion, these differences are due to the differing historical experiences of the two I-E regions. In India, kingship remained central and the well-being of the king was directly related to the well-being of the population at large; in Rome, kingship disappeared very early and it was to "le peuple souverain" that the ritual was directed. In sum, Dumézil concludes that the *Fordicidia-aṣṭāpadī* ritual is derived from an I-E prototype, from a ritual that seems to have emphasized the agrarian aspects of sovereignty as personified in the king or chief. The fact that in Rome these aspects were early transferred to the population as a whole does not, in his opinion, weaken his argument.

It is interesting to note that Frazer, once Dumézil's *vade mecum* (cf. chap. 3), comes in for some criticism here. Dumézil points out that the author of the *Golden Bough* was so certain that the "barbarous Romans" had created their religion wholly independently that he failed to realize that the *Brāhmanas*, with which he certainly was familiar, contained close parallels to this religion and to these usages, and that it is possible to account for this similarity in terms of a common heritage (Dumézil, 1954b, p. 15). In essence, this is a criticism, not only of Frazer, but of all those who cling to the notion that Roman culture, especially Roman religion, was a thing *sui generis*. It is a criticism that is directly applicable to Rose, Wagenvoort, and others who would explain Roman religion in terms of a primitive dynamism or mana.

The other four essays in *Rituels indo-européens à Rome* cover a wide range of phenomena. In "Aedes rotunda Vestae," the 'round house of the Vestals,' the only circular temple in Rome and the site of a sacred and perpetual fire, is related to the circular manner (relative to the cardinal points of the compass) in which sacrificial fires were laid out in Vedic India. In "Albati russati uirides" and "Vexillum caeruleum," Dumézil advances once again the idea that the characteristic colors associated with Roman chariot racing—a quasi-religious ritual reputedly instituted by Romulus which persisted well into Byzantine times—were related to the three fundamental I-E functions: white for the first, red for the second, and blue, green, or black for the third. To prove his point, Dumézil introduces an abundance of comparative evidence, drawn mainly from Vedic, Celtic, Norse, and, interestingly, Hittite materials (cf. de Vries, 1942; Basanoff, 1947). In all instances, the priestly function and its representatives are symbolized by white (cf. the white garments of the *Brahman*, the Druid, and the *Flāmen Dialis*), and red is the color of the warrior gods and their human representatives. The fact that blue was often associated with the Roman *quirites* or people (and their divine representatives as well) is clear from a wide range of ancient sources (cf. Livy 5.25; Virgil 8.663–666).

In the last essay, entitled "Bellator equos," Dumézil points out that the Roman *October equus*, or horse sacrifice, and its Vedic counterpart, the *Aśvamedha*, not only stem from a common I-E ritual, but also reflect symbolically the three I-E functions. At Rome, the relationship between the horse and the human representative of the first function (i.e., the *Flāmen Dialis*) was largely a negative one; as noted earlier, the *Dialis* was forbidden to touch a horse even in the course of its ritual sacrifice. Yet the horse was indeed sacred to Jupiter, as the *quadriga* installed in the pediment of the temple of Jupiter Capitolinus in republican times clearly attests. In India, the connections between Varuna and the *Gandharvas* indicate a similar sacred relationship, one that was indeed signalized in the *Aśvamedha* (Dumézil, 1954b, p. 75). It is with the second function, however, that the horse as a sacred animal really comes into its own. Here, at Rome, the horse becomes the *bellator equos*, the symbol of military prowess; in India, this animal is viewed as the embodiment of *kṣatra-*, "l'essence de la deuxième fonction" (*ibid.*, p. 76; cf. the *Śatapatha Brāhmana* VI, 4, 12). The connection of the horse with the third function is clearly seen

113

in India in the name of the Aśvins, and at Rome the horse takes its place as one of the four-footed beasts used to cultivate the land.

These, then, are "les rituels indo-européens à Rome." In their delineation one see the penchant for detail coupled with an awareness of the overall I-E context so characteristic of Dumézil's florescent phase. Yet, despite the brilliance displayed here—the explanation of the form of the Vestal temple is certainly an outstanding example of this brilliance—there is little that materially advances Dumézil's central thesis concerning the relationship between I-E religion and society. The discussion of color symbolism is, perhaps, an exception.

In my opinion, the most significant passage in *Rituels indo-européens à Rome* is found in the introduction (p. 7), where Dumézil makes quite clear his position on the importance of ritual and the extent to which it is but an expression of an underlying ideology. Underscoring the failures of both the naturists and the ritualists, he points out that today it is necessary to rebuild. Rituals are no more or less important than other aspects of religion, he asserts. Theology, mythology, sacred literature, sacerdotal organization, as well as ritual, all are subordinated to something more profound which unites them into a meaningful whole. This "something more profound" is an *ideology*: "une conception et une appréciation des grandes forces qui animent le monde et la société, et leurs rapports" (*ibid.*, p. 7). Often this ideology is implicit and must be discovered by the analysis of that which *is* clearly stated in mythology and theology, especially that which concerns the character and behavior of divine beings.

Having made a case for the primacy of ideology, Dumézil goes on to sound a warning to those who would construct general theories simply on the basis of ritual similarities. Often, he points out, such apparent similarities have led scholars to create wholly unsound categories, phrased in the name of some general theory (e.g., dynamism or animatism, totemism). As an example, Dumézil cites attempts to classify Aranda totemic ritual and the Christian Eucharist under the common heading of "theophagy." Despite the obvious formal similarities in ritual—in both cases symbolic representations of a divine being are consumed—the Aranda and the Christian "ont conscience d'opérations mystiques radicalement distinctes" and are

114

acting in terms of almost totally dissimilar ideologies (*ibid.,* pp. 7–8).

SOME ROMAN GODDESSES AND THE NATURE OF THE SECOND FUNCTION

In 1956 Dumézil published two significant books: *Déesses latines et mythes védiques* (1956*a*) and *Aspects de la fonction guerrière* 1956*b*). The former, essentially similar in format and purpose to *Rituels indo-européens à Rome,* is concerned with the extent to which four Roman goddesses, Mater Matuta, Diva Angerona, Fortuna Primigenia, and Lua Mater, can be understood in terms of Vedic myth and ritual. *Aspects de la fonction guerrière,* for my purpose the more important of the two books, is concerned with the nature of the second function.

Of the four essays contained in *Déesses latines,* by far the most important is the one that concerns Mater Matuta; it is a model of the Dumézilian method. Mater Matuta, who was celebrated at the festival of the *Matralia* (April 11), has long presented a host of problems both to Latinists in particular and to historians of religion in general. Not the least of these problems are the central features of the *Matralia,* which included (1) forcing a servant woman to enter the sacred confines of the temple, then beating and ejecting her, and (2) ritually regarding one's sister's children as one's own.[9] To explain this curious set of phenomena, scholars have ranged far and wide. Frazer, for example (quoted by Dumézil, 1956*a,* p. 13), suggested that "for certain reasons now unknown it was deemed unlucky for women to pronounce the names of their own children in the rites of Mother Matuta." Rose (1955) went so far as to suggest that the ritual reflected an archaic Roman custom wherein "les tantes maternelles, non les mères, s'occupent des fillettes au moment de la puberté," and that this change of relationship was signalized in the *Matralia.*

---

[9] This aspect of the *Matralia* is perhaps best described by Plutarch in his Life of Camillus (5, 2): "[The women] make a servant girl enter the sacred precincts of the temple, beat her with sticks, and then forcibly eject her; later, in the course of the ceremony, they carry their sisters' children in their arms and honor them instead of their own children" (cf. Dumézil's translation [1956*a,* p. 8]).

Evolution of the System

After citing these and other explanations of the rites involving Mater Matuta, Dumézil proceeds to his own explanation. Pointing out that the word *matuta* is clearly related to a family of words meaning 'good' and, by extension, "dawn" (i.e., the point when the "bad" night is replaced by the "good" day), he asserts that the Roman goddess in question is analogous to the Vedic goddess Uṣas, or 'Dawn.' Furthermore, in the *Atharva Veda*, Uṣas is clearly the sister of 'Night,' the former being characterized as "good" and the later as "bad." Mater Matuta and Uṣas, thus, are sister goddesses par excellence; both reflect an inherited I-E dichotomy of good and bad, a dichotomy expressed in terms of the difference between night and day, or, more properly, perhaps, between the true dawn and the dawn that lingers too long and thereby menaces the cosmic order of things (cf. the *Rig Vedic* account of Indra's attack on the tarrying Uṣas and his breaking of her chariot). The expulsion of the servant woman becomes clear in this context: she is the symbolic representation of the "bad sister," of the lingering dawn, and must be scourged. The honors accorded to sisters' children are symbolic of the fact that the goddess here honored is indeed a "sister" who chooses to recognize her divine nieces and nephews: "l'Aurore, recevant, choyant l'enfant de sa soeur la Nuit" Dumézil, 1956*a*, p. 25). The child of "la Nuit," and therefore the nephew of "l'Aurore," is, in Dumézil's opinion, patently the sun: ". . . aux Matralia ou est honorée la Mère Aurore, les méres [Roman matrons] font avec les infants de leurs soeurs de que cette soeur de la Nuit fait avec le Soleil, enfant de la Nuit" (*ibid.*, pp. 25–26). As added evidence, Dumézil points to the Avestan conception of Bušyasta, a female "démon de l'aube," the demonic character of whom is in keeping with the Zoroastrian reforms (cf. Dumézil, 1945, pp. 92–93; de Menasce, 1947, pp. 10–18; Duchesne-Guillemin, 1948). Dumézil concludes that neither Mater Matuta nor Uṣas was directly inspired by the phenomenon of dawn. Rather: ". . . tous deux supposent d'abord une interprétation anthropomorphique de ce phénomenon, une déesse soeur de la nuit et choyant son neveu le soleil, une déesse tentée de se conduire mal et d'abuser de l'instant qui lui est accordé" (1956*a*, p. 39).

A similar approach is applied to the analysis of the other three Roman goddesses. Diva Angerona, whose feast fell on December 21, is found to be analogous to the Vedic divinity Atri, "restaurateur du soleil enténébré."[10] Both are concerned with the winter solstice, with the end of winter and the coming of spring, with the period when the shadows once again begin to shorten. Fortuna Primigenia, as the "firstborn" or mother of the sovereign Roman gods,[11] is seen to be analogous to Aditi, mother of the Vedic Ādityas (Mitra, Varuna, Aryaman, *et al.*). Lua Mater is related to the Vedic goddess Nirṛti; both are personifications of what might be termed the "destructive principle." Both are appealed to when destruction is socially or ritually necessary: "Dans le seul cas ou nous voyons Lua en service [cf. Livy 8.1, 6], le processus est du type bénéfique et nécessaire et appliqué à la fonction guerrière: il s'agit d'anéantir les armes ennemies." Ritually, "le général romain livre à Lua les armes prises à l'ennemi; le prêtre védique jette à Nirṛti les instruments inutilisables de l'opération rituelle" (*ibid.*, p. 114).

These, then, are the "déesses latines." In their delineation and explanation, Dumézil once again hammers home one of his major themes: that Roman religion can be understood only in a comparative context, only in relation to other ancient I-E religious systems, and that the most fruitful source of comparative materials is the ancient Indic literature. It is interesting to note that here, as in the 1954 volume on Roman ritual, no attempt is made to force matters into a tripartite mold. That these four goddesses derive from I-E prototypes is indeed asserted, but no attempt is made to assign them to one or another of the three I-E functions. Rather, the main emphasis seems to be on vindicating the comparative method as developed by Dumézil and on showing the fallaciousness of the primitivist approach. In no instance, Dumézil points out, can a case be made for the uniqueness or "primitiveness" of these divinities. All have developed independently from common prototypes in much the same fashion as did the linguistic forms employed by their devotees. This point is, of course, fundamental to his larger thesis.

The second major work to appear in 1956, *Aspects de la fonction*

---

[10] Like Diva Angerona, Atri is able to restore the light of the sun by maintaining silence (cf. Dumézil, 1954*b*, pp. 53-57).

[11] Fortuna Primigenia is both mother and daughter of Jupiter (cf. the *Rig Veda* passage wherein Dakṣa is said to have been born of Aditi and vice versa).

guerrière, marks a return to this larger thesis. In previous years Dumézil had devoted much attention to problems relating to the first or sovereign I-E function. He had long since delineated the concept of joint or dual sovereignty (cf. 1940*a*, 1948*b*) and had several times discussed the position of the "souverains mineurs" (Aryaman, Bhaga, Terminus, *et al.*; cf. 1949*b*, 1952*b*). Here, however, for the first time, his attention is focused exclusively upon the second or warrior function, upon the gods, heroes, and others who represent this function: "Utilisant les faits indiens et indo-iraniens, mais aussi, selon les occasions, les faits romains, scandinaves, grecs, nous allons . . . suivre le guerrier jusqu'au terme logique de son épanouissement: dans ses fautes, dans ses forfaits, dans ses malheurs" (Dumézil, 1956*b*, p. 14).

Following a brief introduction, in which the author summarizes his ideas concerning the nature of the first and third functions and underscores some of the unique aspects of the second—in particular the degree to which I-E warrior figures are prone to an "independent" course of action (cf. the Vedic term *svadhā*, 'autonomy,' which is often applied to Indra and the *Maruts*)—the balance of the book is divided into two essays. The first, "La geste de Tullus Hostilius et les mythes d'Indra," is concerned mainly with the extent to which certain episodes in the careers of the warlike Tullus Hostilius (third king of Rome) and his contemporaries (Horatius, Mettius Feffetius) are mirrored in the careers of Indra, Trita Āptya, and Namuci.

Unlike his predecessors, Tullus is manifestly a personification of the warrior ideal: "Dans tous les autres épisodes de sa geste, le premier rôle appartient comme il se doit à Tullus, le roi guerrier, le maître guerrier, celui qui a donné à sa jeune armée une admirable instruction militaire" (*ibid.*, p. 25; cf. Livy, 1.22, 34). He is victorious over the Veiians, the Sabines, and eventually the Albans. It is in this last connection that Dumézil once again analyzes the combat between the young Horatius and the three Alban Curiatii, an episode reviewed earlier (see pp. 78–80) in my discussion of *Horace et les Curiaces* (1942). The Horatii, it will be remembered, were a set of triplets appointed by Tullus to defend the honor of Rome against three Albans, the Curiatii. All three Albans were killed and only one of the Horatii remained alive. The latter, upon returning to the city, slew his sister because she mourned the death of the Alban to whom she was betrothed. Later the Roman champion had to undergo ritual purification.

In India, the slaying of the monstrous three-headed son of Tvaṣṭar (see pp. 61–62) presents some striking parallels to the events just described. The slayer, Trita Āptya, is one of three brothers (the Āptya); the monster is a close kinsman; after the act, ritual purification is required. Although the Vedic and Brahmanic texts vary somewhat—at times, Indra is directly implicated in the slaying—the three Āptya clearly emerge as counterparts of the three Horatii, and Indra's role here seems almost identical with that of Tullus, who "reçoit Horace vainqueur, l'aide à échapper à la conséquence de son excès meurtier, célèbre un triomphe et recueille, avec la soumission d'Albe, le bénéfice politique de la victoire" (*ibid.*, p. 25). A further parallel is seen in the Avestan account of the slaying of the three-headed dragon, Aži Dahāka, by Thraetauna;[12] the Avestan names Thrita (Athwya) and Trita (Āptya) are clearly cognates, and the name Thraetauna is a derivative of Thrita.

Both Horatius and Trita (and by extension Tullus and Indra) perform their respective actions fully in accordance with the demands of the second function, that is, the protection of society through the exercise of physical force. In India the divine scheme of things is threatened by the Tricephalus; in Rome the power of the state is threatened by the Albans, personified by the three Curiatii. Moreover, the motive behind Horatius' slaying of his sister is one of patriotism; her concern for a slain enemy is, in his eyes, tantamount to treason. Yet both heroes are culpable; both have slain kinsmen: Horatius slaughters a sibling; Trita kills a fellow divine being (usually identified as a first cousin) who, to make matters worse, is—despite his demonic aspect—the chaplain of the gods and thus in effect a divine *Brahman*.

In this element of culpability, which must be expiated in both instances, Dumézil sees a most important aspect of the second function; for, unlike (or perhaps to a greater extent than) his fellows, the warrior (or at least the I-E warrior) would seem to have been prone to excesses. His relative autonomy (*svadhā*), coupled with the fury (cf. Lat. *furor*) that served him so well in battle, would appear to have led occasionally to actions contrary to the basic

---

[12] Paralleled in the *Shāhnāmeh* of Firdausi by the slaying of Zohak by Feridun.

norms of the society, such as the slaying of a close kinsman or of a priest. These excesses, even when committed in the name of the society (cf. the patriotic motive behind Horatius' sororicide), could not, of course, be tolerated; and it appears that this ambivalence, this ambiguity as far as the behavior of the warrior was concerned, was projected into myth, into the realm of the sacred. It indeed seems to form one of the fundamental elements of the ideology manifest in the second function.

The parallel between Tullus and Indra does not end with the victories of their respective champions. Later, both are personally involved in actions deemed contrary to public morality; once again there appears the theme of the I-E warrior figure as a "pécheur," as one who sins against the moral order of his society.

After the defeat of the Curiatii and the capitulation of Alba, Tullus reaches an accord with the Alban chief, Mettius Fuffetius; they become *socii*. Later, in the course of a battle, Mettius deserts his new Roman ally and takes his forces with him, thus leaving Tullus in a desperate situation. In order to right matters, the Roman king consults the third-function deities, Quirinus and Ops, who suggest that he pretend to ignore the treason of his Alban ally and thus lull him into a sense of false security. As a result, Mettius is seized while unarmed and eventually executed in a most horrible fashion: he is stretched on a rack until he splits in half.

Like Tullus, Indra also reaches an accord with a former enemy, and a similar sequence of events unfolds. After an inconclusive struggle, the Indic warrior god reaches an agreement with the demon Namuci. The two enemies (as a demon, Namuci is Indra's natural enemy) swear a pact of eternal friendship, to which Indra adds: "Je ne te tue ni de jour ni de nuit, ni avec du sec ni avec de l'humide" (*Maitrāyanī Samhitā* 4.3.4; translated by Dumézil, 1956*b*, p. 42). Thus they become *sakhāyah*, or 'friends' (cf. Lat. *socii*). But true to his demonic nature, Namuci, like Mettius, quickly betrays his pledge. With the aid of *sura*, "la mauvaise liqueur," he deprives Indra of his physical prowess. In his distress, the god consults the Aśvins and Sarasvatī (the canonical gods of the third function) as to how he can dispose of Namuci without violating the contract between them. They advise him (1) to use a weapon made of foam (it is neither wet nor dry, at least in the eyes of the authors of the *Vedas*) and (2) to kill the demon at dawn (i.e., betwixt night and day). As a result, Indra succeeds in decapitating

120

Namuci (i.e., by "battrement, tournoiement de la tête dans l'écume") and thus regains his powers.

There are, of course, some differences between these two accounts. The Roman version lacks the intricate and clearly mythic character of the Indic tale; the Roman king, though employing a ruse, is not forced to find a loophole in his agreement with Mettius. At Rome, there is no question of Tullus' motives in slaying the Alban chief; rather, the fault is seen to lie in the ferocity with which the execution is carried out. In India, however, the fault lies in the nature of the act itself, in the fact that Indra circumvents the letter of a contract and kills one with whom he had sworn a pact of friendship; that Namuci had provoked Indra's action is not seen as significant. Yet despite these differences, which seem to reflect the divergent national characters of the two societies in later times, the essential elements of these two accounts of the slaying of a false friend by a warrior figure are the same. In both instances there is an act of treachery; in both, the traitor, the false friend, is slain only after consultation with third-function figures; in both, a ruse is employed. In both instances the victim is dismembered, and both Rome and India surround the slayer with a mantle of guilt.

Underlying these Roman and Indian accounts of the untoward behavior of warrior figures is a deeply rooted opposition between the first and second functions (Dumézil, 1956b, pp. 54–57). The acts committed by Tullus, Indra, and their cohorts are clearly in violation of the rules laid down by the sovereign gods of the first function; these acts, which must be expiated, are, in a very real sense, tantamount to a rebellion against first-function authority and must be shown to be in error, regardless of the immediate motives that prompted them. That this reflects what must have been a fact of early I-E social life seems highly probable, in my opinion; for, if Dumézil is correct in his assumption that Proto-I-E social organization was tripartite, then a structural opposition between the two dominant strata would seem to have been inevitable. Indeed, the known history of Indian society, a society that, in many respects, has remained truer to the archaic I-E pattern than any other, provides numerous examples of such an opposition. One that comes immediately to mind is the career of the Buddha. Born a *Kṣatriya*, a prince, the sage of the Sakyas sought to overthrow the authority of the *Brahmans* (i.e., of the first function) by asserting that all men were brothers and that caste was thus untenable. A similar

121

movement was led some 2,000 years later by *Kṣatriya*-born Nanak Dev, the founder of Sikhism. In both instances there was a clear defiance of the moral and religious authority wielded by the human representatives of the first function.

While these historic Indian examples do not include the sort of violence contained in the mythic accounts of the behavior of Tullus and Indra, they do involve opposition to the sovereign magico-religious order, the basic sort of social conflict experienced by Indra and Tullus.[13] It is not unreasonable to assume that, among the less civilized Proto-Indo-Europeans, this opposition did indeed lead to violent actions; at least the threat of violence, of the warrior's fury, must always have been present. Such internecine strife is, of course, socially disruptive and must be avoided if the society is to remain vigorous; the folly of rebellion against the sovereign order of things must necessarily receive expression in sacred literature. In sum, it seems to me that once again the fundamental Durkheimian axiom that ongoing social and cultural realities are inevitably projected into the realm of the sacred, into myth, upon which so many of Dumézil's theoretical interpretations are based, is amply demonstrated here. The conflict between warrior and priest, phrased in terms of their respective collective representations, is certainly an integral part of I-E ideology.

In the second essay in *Aspects*, "Les trois péchés du guerrier," Dumézil builds upon the foundation laid in the previous essay. Having shown the conflict inherent in the relationship between representatives of the first two functions, he proceeds to demonstrate the extent to which the I-E warrior figure is conceived of as behaving in a manner inconsistent with the demands of all three functions—including the second! His examples are drawn from the literature concerning Indra and Vāyu (together with their heroic

---

[13] That some elements of the archaic opposition between priest and warrior were present in the medieval struggle between the papacy and the Holy Roman Empire seems to me wholly possible. It must be remembered that European society of the eleventh and twelfth centuries, though professing belief in a religious system having its roots in the Semitic tradition, was nevertheless an I-E-speaking one and, as such, heir to the common I-E ideology. Moreover, many of the component elements of this society—the Germanic-speaking elements, at least—were still much closer to a form of social life more in keeping with what is known of our remote I-E ancestors (see chap. 1) than were the Romans, even in the earliest days of their Republic. See also chapter 7.

counterparts), Heracles, and the Norse hero Starkadr (or Starcatherus).

The sins Indra committed against the first two functions are those discussed previously: complicity in the murder of a *Brahman* (the son of Tvaṣṭar) and the abrogation of a treaty or contract resulting in the injudicious and cowardly use of physical force. The sin committed against the third function was an adulterous act perpetrated by the god while in the guise of another; that is, he assumes the form of the figure Gautama (no kin to the Buddha) and violates the latter's wife, Ahalyā.

In order to understand the full import of these acts, it is necessary to consider in some detail Dumézil's interpretation of Wikander's thesis concerning the origin of the Pāṇḍavas, the five heroic brothers who are the central characters in the *Mahābhārata*, for this thesis plays an important part in Dumézil's theory. Wikander (1947), as noted elsewhere, has demonstrated that these heroes are all projections or transpositions of the canonical Vedic gods and are thus representations of the three functions in their own right. As Dumézil sees it, their births are directly related to Indra's sins.[14] As a result of the first misdeed, the later loses his *tejah*, or "force spirituelle" (Dumézil, 1956*b*, p. 74), that aspect of his divine personality which is closest to the first function; as a result of the contract violation, Indra is divested of both his physical force and his vigorous manhood; because of the third sin, he loses his physical beauty, a trait generally associated by Dumézil with the third function (*ibid.*, p. 75). Indra's lost *tejah* enters into the body of Kuntī, wife of King Pāṇḍu, and gives birth to the Mitra-like figure, Yudhiṣthira, eldest of the five brothers and an incarnation of the principle of *Dharma*, or "Loi, Justice" (cf. the fundamental characteristics of Mitra as discussed earlier; Pāṇḍu himself, "pale and impotent," yet ultimately exercising sovereignty over his offspring, is equated with Varuna). From his vigor is born (via Kuntī) the "perfect warrior" figure, Arjuna. The course taken by Indra's physical force is more devious. First it enters into the person of the god Vāyu, or 'Wind,' and then gives birth to the brutal and bestial figure, Bhīma. Finally, his beauty gives birth to the twin heroes, Nakula and Sahadeva, who are clearly incarnations of the third-function Aśvins. In this "Wikander-Dumézil" theory, the relationship be-

---

[14] Wikander (1947) originally asserted simply that the Pāṇḍava derived from Dharma, Indra, Vāyu, and the two Aśvins.

tween Indic myth and epic is geared to the three sins of Indra, which serve as mechanisms whereby collective representation of the three functions is transferred from the gods of the *Vedas* to the heroes of the *Mahābhārata*. To Dumézil, this transference, as well as the sins associated with it, is a fundamental I-E characteristic.

A fairly close parallel to the sinful behavior of Indra is seen by Dumézil in the career of the Norse hero Starkadr, who, as Starcatherus, figures prominently in Books VI-VIII of the *Gesta Danorum* of Saxo Grammaticus. Like Indra, Starcatherus is an ambivalent figure; he is a hero who commits unheroic acts. He is specifically said to have committed three such acts. First, he is reputed to have strangled the Norwegian king, Wicarus, after gaining the latter's confidence and trust. Second, as a warrior in the service of Sweden, he displays cowardice in battle and causes a war to be lost. Finally, he commits another regicide, this time for purely venial reasons. Having agreed, for a price, to kill the Danish king, Olo, he obtains the latter's confidence and succeeds in killing him while Olo is in the act of bathing and thus unable to defend himself. Although there are some important differences here, Dumézil sees these three acts as analogues to those committed by Indra. The first is clearly an offense against sovereignty, though it is coupled with deceit (cf. Indra's second "péché"). The second is manifestly involved with the second function; the most powerful warrior in a battle suddenly turns coward and, in effect, loses his prowess. The third, though it lacks the sexual element, does involve both money and bathing, and the act of bathing is conducive to a sense of physical relaxation and well-being. To kill a bather is to kill one who, for the moment at least, is neither a sovereign nor possessed of effective physical prowess, and would indeed seem to relate to the third function.

There is yet another aspect of the Starcatherus account which bears on the comparison here. Like Indra, the Norse figure suffered a loss each time he sinned. As a youth he had been favored by Othinn, who had granted him great physical strength and a gift of three lives. After each offense he lost one of these lives, and at the end, after killing Olo, he committed suicide. That this is broadly analogous to Indra's progressive decay seems obvious, despite the fact that Starcatherus' disintegration occurs on the epic rather than on the mythic plane.

The third example of a warrior figure who commits three sins is drawn from Greek myth and epic, an otherwise rather barren field from Dumézil's point of view. The figure in question is Heracles, "le seul heros panhellénique" (Dumézil, 1956*b*, p. 93). Drawing upon the work of Schröder and Wilamowitz-Moellendorff, who had contended that the Theban hero bears certain resemblances to Indra, and following Diodorus Siculus (IV, 9–11, 31, 37–38), Dumézil divides Heracles' career into three major phases, each of which is commenced by a "péché." The first phase begins with the murder of his children, an excess committed in a blind rage that came over him after the Delphic oracle confirmed Zeus's command that he perform the twelve labors set by Eurystheus. The labors had been imposed upon Heracles in large measure because he had defied the power of his king; the murderous act was thus related to his frustration at having to obey the commands of those who represented the sovereign order of things, Eurystheus and the chief of the gods (who was also, of course, his father). It is another case of the warrior's *furor* gone amuck. As a result of this misdeed, the hero is reduced to the status of a menial, a laborer, and thus loses any trace of sovereignty he might have possessed (cf. Indra's loss of his *tejah*).

The second phase of Heracles' career begins after the labors are completed. Convinced that his wife will have no more children, Heracles seeks to ensure his posterity by taking a second wife. He asks for the hand of Iole, daughter of King Eurytos of Oichalia. The girl's father hesitates, mindful of his prospective son-in-law's earlier actions. Highly insulted by this hesitation, Heracles steals the king's broodmares. Iphitos, the king's son, suspects who has stolen them and searches out Heracles. Inviting the prince to view his herds from the vantage point of a high tower, Heracles, who has cleverly hidden the stolen animals, asks Iphitos if he can spot the royal mares. He is unable to do so. The Theban hero then declares that he has been unjustly accused and, without warning, hurls Eurytos' son from the tower. After this, his second murder, Heracles falls ill, losing the physical prowess that heretofore had sustained him. Once again he consults the Delphic oracle and is told that, in order to be relieved of his affliction, he must sell himself into slavery.

Thus Heracles commits an offense against the second function, the function of which he is a prime representative. Like his Indic and Nordic counterparts, he has behaved contrary to the spirit inherent in the ideology of the second function. His actions, of

125

course, more closely recall those of Indra (cf. the slaying of Namuci) than they do those of Starcatherus. Nevertheless, Dumézil concludes that the same basic wrong is committed in all three instances: a violation of "le devoir et l'honneur du Fort" (1956b, p. 97). In effect, all three heroes display cowardice, which is the antithesis of the second function: Starcatherus displays it in battle; Indra and Heracles display it in the murder of one who is disarmed and unsuspecting and therefore unable to defend himself. And, as a result, all three suffer a diminution of their physical abilities.

The third and final phase of Heracles' career begins after his desertion of his second wife, Deianeira, daughter of King Oineus of Calydon. Finding himself in the Pelasgiotis, he encounters King Ormenos and demands the latter's daughter Astydamia. "Mais comme il avait déjà pour épouse legitime Dejanire, fille d'Oenée, elle lui fut refusée. Il attaqua alors Ormenos, prit sa ville, le tua et emmena captive Astydamie, dont il eut un fils, Ctésippos" (*ibid.*, pp. 97–98). After this episode, Heracles decides to seek further revenge against the house of Eurytos for having denied him access to Iole. He succeeds in killing the king's remaining three sons and carries off Iole into Euboea, an act that ultimately brings about his downfall. Desirous of offering a sacrifice, Heracles sends word to Deianeira to send him the tunic he habitually wore while engaged in such a ritual. She complies, but, before sending the garment to him, impregnates it with the blood of the centaur Nessos, a vial of which the latter had given her with the assurance that if ever her husband's passion for her should diminish she could rekindle it by rubbing some of the blood into his clothing. Nessos, however, had deceived her, for, when Heracles puts on the tunic, the effect is disastrous. The centaur's blood causes him to contract a loathsome and most painful disease. After a last consultation with the Delphic oracle, Heracles causes himself to be burnt on a funeral pyre and thus, like Starcatherus, voluntarily puts an end to his mortal existence.

"Tel est le drame en trois actes," Dumézil (*ibid.*, p. 98) observes, "—trois péchés, trois maladies, scandés par les trois oracles delphiques—que se développe dans l'ordre hiérarchique descendant, à travers les trois fonctions." It is, of course, possible to accuse Dumézil of imposing a preconceived scheme upon the data, of twisting the facts until they fit the system; but the extent to which the behavior of Heracles agrees in its essentials with that manifested by Indra and Starcatherus cannot be ignored. The differences are no greater than might be expected after several millennia of independent development. In sum, I feel that in the figure of Heracles, no less than in those of Indra and Starcatherus, one can see elements of a common I-E representation of the warrior and his antisocial proclivities.

Aspects de la fonction guerrière must indeed be ranked among Dumézil's most significant publications, for in this delineation of the ambivalent position of the I-E warrior, an ambivalence clearly expressed in myth and saga, he touches upon what appears to have been a fundamental element of I-E ideology. More than any single military implement, the I-E warrior band, or *Männerbund*, organized around the person of a fearless leader (cf. Finn and the *fianna*, Indra and the *Maruts*), seems to have been the "secret weapon" that facilitated the I-E expansion. The warrior was thus the prop and, in many respects, the pivot of the social system. Yet the very separateness of the warrior class, the extent to which the warrior role was clearly distinct from that of priest or cultivator, seems to have led inevitably to a structural opposition between this class and the others; especially does this appear to have been true of the sovereign priest class. Such an opposition, if unchecked, could easily produce a state of disorganization fatal to the society, and thus mechanisms seem to have developed which served to keep the warrior in bounds. The tendency on the part of the I-E warrior to oppose the interests of the other strata of his society and to compromise, in the long run, the best interests of the stratum to which he himself belonged, the tendency for him to behave in ways that were clearly dysfunctional, became an integral part of the ideology and received expression in myth and saga; it was built into the collective representation of the warrior stratum. Here again one can see the extent to which the fundamental Durkheimian assumption—that important social and cultural realities are inevitably represented in myth—underlies Dumézil's approach to I-E materials.

SOME ARTICLES, 1956–1957

In addition to *Déesses* and *Aspects*, Dumézil published a number of fairly significant articles in 1956. Among them was one (1956c) devoted to further elaboration of Wikander's thesis concerning the

127

origin of the heroes of the *Mahābhārata*. In it Dumézil concerns himself with relatively minor figures such as Krṣṇa, Arjuna's faithful friend and charioteer, whom he identifies with Viṣṇu. A second article (1956*d*) is concerned with the extent to which the Roman *Ius Fetiale* is related to the Vedic concept of *dhātu-*, or 'base, foundation.' Equating Latin **fēti-*, the probable source of *Fētiālis*, with *dhātu-*, Dumézil attempts to demonstrate a correspondence between the Indic and Roman devices for justifying a claim to disputed territory. Needless to say, this justificatory technique involves tripartition. In India the mythic justification is seen in the account of Viṣṇu's three steps which brought the whole world (i.e., the *tridhātu-*) into the position of being a place where victorious campaigns might be waged, especially by Indra and his cohorts. A further Indic example of this concept may be seen in the account of the priest Vasiṣṭha, who secured the success of a military engagement by offering a sacrifice of *soma* to Indra and thus rendered the disputed territory *sudhātu-*, or 'well supported, well based,' that is, subject to the sovereignty of those who claimed it. Among the Romans, the *Fētiālis* served a similar function; their priestly duties were exclusively concerned with justifying the city's claims upon disputed territory (their services were not needed within the *urbs* itself as it had been "well based" ritually since its foundation). Another correspondence may be found, Dumézil claims, in the nature of the ritual involved. In both instances, bouquets of sacred herbs figure prominently. In India they are spoken of as the "ornament of the head of Viṣṇu" (cf. his three steps and their significance in this "basing" process), and at Rome the herbs are touched to the heads of horses. Dumézil concludes by observing that the Roman *Ius Fetiale*, when employed in the conclusion of treaties, preserves in its invocation of Jupiter, Mars, and Quirinus a clear example of tripartition.

Two 1957 articles deserve mention. The first, "Remarques sur *augur, augustus*" (1957*a*), is largely concerned with an investigation of the relationship between the Latin term *augur* and the Indic noun *ojah*. The accepted translation of the latter is 'physical strength,' but Dumézil examines the occurrences of the word in the *Vedas* (where it is usually applied to Indra and the second function) and, in the light of certain passages, refines the definition to indicate, not immediate and active force (that personified by Indra), but rather a well or repository of such force upon which the agent

128

may draw in time of need. At Rome the term *augur* seems originally to have designated a similar repository of power and then to have been applied to a person or priest. In primitive times, Dumézil asserts, this priest was probably conceived of as possessing this power or force and allocating it ritually to those who needed it. Later, however, as sophistication developed, the *augur* came to be regarded as one who merely had access to information about divine decisions; in other words, his function was to ascertain whether or not this force could be drawn upon in given situations, whether the repository was present or absent in relation to matters at hand. The adjective *augustus* was originally applied to objects or persons possessing this force; later it became merely an indication of rank. It is interesting to note that this shift in the definition of *augur* was from the second to the first function. The character of the force or power changed from that which is purely physical (second function) to that which is associated with sovereignty and divine decisions regarding the course of events (first function).

The second article (1957*b*) discusses the extent to which third-function divinities, such as Quirinus, are not wholly divorced from things military. (Dumézil's conception of Quirinus as a third-function figure has been criticized on the basis of the latter's affinities with Mars.) Such deities, he asserts, though primarily concerned with tranquillity and the maintenance of physical well-being, are often defined as armed in a protective capacity; typically, they do not instigate conflicts, but are not exempt from them should they arise or should the domestic peace be threatened. Quirinus is referred to often as *Mars qui praeest paci*, and there are *arma quirini*. The Norse Freyr is armed with a sword, and the Indian epic heroes Nakula and Sahadeva (projections of the Aśvins) carry weapons and engage in battle.

THE SECOND GENERAL SYNTHESIS: *L'idéologie tripartie des Indo-Européens* (1958)

The second and, in many ways, most important general synthesis yet to be published by Dumézil in his still ongoing florescent phase appeared in 1958. *L'idéologie tripartie des Indo-Européens* (1958*a*) is, in one sense, the summation of a lifetime of research into the nature of things Indo-European; in another sense, it is but a guide to the labyrinth of particular theories and interpretations

129

that constitute its author's general thesis. It also serves as a guide to the relevant literature, which, by 1958, had become extensive indeed.

The book is divided into three parts. The first, "Les trois fonctions sociales et cosmiques" (1958a, pp. 7–33), reviews the now familiar evidence relating to social tripartition (i.e., the three strata or "fonctions") in Vedic, Roman, Celtic, Scythian, and other ancient I-E societies heretofore considered by Dumézil; emphasizes the extent to which this pattern was uniquely I-E; rapidly surveys a host of specific expressions of tripartition in the form of triads of possible disasters and threefold sets of things such as "sins" and colors; and generally points up the degree to which tripartition was embedded in the *Weltanschauung* of the I-E community. Having laid the basis for the assumption that the ancient Indo-Europeans were indeed characterized by an "idéologie tripartie," Dumézil proceeds to the next section, "Théologies triparties" (*ibid.*, pp. 34–61), wherein the evidence pertaining to the mythological expression of this tripartite ideology is reviewed. The Vedic, Zoroastrian, Roman, and Germanic pantheons are surveyed, and their tripartite character is clearly delineated. The importance of the war between representatives of the first two functions and the third function (e.g., the war between the *Aesir* and *Vanir*) is duly noted. The final section, "Les diverses fonctions dans la théologie, la mythologie et l'épopée" (*ibid.*, pp. 62–89), includes a discussion of the joint sovereignty, the role of the "souverains mineurs," and a survey of the work of Wikander and others (himself included) relative to the transposition between myth and epic.

Little that is new in the way of data or interpretation is presented here, and no one subject is discussed in any detail or depth. Yet the very succinctness of the book is important, for it emphasizes that the new comparative mythology has indeed come of age and demonstrates that this approach to I-E mythology, despite its complexity, has achieved a degree of internal consistency which renders it amenable to a general synthesis. *L'idéologie tripartie* is by far the most systematic of Dumézil's major publications. While the first major synthesis, *Les dieux des Indo-Européens* (1952b), perhaps contained more that was original and thus represented a more significant advance in the system per se (see pp. 104–106), *L'idéologie tripartie* is also significant for the reasons just discussed. Perhaps even more important is the fact that in the latter, more than in any other earlier work, major or minor, Dumézil adopts a strictly sociological attitude. This is made explicit in the "Historique des études et bibliographie" (1958*a*, pp. 90–92) which follows the third section. Tracing the development of his own thinking, Dumézil entirely rejects his earliest, Frazerian phase and emphasizes the debt owed by him to sociology and ethnology, to say nothing of comparative philology. As he puts it, in what is perhaps the most significant single statement of his theory and method (*ibid.*, p. 91):

Cette enquête ne se réclame d'aucun système préconçu d'explication, mais utilise les enseignements de la sociologie et de l'ethnographie comme elle a recours à l'analyse linguistique des concepts. Elle n'a que deux postulats: elle admet que tout système théologique et mythologique signifie quelque chose, aide la société qui le pratique à se comprendre, à s'accepter, à être fière de son passé, confiante dans son présent et dans son avenir; elle admet aussi que la communauté de langue, chez les Indo-Européens, impliquait une mesure substantielle d'idéologie commune à laquelle il doit être possible d'accéder par une variété adéquate de méthode comparative.

In these two postulates—(1) that mythological and theological systems, as the primary vehicles wherein values are expressed, function to maintain and enhance social cohesion, and (2) that a demonstrable linguistic unity (such as that manifested by the ancient Indo-Europeans) necessarily implies a substantial measure of ideological unity understandable in terms of the comparative method—Dumézil succinctly sums up his fundamental methodological and theoretical position, a fusion of the sociological and comparativist traditions. It is this fusion that makes Dumézil unique among contemporary students of either myth, social organization, or ideology. His approach is neither wholly functional (although he is very much concerned with the concept of function) nor wholly historical (although the historical or comparative method is a cornerstone of his methodology); nor can it be classed among the "pattern" theories (his conception of I-E ideology, rooted as it is in the concept of "collective representation," is quite distinct from Benedict's conception of the Apollonian and Dionysian patterns). In short, it is, as I have said, unique.

Although there are indeed times when Dumézil fails to follow these two precepts, especially when he is analyzing very specific

131

materials, the fact that they serve generally to guide his research cannot be overlooked. If there are errors in his analyses, if on occasion he imposes a preconceived scheme upon data that might possibly admit of alternate interpretation, if his use of either the sociological or comparative method is sometimes less than perfect, these lapses are forgivable; for no one else has as yet devised a more effective or more strategic approach to I-E mythology—his critics to the contrary notwithstanding.

1958 TO THE PRESENT

In addition to *L'idéologie tripartie*, Dumézil published several significant articles in 1958. Perhaps the most important of these is "La *Rigsþula* et la structure sociale indo-européenne" (1958*b*), concerned with the apparent absence of the first function in historic Germanic society (i.e., the function or stratum of which Othinn and Týr should have been the representatives). After a careful analysis of the *Rigsþula*, a tale of the wanderings of the god Heimdallr and his children, Dumézil finds evidence of what indeed must at one time have been a full tripartite social system. The god had three children: Þraell (slave), Karl (peasant), and Jarl (noble). Here, of course, the priest class is lacking and in its place there is the slave, equivalent to the Śūdra of classical Indian society; Karl is compared to the *Vaiśya* class and Jarl to the *Kṣatriya*. Yet in the person of Konr-ungr, the magician-king, son of Jarl, Dumézil sees the remains of the first function. His conclusion is that at a very early phase in the evolution of Germanic society, and for reasons not entirely clear, the first function was assimilated to the second and only traces of its independent existence, such as in the person of Konr-ungr, can be found. That this change in the nature of Germanic social organization had little or no effect upon the nature of the first function as conceived supernaturally (i.e., in the differentiation among Othinn, Thōrr, and Freyr) is most interesting; it demonstrates, perhaps, the conservatism of theological systems which, once generated, are highly resistant to change. This, of course, was also true at Rome, where evolution of the social system so that social tripartition was largely eliminated seems to have taken place in the early days of the Republic, while supernatural tripartition (i.e., the distinctions between Jupiter, Mars, and Quirinus) remained intact for many centuries.

132

Although Dumézil's evidence is admittedly slender, drawn, as it is, from a single narrative, I am inclined to go along with him. It seems inconceivable that, given the rest of his evidence for the I-E community as a whole, and given the clear distinction between noble and commoner (i.e., between Jarl and Karl) which was so characteristic of Norse society in its earliest historical phases, the first or priestly function never existed in Germanic society.

In a second article written in 1958, "L'idéologie des trois fonctions dans quelques crises de l'histoire romaine" (1958c), Dumézil singles out from Roman history three episodes wherein one of the functions predominates over the others. The predominance of the first function is seen in one of the legends attaching to the Punic wars: a human head was found buried in ground being prepared for a temple of Jupiter (first function), whereas at Carthage, the defeated city, the heads of a horse (second function) and a cow (third function) were found. In the story of Coriolanus, the third function is predominant: Coriolanus, after the futile efforts of the warriors and priests, is finally won over by the entreaties of the women carrying their children. The second function stands out in the episode of the Lacus Curtius, wherein a chasm that opened in the Forum was closed only after the warrior Marcus Curtius rode into it. Dumézil concludes by seeking evidence of the tripartite ideology in three attempts to reestablish absolute monarchy during the lifetime of the Republic: Camillus and Manlius aimed at the position of *rex*, with its Jovian characteristics; Caesar sought the martial glories of the *imperator*; and Octavian finally achieved the peace, prosperity, and abundance of Quirinus.

Although Dumézil's analysis of the predominance of one or another of the three functions may be correct when legendary materials or augural interpretations are involved (cf. Gerschel, 1950), I feel that this last attempt to explain clearly historical events in terms of tripartition is pushing things a bit too far. It is extremely doubtful that either Camillus, Caesar, or Octavian was acting consciously in terms of the tripartite ideology. If, indeed, a later Roman historian were to have viewed their actions in this light, then this would be most important; but Dumézil's assuming such a role is an unfortunate example of the extent to which he sometimes violates the canons of procedure he himself has laid down (cf. 1958a, p. 91).

133

Evolution of the System

Two major publications of 1959 should be mentioned. In *Les dieux des Germains* (1959*a*), an updated edition of *Mythes et dieux des Germains* (1939*b*), much of Dumézil's recent thinking about the nature of ancient Germanic myth and society and its I-E roots is summarized. The second publication, a German translation (by Inge Köck) of *Loki* (1959*b*; cf. 1948*c*), has a laudatory introduction by Otto Höfler, a new preface by the author, and substantial revisions in the text, especially in regard to the nature of the Ossetic trickster figure, Syrdon. These revisions are based upon more recent researches by Dumézil and others in the Caucasus area. Of greater significance, however, are two 1959 articles, both concerned to a large extent with the problem of transposition between Indic myth and legend. One, entitled "La transposition des dieux souverains mineurs en héros dans le *Mahābhārata*" (1959*c*), is devoted to an analysis of the extent to which the two brothers of Pāṇḍu (father of Yudhiṣṭhira, *et al.*), Dhṛtarāṣṭra and Vidura, are transpositions of the Vedic "souverains mineurs" (i.e., Bhaga and Aryaman). Just as Bhaga and Aryaman are helpers of Mitra, so Dhṛtarāṣṭra (who, like Bhaga, is defined as "blind") and Vidura are counselors of their nephew Yudhiṣṭhira (the incarnation of *Dharma*, i.e., Mitra) after the final victory over the *Kauravas* is won. Early in the epic, Dhṛtarāṣṭra oversees the distribution of booty (cf. Bhaga, whose name literally means 'Divider'), and Vidura is consulted on the occasion of his brother's marriage (a function of Aryaman); later, Dhṛtarāṣṭra appears in the role of "blind fate" (cf. Bhaga) and Vidura, in Aryaman-like fashion, serves as a mediator and peacemaker.

It is interesting to note that in this article Dumézil retracts his earlier position, first annunciated in the last chapter of *Mitra-Varuna* (1948*b*), that Bhaga could be compared to the one-eyed, magico-religious sovereign (i.e., "le dieu borgne"; cf. Othinn, etc.), and that the handless Savitar corresponded to his "jurist" counterpart (i.e., "le dieu manchot"; cf. Tȳr, etc.). Blindness, he now asserts, is not synonymous with the state of being "eye-eyed," and he claims to have uncovered examples of the same I-E pair (i.e., the pair typified by Aryaman and Bhaga) in the Norse brothers, Baldr ('Peaceful') and Hödr ('Blind'), and in the Roman Iuventas and Terminus (cf. Dumézil, 1952*a*). Just as the Indic transpositions of the "souverains mineurs" emerge as leaders only after the great battle on which the *Mahābhārata* turns, so Baldr and Hödr are defined as ruling the new order that will come into existence after *Ragnarök*.

Here is yet another example of the mutability of Dumézil's thinking. Although retractions of this sort can perhaps be defended on the grounds that any such interpretive system must necessarily be continually refined and reshaped as new materials come to light, it should be noted that they (cf. his retraction [1948*b*] of the idea that Ouranos and Varuna could be equated in terms of their assumed proclivities for "binding") have been cited on more than one occasion by Dumézil's critics as evidence of the instability and therefore of the untenability of his position (cf. Thieme, 1957*c*; Gonda, 1960*b*).

The second 1959 article, "Remarques comparatives sur le dieu scandinave Heimdallr" (1959*d*), concerns (1) the extent to which the Indian epic hero Bhīṣma is an incarnation of the Vedic god Dyauh and (2) the extent to which the latter divinity is comparable to the Norse god Heimdallr. Dyauh, or 'Heaven,' is defined as "non pas souverain . . . mais procréateur et observateur vigilant, bien qu'inactuel, des dieux actuels." Heimdallr, whose name means 'Ram' (cf. *heimdali*), is similarly defined in Norse myth. He is said to have nine mothers, who are conceived of as sea waves (i.e., the "nine daughters of Aegir"); both the ram and the idea of nine waves have exact analogies in Welsh folklore. Dyauh, though unconnected with the ram, is indeed linked to water; he and his seven brothers (the Vasus) are temporarily incarnated with the river goddess Gaṇgā (cf. Ganges). The goddess drowns seven of eight siblings and only Dyauh reaches maturity (cf. *Mahābhārata* 1.3843–3963). From these traditions surrounding the births of Dyauh and Heimdallr, Dumézil concludes that Proto-I-E theology possibly included a tradition that Heaven was the last and only surviving offspring of a great water deity (probably female), who drowned all but one of her children as soon as they were born.

This is one of Dumézil's few excursions into the realm of I-E cosmology and it bears some attention. Admittedly the evidence is rather slender: Heimdallr has nine mothers, whereas Dyauh is one of eight brothers; one is connected with the ocean, the other with a river. Yet, slender as it is, the evidence certainly suggests a possible relationship. That the Proto-I-E community conceived of Heaven

135

as an otiose figure whose main function was to procreate the more immediate sovereign gods is not at all out of phase with what is known of the several ancient I-E cosmogonies (e.g., the Greek Theogony, the Norse *Völuspa*, the Hittite Kumarbi myths, etc.); that this figure, in turn, emerged from waters of some sort (the sea, a river or set of rivers) which claimed the lives of his siblings, though certainly less clearly attested, is also not wholly out of phase with these cosmogonies (cf. Brown, 1942, who discusses the great importance of water, its captivity and release, in Vedic cosmology; cf. also Gr. *okeanos*, 'origin of the gods,' and Ouranos).

A third 1959 article (1959c) is focused upon one of Dumézil's earlier areas of interest: the Roman *Flāmines Maiores* (cf. Dumézil, 1935). Here he is concerned with the manner in which the cults presided over by the *Flāmen Dialis*, *Flāmen Martialis*, and *Flāmen Quirinalis* were fused together in the person of the *rex*. The *Flāmines* themselves, however, were conceived of as representatives of the several gods they served and, therefore, as incarnations of the three functions.

A fourth article published in the same year (1959f) is concerned with Roman and Vedic rituals relating to sacred fires.

Although no new major theories or monographs have as yet appeared—a work Dumézil refers to as his "bilan roman" is now in press and, as this book goes to press, a summary volume dealing with his Caucasian studies has just been released—the last eight years have seen a steady flow of articles, reviews, and replies to criticism (discussed in chap. 6). Among them is a continuing series of very specific comparative studies of Roman and Vedic ritual ("Quaestiunculae Indo-Italicae," appearing in the Belgian series *Collection Latomus* [1960a], *Latomus* [1961a], and elsewhere); a recapitulation of Dumézil's tripartite interpretation of Ossetic folklore (1960b); a discussion of the controversy between Dumézil and Benveniste regarding the nature of the three Scythian tribes (1962); an addendum to Dumézil's study of Roman goddesses (1960c; cf. 1955a), wherein the obscure goddess Carna is explained as the divinity responsible for proper digestion and the maintenance of alimentary metabolism; and an examination (1965) of *Yasna* 29, wherein the division of labor between the two Iranian representatives of the first function, Aša and Vohu Manah, is clarified in terms of their respective reactions to the demand of the Soul of the Cow (*Gēuš Urvan*) that it be protected from mistreatment and given a divine patron.[15]

Of the several articles alluded to above, perhaps the most significant is the one concerning the nature of the Scythian tribes: "La société scythique avait-elle des classes fonctionelles?" (1962). In 1930, it will be remembered, Dumézil (1930*b*) first set forth his now familiar interpretation of the Scythian origin myth as given by Herodotus. At that time, the four Scythian tribes were seen by him as strata corresponding to the general I-E tripartite social system. The agricultural *Katiaroi* and *Traspies* were descended from the eldest son of Targitaos, Lipoaxaïs; the military *Aukhatai* were descended from the middle son Arpoxaïs; and the royal *Paralatai* were descended from the sovereign youngest son, Kolaxaïs, the recoverer of the burning golden objects that fell from heaven. This thesis was rejected by Benveniste (1938) in favor of a purely ethnic argument. The tribes were indeed tribes and not social classes. Dumézil persisted in his position (cf. 1941*a*) but finally yielded to his colleague's interpretation in the late 1950's (cf. 1958*b*; 1960*b*). Yet his doubts have remained. In the present article he attempts a new interpretation of the tribal names: *Paralatai* can be connected, he now feels, with the Avestan *paraoāta* ('placed in front'), an epithet of King Haoyaŋha who, with his successors, Taxma Urupi and Yima Xšaeta, forms a trifunctional unit in *Yašt* 19.27–33; *Aukhatai* corresponds to the Avestan *aegah-*, *aojah-* ('strength, force'); and *Traspies* and *Katiaroi* correspond, respectively, to the Avestan **dravasp(i)ya-* ('with fine horses') and *gau-čahra* ('with cow pastures'). Thus there appears a hierarchial order here corresponding to the three I-E functions, and, in spite of himself, Dumézil seems to have returned to his former tripartite view of Scythian social organization.

---

[15] The Cow addresses itself first to Aša, the incarnation of Order, and asks whether in the initial ordering of things it had been provided with a patron. The answer being no, the Cow then petitions Ahura Mazdah, who points out that the Cow had been created to serve mankind and thus had no divine patron. Finally, the Cow addresses itself to Vohu Manah, or 'Good Mind,' fully conscious of the latter's close connection with the affairs of mortals; but all Vohu Manah can do is to suggest that the Cow place itself under the protection of Zoroaster, who has proved himself to be a staunch opponent of Evil and a devoted follower of the way of Ahura Mazdah. Dumézil sees here a further indication of the difference between the two representatives of the first function: Aša is remote from human affairs and thus can do little to help the Cow, while Vohu Manah puts the beast under the protection of the one human being who most closely approximates the concept of "Good Mind," Zoroaster. Cf. Dumézil, 1945, pp. 119-124.

Evolution of the System

SUMMARY

In 1949 Dumézil began the long and still unfinished process of synthesizing and elaborating the ideas he had developed in the course of the previous decades. The first general synthesis, *Les dieux des Indo-Européens*, appeared in 1952; a second and more complete synthesis, *L'idéologie tripartie des Indo-Européens*, appeared in 1958. The title of the latter work gives a clue to the general direction that Dumézil's thinking has taken as the last eighteen years have unfolded. More and more he has come to conceive of social, mythological, theological, and symbolic tripartition as manifestations of a single, underlying *ideology* which manifests itself in nearly all areas of systematic classification, thought, and behavior engaged in by I-E speakers. The germs of this conception were already present in his inaugural lecture as occupant of the Chair of Indo-European Civilization in the Collège de France: ". . . tout, dans les représentations humaines, ou du moins tout l'essentiel, est système" (1951*a*, p. 223).

In pursuing this concern with ideology and system, Dumézil has ranged far and wide, and it is largely for this reason that the current phase in his scholarly career has been labeled "florescent." His ideas have flowered in many diverse areas. Indeed, one of the major characteristics of the phase in question has been an increasing concern with detail, with nuance. Examples of this can be seen in his studies of Roman and Vedic rituals (1954*b*), in his analysis of various Roman and Vedic goddesses (1955*a*; 1960*c*), in his series of works devoted to the nature of the second function and the extent to which I-E warrior figures are structurally opposed to those representing the other two functions (e.g., 1956*a*), and in the extent to which he has continued to study Ossetic folklore (1960*b*) and has followed up Wikander's ideas regarding the transposition between myth and epic (cf. 1959*a*; 1959*b*). Yet, despite this tendency toward diversity, despite this tendency to focus upon minutiae and to follow up numerous side paths,[16] Dumézil has never completely

---

[16] Sometimes these side paths have taken Dumézil far outside the I-E-speaking realm, ancient or modern. For example, in 1955, while a visiting lecturer at the University of Lima, Peru, he turned his attention to the study of Quéchua linguistics and folklore (cf. Dumézil, 1955*b*, 1956*e*).

lost sight of his central objective, which is a deeper understanding of the nature of I-E myth, society, and ideology.[17]

Thus far the florescent phase has been characterized by two complementary tendencies: one in the direction of synthesis, stressing ideological unity and common heritage, and the other in the direction of intensive and detailed research into very specific problems. That these tendencies will continue seems quite likely.[18] Whether or not any wholly new or startling interpretations (or reinterpretations) of I-E myth will accompany them is another matter, for it seems to me that Dumézil has pushed his approach to I-E matters about as far as it can go, and it is doubtful whether any drastic changes will occur in the system as it now stands. But science has a way of mocking such predictions.

Having surveyed the evolution of Dumézil's ideas, I now wish to look briefly at the impact these ideas have had upon the scholarly world, to survey the contributions made by those who have taken these ideas to heart and the criticisms lodged by those who have not, and to assess the whole in terms of contemporary social anthropology. These are the tasks of Part III.

---

[17] Cf. the dialogue between Dumézil and Pierre Sipriot (Dumézil and Sipriot, 1961), wherein the former points up rather clearly the general importance (i.e., to I-E studies as a whole) of his seemingly overly detailed Roman studies.

[18] It should be noted that in a recent communication Professor Dumézil himself suggests that at present (1966) he is perhaps entering a fourth phase, a "phase de bilan," as he terms it. If this is indeed true, then it is likely that the emphasis upon broad syntheses, so characteristic of what I have labeled his "florescent phase," will continue.

PART III

Disciples, Critics, and an Anthropological Assessment

6

The Disciples and the Critics

Most of the scholars who have concerned themselves with Dumézil's ideas regarding the nature of I-E myth, society, and ideology fall into one of two broad categories: disciples and critics. A few, of course, have remained more or less neutral, affirming or denying the validity of specific constructs and interpretations in the light of their own particular research problems.[1] For the most part, however, Indo-Europeanists, classicists, Indologists, Iranianists, Celticists, Germanicists, Latinists, and the like have been either markedly favorable or severely critical. Some, indeed, like Benveniste, Wikander, and Gerschel, have made significant contributions to the system in their own right; others, like Thieme, Rose, and Brough, have consistently sought every opportunity to discredit it and its supporters. In this chapter, some examples of this twofold reaction to Dumézil's theories and methods are examined.

THE DISCIPLES

BENVENISTE

By far the earliest of Dumézil's supporters—he cannot truly be labeled a "disciple" for he has at times been rather critical of Dumézil's work—is E. Benveniste, some of whose contributions to the formative and developmental phases have already been noted. Benveniste (1932), it will be remembered, was the first to follow

---

[1] These "neutrals" are categorized as disciples or critics on the basis of their reactions to specific theories and ideas.

up Dumézil's suggestion (1930*b*) that the ancient Iranian class structure was tripartite, that it was composed of priests (*athravan-*), warriors (*rathaēstar-*), and cultivators (*vastriyō.fšuyant-*), with a class of artisans (*hūitiš-*) being added later. This independent confirmation of Dumézil's pioneering researches had a profound effect upon the latter's thinking. Later, in his "Traditions indo-iraniennes sur les classes sociales" (1938), Benveniste expanded this thesis to include Indic and Scythian society as well as that of ancient Iran. Thus, coupled with Dumézil's researches, the tripartite thesis—at least as far as Indo-Iranian society is concerned—was firmly established.

But all was (or is) not total agreement. In "Traditions indo-iraniennes sur les classes sociales," Benveniste takes issue with Dumézil's assumption (cf. Dumézil, 1930*b*) that the sons of Targitaos represent, respectively, the three inherited I-E strata as reflected in Scythian society. He sees them rather as simply the legendary ancestors of the several Scythian ethnic or tribal divisions, though he does support Dumézil's interpretation of the golden objects fallen from the sky as symbolic of the tripartite division of Scythian society as a whole, and sees it as evidence for an archaic Pan-Indo-Iranian *Weltanschauung*. The argument over the role played by the sons of Targitaos still continues. As noted earlier, Dumézil persisted in his interpretation of Kolaxaïs, his two elder brothers, and the three objects of burning gold until 1958 (cf. 1958*a*, 1960*b*), but he has recently returned to his original position (cf. 1962).

Among the other contributions of Benveniste to the development of tripartite system are two noteworthy articles he published in 1945. One, "La doctrine médicale des Indo-Européens" (1945*a*), was concerned with the extent to which there existed a tripartite medical doctrine among the ancient I-E speakers, a tripartite doctrine pertaining to the cause and cure of illness and other bodily afflictions. Linguistically, such a doctrine is attested in the I-E root *med-* (Greek μέδομαι, 'take care of'; Old Irish *midiur* 'I judge'; Gothic *mitan*, 'measure'; Armenian *mit*, 'thought'; *cf.* Avestan *vimad-* and Latin *medeor*, which have a special connotation of "care for the sick"). Further evidence is seen in the Avestan division (*Vidēvdāt* 7.44) of medicine into 'knife-medicine' (*keretobaešāza-*), 'herb-medicine' (*urvarō-baešāza-*), and 'spell-medicine' (*manthrō-baešāza-*), and in Pindar (*Pythian Odes*, 3.40–55), wherein Asklepios treats sufferers from sores, wounds, and exhaustion by spells, incisions, and potions. In *Rig Veda* 10.39.3, the Nāsatyas are said to be healers of the blind, the emaciated, and the fractured. All this adds up, in Benveniste's opinion, to a tripartite distribution of both afflictions and cures according to the three functions: sores, blindness (especially that of prophets), and other similar afflictions are treated by spells and belong to the first function; wounds, fractures, and the like are cured by incisions and belong to the second function; exhaustion, emaciation (i.e., lack of nourishment), and most wasting diseases are cured by drugs, herbs, potions, and so on, and belong to the third function. Here is further evidence of I-E ideological tripartition, evidence that has indeed been utilized by Dumézil (cf. 1958*a*, p. 21).

The second 1945 article, "Symbolisme social dans les cultes gréco-italiques" (1945*b*), augmented the then already considerable amount of data concerning Roman tripartition which had been amassed by Dumézil (cf. 1949*a*). Examining the famous Umbrian tablets found at Iguvium, Benveniste points out that the enumeration *nerf* ('rulers'), *arsmo* ('priests'), *ueiro* ('men'), *pequo* ('flocks'), *castruo* ('fields'), *frif* ('fruits'), lists in canonical order persons and phenomena representative of the three functions. Likewise, the Umbrian divine triad Juu-, Mart-, Vofion(o)- coincides exactly with the Roman triad Jupiter, Mars, Quirinus because *vofion(o)-* (from I-E **leudhyon-*; cf. German *Leute*, 'people') is of the same meaning as Latin **co-uir-* (cf. Quirinus), 'people, collectivity.' While Dumézil had previously come to much the same conclusion concerning the relationship of the Roman and Umbrian triads (cf. 1938*a*), once again Benveniste covered the same ground independently and arrived at a similar conclusion.

Turning next to "la lustration agraire à Rome," Benveniste analyzes a prayer in Cato's *De agricultura* (141) which asks Mars to *prohibessis defendas averruncesque* ('forbid, repel, sweep away') three functionally classifiable disasters:[2] plague (first function; i.e., to be averted by spells), depopulation and devastation (second function; i.e., to be averted by armed might), and crop failures and blights (third function; i.e., to be averted by proper husbandry).

---

[2] In his 1938 article, Benveniste noted a similar triad of calamities in ancient Iran, i.e., the famous Behistun inscription, which asks Ahura Mazdah to protect the society against political subversion (an offense against sovereignty), invasion, and crop failure.

Finally, he points out that in Roman religion the pig is sacred to Tellus ('Earth,' a third-function figure), the bull to Mars, and the sheep to Jupiter (cf. the *suovetaurilia*, which parallels the Greek τριττύς, a sacrifice offered notably to Poseidon, but also to Apollo, Asklepios, the Dioscuri, etc.), and that the Greek χοή consisted of wine, honey, and milk, the sacred beverages, respectively, of the warrior, the priest, and the shepherd or farmer.

In the last two decades Benveniste has published relatively little that is germane to Dumézil's work; his contributions belong largely to the earlier phases in the evolution of the system in question. Yet it should be emphasized that he and Dumézil have been close colleagues since the days when both were students of Meillet; thus the influence exerted by him upon Dumézil, especially in the formative phase, cannot be overestimated. Indeed, it seems fair to say that without Benveniste's support, without his acceptance of the fundamental principle of social and mythological tripartition, Dumézil's theories would not have crystallized so rapidly as they did; nor, I might add, would they have been so widely accepted as they are today.

WIKANDER

The earliest and by far the most original of Dumézil's true "disciples" (i.e., those who have oriented their work largely or wholly to his precepts) was the Swedish mythologist Stig Wikander,[3] some of whose major contributions have already been discussed (see pp. 123–124). Wikander's contributions to the system in question began in 1938 with the publication of his *Der arische Männerbund*. In this monograph, which has taken its rightful place as one of the basic documents of the "new comparative mythology," the Swedish scholar sought to demonstrate that the ancient I-E-speaking communities were characterized by the presence of a *Männerbund*, a band of young warriors led by a chief or king which was distinct from the other strata of society (i.e., the priests and the cultivators) and which exhibited in batle a remarkable recklessness and esprit de corps. As the prime examples of this uniquely I-E institution,[4]

---

[3] Wikander, though certainly a "disciple," was not, in the strict sense of the term, one of Dumézil's students.

[4] That is, in the ancient Near East and its environs. Such bands are, of course, commonly encountered in East Africa (e.g., among the Masai), but

the author chose the *Maruts*, as described in the *Rig Veda* and else-where, and the *maryannu*, or 'chariot warriors,' who established and maintained, for a time, I-E-speaking authority in northern Syria (i.e., in Mitanni), around 1600 B.C. Also included here were other I-E examples of warrior bands, especially as delineated in Germanic and Celtic myth (cf. Höfler, 1934; Lommel, 1939). Needless to say, Dumézil has more than once drawn upon this fundamental piece of research on the part of his disciple, especially in his delinea-tion of the ideology of the second function[5] (cf., for example, Dumézil, 1956*a*).

Perhaps the most important single contribution yet made by Wikander is the previously discussed theory of transposition be-tween myth and epic, first annunciated in his 1947 article, "Pāṇḍava-sagan och Mahābhāratas mytiska förutsättningar," published in the Swedish annual *Religion och Bibel*. Here he presented the re-sults of a long and detailed investigation of the central figures of the *Mahābhārata*, the Pāṇḍavas, and came to the conclusion that the latter were projections of the canonical gods of the Vedas, that they reflected the same tripartite division of functions Dumézil had de-scribed for Varuna, Mitra, Indra, and the Nāsatyas. To say that this breakthrough has had a profound effect upon Dumézil's thinking is an understatement (cf., for example, Dumézil, 1954*a*, 1956*a*, 1959*b*). For one thing, it demonstrated that the I-E tripartite ideology was so deeply rooted that it could pass from myth to epic without serious alteration.

---

membership in them is based largely upon an age-grade principle. Whether or not the Proto-I-E *Männerbund* was related to an explicit age-grade system is still a moot point, though the evidence seems to indicate that it was a firmly established, permanent social class (i.e., the second function), rather than an age-grade into which boys passed at a certain age. The *Männerbund*, thus, would seem to have included *all* able-bodied members of the warrior class, though the younger of these would naturally have formed the most active contingent.

[5] Dumézil points out, however (1958*a*, p. 95), that "une des grosses dif-férences entre le 'Männerbund' des Indiens et celui des Germains est que le premier est d'Indra (non de Varuna), tandis que le second est d'Odinn (non de Þorr): effet de l'évolution de la 'fonction guerrière' chez les Germains" (cf. Dumézil's theory [1958*b*] that, although the distinctions between the functions are clear enough at the supernatural level, the ancient Germanic priestly class seems to have merged with that of the warriors). In the course of this evolution, Othinn would seem to have been substituted for the tra-ditional warrior figure (Thōrr) as the patron of the *Männerbund*. In most other situations, the distinction between Othinn and Thōrr corresponds to the overall I-E pattern.

Wikander has followed up this original research in a number of subsequent papers. One, entitled "Sur le fonds commun indo-iranien des épopées de la Perse et de l'Inde" (1950), is concerned with the extent to which the Iranian *Shāhnāmeh* reflects a transposition similar to that reflected in the *Mahābhārata*. Rejecting Darmesteter's (1902) conclusion that the Iranian epic profoundly influenced the Indian one, he accounts for the similarities between Firdausi and the *Mahābhārata* in terms of a common Indo-Iranian and I-E heritage. An example of tripartition in the Iranian "Epic of Kings" can be seen in the institution of the three great sacred fires: *Atur Farnbag* (the 'priestly fire'), *Atur Gushnāsp* (the 'warriors' fire'), and *Atur Burzen Mithr* (that of the "third estate"). Of these three fires, the second was instituted by the thirteenth king, Kai Chosrau, and the third, by the fourteenth king, Luhrāsp. There is a significant dynastic break here. In the *Avesta*, a sharp break appears between the reigns of Aurvataspa and Vishtāspa and those who had preceded them. Similarly, the succession of Luhrāsp and Gushtāsp (the fifteenth king) to the throne of the Kayanids marks a definite break; Kai Chosrau, the last of the Kayanids, is of a wholly different order from his two successors. Moreover, in both myth and epic, this new era is one characterized by peace and physical well-being, a clear contrast to the preceding period.

Luhrāsp and Gushtāsp are, in fact, little differentiated; they are, indeed, almost twins and can be equated, functionally and etymologically, with the Indic Aśvins (Iranian *aspa-*, 'horse,' corresponds to Skt. *aśva-*). Their third-function identification is completed by Gushtāsp's wife, Nāhid (i.e., Anāhitā), who appears as a typical third-function consort (cf. Sarasvatī, Freya, Anāhitā, etc.). Opposition to Luhrāsp's succession to the kingship is the Iranian counterpart of Indra's attempt to keep the Aśvins from the *soma*-sacrifice. Thus, as Wikander sees it, the fourteenth through the seventeenth kings on Firdausi's list are third-function figures; the warlike Kayanids belong to the second function, and the earliest kings, to the first function.

Another parallel between the *Shāhnāmeh* and the *Mahābhārata* is seen in the degree to which the Indic Bhīma, son of Vāya, approximates the Iranian epic hero Rustam, kinsman of Keresāspa (who himself is closely associated with the Iranian Vāyu and resembles the mace-wielding Bhīma). Both are clearly incarnations of the second function.

148

In sum, Wikander finds clear-cut evidence of a common background in myth and a common tendency to transfer the inherited tripartite ideology into epic literature. The differences between the *Shāhnāmeh* and the *Mahābhārata* are due to the differing historical milieus in which the two epics emerged.

A more recent article, "Nakula and Sahadeva" (1957), is concerned with a detailed analysis of the epic twins Nakula and Sahadeva, sons of the third-function Aśvins. The former are more differentiated than their Vedic fathers, Wikander asserts, pointing out that Nakula is handsome and warlike and often associated with Bhīma (second function), whereas Sahadeva is intelligent, pious, and has distinct connections with Yudhiṣṭhira (first function). Yet in the persons of their mythic counterparts, one can still see the same distinctions mirrored in the names Nāsatya and Dasra, the first of which corresponds to the single Avestan Naṇhaithya, who, along with Indra, was consigned by Zoroaster to the realm of the demons. At the court of Virāta, Nakula becomes a groom, while Sahadeva is employed as a stockman; thus the name Aśvin ('Horseman') may originally have been applied to only one of the mythical twins (Nāsatya). Wikander connects the pastoral Sahadeva (mythical 'Son of Heaven' or Dasra) with the Avestan epithet *yazush puthrō* for Atār ('Fire') and with the Vedic epithet *sahasas yahuh*, '(youngest) son of *sahah*,'[6] applied to the fire god, Agni. He concludes that Sahadeva (and Dasra) may, like Agni, reflect an archaic Indo-Iranian anthropomorphization of the sacred fire and, in this sense, have definite connections with the first function.

Although I do not have the data to confirm it, it appears to me that a similar distinction may well have been present between the Roman pair Quirinus and Ops. That the former, although certainly a third-function figure, had some connections with Mars is quite clear; as noted earlier, Ops is often referred to as one of the *arma quirini* (i.e., a military aspect of Quirinus), and Quirinus is referred to as *Mars qui praeest paci* (cf. Dumézil, 1957b). This relationship may well parallel that between Nakula and Bhīma. Whether or not Ops has any connections with a sacred fire is a moot point, but one that, in the light of this research, might be well worth investigating.

In 1950, Wikander (1960a, 1960b) widened his scope to in-

---

[6] I.e., first-function power as opposed to brute force (cf. Dumézil, 1948a, pp. 106 ff.).

clude a comparison of the Indian epic and certain aspects of Scandinavian pseudohistory as related by Saxo Grammaticus. The background and circumstances of the great battle fought at Brávellir (*Gesta Danorum*, 8) bear striking resemblances, he suggests, to the plot of the *Mahābhārata*.[7] In both instances, the action centers in a fight between two branches of a royal house, and the genealogical relationships present many analogies.

The Scandanavian situation is as follows: King Gunnarus of Sweden marries Drota, queen of Norway, and has a son named Hildigerus. Bocarus the Dane kills Gunnarus, takes Drota, and by her fathers a bastard son, Haldanus, who eventually kills his legitimate half brother. Haldanus then seeks the hand of Guritha, a Danish princess and the last of her dynasty. At first she rejects him because of a festering facial sore, but at last he wins her by slaying a rival. They in turn produce a son, Haraldus Hyldetan, who rebuilds Danish power. The latter fights with his nephew Ringo, king of Sweden, at Brávellir. Haraldus has become blind, but participates in the battle riding in a chariot. Finally he is clubbed to death by his retainer Bruno (Othinn in mortal form).

In India the sequence of events is as follows: Satyavatī gives birth to a bastard son, Vyāsa, fathered by the ascetic Parāsara. Later she marries King Śantānu. Their two legitimate sons die, and Vyāsa is entitled by levirate to perpetuate the dynasty with the only two surviving widows of his younger half brother. But he is ugly and smelly, and the queens find him repulsive; one closes her eyes and the other blanches. The resulting sons are Dhṛtarāṣṭra and Pāṇḍu, 'Blind' and 'Pale,' respectively. Their story leads to the central conflict of the *Mahābhārata*, the fight between Dhṛtarāṣṭra and his nephew Yudhiṣṭhira.

The similarities between these two genealogies are too close to permit one to explain them in terms of chance; as it is doubtful whether Saxo ever heard of the *Mahābhārata*, the only possible explanation is that offered by Wikander: a common I-E mythological inheritance. There are some other concordances that make this conclusion even more inescapable. For example, the greatest champions in the two battles, Bhīṣma and Ubbo Fresicus, are both

---

[7] Cf. Dumézil (1959*b*, pp. 78-105), who compares Iranian eschatology and the *Mahābhārata* to the killing of Baldr and the coming into existence of *Ragnarök* in Scandinavia.

overwhelmed by countless arrows, whereas Indic and Norse heroes usually die in single combat.

In addition to his work on the transposition from myth to epic, Wikander has analyzed certain etymological aspects of the name Mithra (1952*a*), and has attempted to demonstrate (1951, 1952*b*) that the so-called kingship-in-heaven theme (i.e., the three-generational sequence of gods characteristic of Greek, Hittite, Iranian, and Phoenician mythology) is I-E in origin. Discounting Güterbock's (1948) assumption that the Greek figures Ouranos, Kronos, and Zeus were derived from Hurrian (and ultimately Babylonian) prototypes by way of Phoenicia, Wikander points out that the theme occurs in the *Shāhnāmeh* (Jamshid, Zohak, and Feridun), and that the Hittite version (Anu, Kumarbi, and Tešub) is not necessarily Hurrian in origin, as Güterbock had suggested. Wikander concludes that this theme is, instead, part of an underlying, inherited I-E myth complex.[8]

These are, briefly, some of the contributions of Stig Wikander. They loom large indeed in any consideration either of the system in question or of I-E mythology in general. That he will continue to support and expand Dumézil's theories, especially in regard to the depth to which the tripartite ideology is rooted in what otherwise might appear to be straightforward accounts of early Scandinavian, Iranian, or Indian history, seems certain.

GERSCHEL

Since the end of World War II, Dumézil, in his capacity as director of studies at the École des Hautes Études, has attracted a number of students who have worked closely with him on various projects relating to I-E myth. By all odds the most brilliant and devoted of these has proved to be Lucien Gerschel. The latter's contributions began in the late 1940's. In 1950 he published an article ("Saliens de Mars et Saliens de Quirinus") concerned with the problem, referred to several times previously, of the relationship between Mars and Quirinus. Here, Gerschel focuses upon the order of Roman priests known as the *Salii*. The *Salii* were warlike (with magic shields, or *ancilia*), yet there were *Salii*, not only of Mars Gradivus,

---

[8] As noted elsewhere, most of the evidence and the balance of scholarly opinion is against Wikander here (cf. Littleton, in press).

but also of Quirinus, who is often referred to as *Mars qui praeest paci*. The two kinds of *Salii* are seen by Gerschel to be in charge of two different types of passage rites: those of Mars Gradivus (reputedly founded by Numa) conferred the *furor* of war (cf. Dumézil, 1942); those of Quirinus (reputedly founded by Tullus Hostilius) effected demobilization, return to peace, and lustration of arms.

Two years later, in 1952, Gerschel published a much more significant article, "Structures augurales et tripartition fonctionelle dans la pensée de l'ancienne Rome,"[9] in which he attempts to show that Roman augural thought, so important in the early history of the city, reflected the tripartite I-E ideology. He first concerns himself with omens relating to the ultimate triumph of Rome over Carthage. Drawing principally upon Servius' exegesis of the *Aeneid*, Gerschel outlines what appears to be a purely Roman version of certain events supposedly surrounding the founding of Carthage: while preparing the ground for a temple to Juno, Dido uncovers (or her workmen uncover), in succession, two heads, the first being that of a cow and the second, that of a horse. The former is an omen according wealth and prosperity to the city (third function), and the latter promises military power (second function). It is only at Rome, however, that an omen according sovereignty (first function) is uncovered: Tarquin, while preparing ground on the Capitol for a temple to Jupiter, uncovers a bloody human head; this, the augurs claimed, was symbolic of the Italian city's future triumph over its African rival. Thus the I-E triad of functions is complete, and Gerschel compares this sequence of heads to a sequence of five sacrificial victims mentioned in the *Śatapatha Brāhmana*, the first three of which are a man, a horse, and a cow.

The rest of the article is devoted to a detailed analysis of three omens which Gerschel terms "présages mobiles." They are "mobile" in that they may be passed from one community to another, although it is implied that Rome is destined to acquire all three. These include the "Sabine heifer" (third function), the baked earthen quadriga (a type of chariot) of the Veiians (second function), and, once more, the "Capitoline head" (first function).

If Gerschel is correct, and I have reason to believe that he is, then the tripartite ideology is capable of persisting, not merely into

---

[9] The article is preceded by a brief note by Dumézil (1952c) in which he introduces and "gives his blessing to" his student's research.

the realm of epic (cf. Wikander, *et al.*), but indeed into the interpretation of what are, by all objective criteria, historical facts: the fall of Carthage and the subsequent world domination by Rome. That the augurs of Rome in the first century B.C., members of a society vastly more complex and sophisticated than that of their I-E ancestors, should interpret what were then relatively recent historical occurrences in terms of this ideology is eloquent evidence of the depths to which it had penetrated the Roman character, despite the disappearance of the social forms upon which it had originally been based (i.e., a clear-cut tripartite stratification pattern).

Gerschel has continued his investigations of Roman ideology and the extent to which it followed the pattern first discovered by Dumézil. In 1953 he analyzed the second-function characteristics of the quasi-historical figure, Coriolanus, and compared him with the sixteenth-century German *Raubritter*, Goetz von Berlichingen, as portrayed by Goethe. As with Coriolanus, Goetz displays most of the salient characteristics of the prototypical I-E warrior: great personal courage, a strong sense of class distinction, loyalty to military rather than national ideals, and so on (cf. Dumézil, 1956*a*). In 1958 he concerned himself with the extent to which Varro's *De lingua latina* (5.80–94) reflects the three functions as well as the concept of joint sovereignty; the Latin author's *De hominibus* is subdivided into *De honore publico*, *De sacerdotibus* (respectively, the juridical and magico-religious aspects of the first function), *De re militari* (second function), *De fortuna* (third function), and *De artificibus et scientia* (an appended "artisan" class paralleling the Iranian *hūitiš-*; cf. Benveniste, 1932, etc.). Here again, a remarkable persistence of tripartition in Roman thought can be seen.

Perhaps stimulated by his own suggestion that Goethe's picture of Goetz von Berlichingen reflects the second function, Gerschel published, in 1956, a most interesting, albeit exploratory, paper. Entitled "Sur un schème trifonctionnel dans une famille de légendes germaniques," the paper is concerned with the possible existence of a tripartite scheme in a series of German and Swiss legends wherein a man or a woman performs some service for the "little people" (fairies, elves, etc.) and, in return, receives three gifts (e.g., a ring, a sword, and a loaf of bread) which are to be passed on to three sons. So long as these three items are preserved, the three branches of the family will prosper. These gifts, of course, are seen

153

by Gerschel as symbolic of the three functions, and the prosperity of the three sons so endowed varies accordingly: the eldest son receives a gift symbolizing the third function (e.g., a loaf of bread; cf. the third-function identification of Lipoxaïs, eldest son of the Scythian Targitaos) and becomes a successful farmer and the father of many children; the second son receives a gift symbolic of the second function (e.g., a sword) and becomes a successful warrior; the youngest son receives a gift symbolic of the first function (e.g., a ring or a cup) and becomes a priest, an abbot, or the governor of a province. Should these objects be lost or destroyed, then the three branches of the family will cease to prosper in their respective ways. Often the first and second sons lose their talismans, while the youngest, who holds the gift symbolizing sovereignty, is able to preserve his by sequestering it in an abbey and thus continues to prosper. Gerschel concludes that these modern (fifteenth- to eighteenth-century) South German and Swiss legends, many of which are tied to existing families in the area and are used to explain the differing fortunes of various branches thereof, "sont susceptibles de récéler une matière d'origine indo-européenne: la légende est ici héritière du mythe" (1956, p. 92).

This interpretation, if correct, is, in my opinion, of the highest significance; it implies that the tripartite ideology has persisted far beyond the phase in which epics were composed, that it transcended the era of classical historical interpretation, and that, despite well over a thousand years of Christianity, it still forms a part of the European world view (at least in Bavaria and some Swiss cantons). As I see it, even if these legends are but isolated examples, Gerschel's work, coupled with that of Dumézil, opens up some most interesting avenues of research, ones that have perhaps some important theoretical implications as far as the relationships among language, society, and ideology are concerned.

Another matter that this article brings into focus is the extent to which Proto-I-E society was characterized by ultimogeniture. I have alluded above to Lipoxaïs, who, as the eldest son, received the lowest rank; conversely, his youngest brother Kolaxaïs became sovereign. In these German and Swiss legends, the same thing happens. Elsewhere the evidence is not clear-cut, but hints of ultimogeniture can be found throughout ancient I-E literature (although the case of Yudhiṣṭhira in the *Mahābhārata* seems to be an exception). One such example can be seen in the kingship-in-heaven theme mentioned previously in my discussion of Wikander's work (cf. Wikander, 1951, 1952*b*); here again, the youngest son inherits the sovereign position (cf. the positions of Zeus, Feridun, Tešub, etc., relative to their respective siblings). That this was indeed the Proto-I-E pattern is still an open question, but I feel that a good case for it can be made on the basis of the evidence presented above.

Among some of Gerschel's other contributions to the system is an article (1960) in which he isolates some evidence of tripartition in an episode of the Norse saga of Hrolfr Kraki. In this particular episode, three sons choose careers commensurate with the three functions, and Gerschel compares this to the situation wherein the three sons of the Iranian figure Thraetauna (Feridun in the *Shāh-nāmeh*) choose their careers (cf. Molé, 1952, pp. 456–458). In both cases the functions appear in the order 3–1–2, which is precisely the order of appearance of the functions at Rome. Romulus and Remus, it will be remembered, seem to have undergone a change in functional identification from the third to the first function (cf. Dumézil, 1953*b*; see pp. 107–109, above). Commenting upon the apparent primacy, at least in time, of the third function in Rome and elsewhere, Gerschel notes that "dans la perspective indo-européenne, la troisième fonction, en effet, sert de base aux deux autres" (1960, p. 115). In support of this, one could perhaps bring to bear the ultimogeniture pattern discussed above; the eldest son is clearly identified with the third function.

Yet, as I see it, there is something of a hiatus here. If one views this matter from the perspective of the Sabine War, the war between the *Aesir* and *Vanir*, and so on, one sees the third function as the *last* to be admitted to the social system. That the third function or stratum, comprising as it does those who produce the food that nourishes the society as a whole, "sert de base aux deux autres," is clear enough, but to assume that the warrior and priestly strata of Proto-I-E society emerged out of the producing class and received definition only at a later stage in the development of this community is to assume something that cannot be clearly attested. It is possible, as I have said earlier, that the Proto-I-E society was heterogeneous in origin, that it was the result of a victory by a nomadic hunting and gathering people over one possessed of a more sedentary, Neolithic type of economy. The apparent temporal primacy of the third function and its representatives may thus be due to

155

a symbolic expression of its lowly, but nevertheless fundamental, importance to the society; the order 3–1–2 may reflect social rather than historical reality.

Finally, I should mention a brief (seven-page) article published by Gerschel in 1957 and translated into English by the American folklorist, Archer Taylor. Entitled "Georges Dumézil's Comparative Studies in Tales and Traditions," and appearing in *Midwest Folklore*, it is one of the very few favorable (or, indeed, objective) discussions of Dumézil which have so far appeared in English.[10] Unfortunately, the article's contents do not live up to the promise of its title. Gerschel's focus is upon Dumézil's comparative method and upon the ways in which this method can make sense out of such seemingly divergent phenomena as the Roman injunction in the Twelve Tables against a *malum carmen* and the fact that the Celtic hero Ferdead (*Tain Bó Cualnge*, 20) "chooses death by the spears (mythical) that 'the authors of magical satire, insults, and abuse' [cf. *malum carmen*] will hurl at him" (1957, p. 143). Only passing mention is made of the tripartite ideology, though Gerschel does indeed emphasize that Dumézil is attempting to reconstruct a common I-E folklore and mythology, and appends a selected bibliography of his mentor's works. In addition, he makes a useful, if not original, distinction between tales (*Märchen*) and traditions (*Sagen*). The latter, he feels, always serve a purpose; they "explain something." Tales, however, may serve simply as entertainment. Although Gerschel rightly (in my opinion) claims that there is no absolute distinction between the two categories of narrative,[11] he is a little unclear in his further distinction between myth and tradition; apparently myths are "ancient traditions," for he claims that "perhaps one believed more in a myth than in a tradition" (1957, p. 145).

Like most "true believers," Gerschel tends to push his interpretations even further than the master. Yet, on occasion, this very failing, this seeming lack of scholarly caution, may prove to be an asset; for, in seeking a wider range of applicability for the tripartite thesis, Gerschel has, in my opinion, materially widened the possible dimensions of the system. Especially is this evident in his

---

[10] See also Duchesne-Guillemin (1958, pp. 32-41); Rees and Rees (1961, pp. 112-117).

[11] For a discussion of the typological differences among myths, *Sagen*, *Märchen*, and other forms of traditional narratives, see Littleton (1965).

work with Roman historical interpretation and with modern European folklore.

THE CELTICISTS

Among Dumézil's students and disciples have been a number of scholars concerned primarily with Celtic myth and saga. One of the first of these was the late Marie-Louise Sjoestedt, whose *Dieux et héros des Celtes* appeared in 1940. In it she attempted to apply the tripartite scheme, as it had then evolved, to the great mass of Celtic data (the bulk of which is Irish), and to make sense out of the relationship between such figures as Lug and the Dagda. Unfortunately her effort, though brilliant, did not shed a great deal of light on the subject.

In 1948 two scholars, both of them Irishmen, approached the problem using Dumézil's framework. One, T. G. E. Powell ("Celtic Origins: A Stage in the Enquiry"), developed not only a theory of Celtic origins, but also one of I-E origins in general. Powell concludes that there were probably *two* major I-E migrations. The earliest, he asserts, beginning about 2000 B.C. in the East European steppes, saw (1) the advance up the Danube Valley into Central and Northern Europe of the so-called battle-ax folk, the descendants of whom emerged into history as the Germanic peoples; (2) the appearance of the Hittites and others in Anatolia; and (3) the arrival of the earliest Greek speakers in Greece. The second wave, beginning somewhere south of the Caucasus mountains after about 1500 B.C., included the ancestors of the Celts, Italic peoples, and Indo-Iranians. Powell postulates a period of "Aryan-Celtic-Italic" linguistic and cultural unity, perhaps somewhere in northeastern Anatolia. In the West, bypassing Greece and, for the most part, the battle-ax folk already settled in northern Europe, the Italo-Celts pushed up through the Balkans into Central Europe, bringing with them chariots, cremation (i.e., the urnfields), *and* a threefold social structure of the sort Dumézil has delineated.

Thus, while accepting Dumézil's evidence for socioreligious parallels between Ireland, Rome, and Vedic India, Powell nevertheless feels that this was a *later* I-E development, stimulated, perhaps, by contact with the older civilizations (including that of their I-E-speaking cousins, the Hittites) of the ancient Near East; he infers that neither the battle-ax folk (i.e., the Germans), the Hittites, nor

157

the earliest Greeks were culturally complex enough to sustain a tripartite social system, and that therefore such a system was not a Proto-I-E characteristic. He disagrees with Dumézil's conclusion that the Germanic peoples possessed this system, pointing out that had a sacerdotal "sage-magician" class existed, it would have been preserved, at least down to the earliest historic times.

Needless to say, Powell's theory of I-E origins and migrations is somewhat out of phase with current research (cf. Gimbutas, 1963), and his suggestion that the Celts, Indo-Iranians, and Italic speakers shared a period of common development in Anatolia must be completely discarded. Also, his conclusion about the nature of Germanic and Greek society does not stand up in light of more recent research (cf. Dumézil, 1958b). Yet despite his criticisms, I include Powell as a disciple for the reason that he does attempt to view ancient Celtic religion and society in tripartite terms. That he fails to solve any important problems is perhaps indicative of the sorry state of our knowledge of Celtic myth (as opposed to legend or folklore).

The second 1948 approach to Celtic problems mentioned above was that of Myles Dillon (*The Archaism of Irish Tradition*), who discusses analogies between the mythical traditions of Ireland and India with a view to discovering common I-E survivals. In doing so, he makes constant reference to Dumézil's work (especially to 1941a and 1943a). Many aspects of ancient Irish law and custom have very specific parallels in Vedic India, Dillon asserts, to say nothing of the clear analogy between the Druidic and Brahmanic classes. In the realm of epic, he points to the correspondence between Nala and Damayantī, and Serglige Con Culainn, and between Śunahśepa and Art, son of Conn, in the Book of Fermoy. No attempt is made, however, to "tripartize" the ancient Irish pantheon.

It remained for another of Dumézil's disciples, the late Jan de Vries, a Germanicist (cf. 1951, 1952) turned Celticist, to attempt this feat (cf. 1958, 1960a, 1960b, 1960c, 1961). De Vries' contributions to the system began in the early 1950's. In an article published in 1951, "Der heutige Stand der germanischen Religionsforschung," he claims that ethnology and its "jüngere Schwester," sociology, can and should be profitably employed by specialists in Germanic mythology. After concluding that "Wenn wir die indogermanische Götterwelt verstechen wollen . . . als eine wirklich organische gegliederte Welt, so müssen wir versuchen ihre Fonctionen zu bestimmen . . ." (1951, p. 9), de Vries goes on to cite Dumézil's system, toward which he expresses "grosse Bewunderung und Anerkennung" (p. 10). For example, following Dumézil, he points out that it is now possible to conceive of Indra and Thōrr, not as personifications of lightning or the weather (naturism dies hard!), but rather as personifications of the warrior ideal or function as it existed in ancient I-E social life. In a second article (1952), de Vries attempts to revive a previously discredited comparison between the Germanic stem *irmin*, which appears in a wide variety of names and words, and the Sanskrit *aryaman-*. Brushing aside linguistic difficulties, he points to the fact that many mythical persons bearing names containing the stem in question (e.g., Iörmungardr) are functionally similar to the "troisième souverain," Aryaman, as interpreted by Dumézil (cf. 1949*b*).

De Vries' ideas regarding the nature of the Celtic pantheon began to take shape in 1953, when he undertook an interpretation of the Gallic god Esus in light of the scenes depicted on the so-called Paris Altar. In one scene, the god is portrayed cutting a tree with an ax; in another, there appears the *tarvos trigaranus*, or 'bull with three cranes.' De Vries' interpretation here closely parallels that of Dumézil (1942), who linked Esus' behavior as depicted on the altar with Indra's (or Trita Āptya's) slaying of the three-headed son of Tvaṣṭar. According to Yajurvedic and epic tradition, Indra was exhausted by the fight and enlisted the services of a passerby, a carpenter, who completed the slaying by severing the three heads with his ax, upon which three birds (cf. the three cranes) escaped from each hollow. The foregoing Indic-Celtic parallel,[12] coupled with the Roman tale of Horatius and his slaying of the three Curiatii, led Dumézil to the conclusion that there may have been a Proto-I-E (or perhaps even more ancient) initiation ritual, applied to warriors, in which the initiate engaged in a mock battle with a three-headed wooden dummy (cf. Dumézil, 1942, pp. 131–135). Whether or not this ritual actually existed, the association here of an ax-wielding Esus with the *tarvos trigaranus* would, in light of the Indic and Roman materials just mentioned, seem to

---

[12] In the Gallic domain, there is the mythic tyrant Tauriscus, coeval with the threefold Geryon in Spain and inseparable from the Gallic three-horned bull statuettes and another sculpture (from Trèves) showing Esus felling a tree with a bull's head and three birds in the foliage. Cf. Pettazzoni (1954, pp. 125-135).

indicate that the Gallic god in question is indeed a representative of the second function.

A further step was taken in 1958, when de Vries attempted to demonstrate that Lug was the Gallic equivalent of Othinn (or Wodan), that both were typical representatives of the magico-religious (or Varunian) half of the first function. Both gods are the supreme beings of their respective pantheons (Gallic and Norse); both have only one eye; both are leaders in war (cf. the battle of Mag Tured and the war of the *Aesir* and *Vanir*) but do not themselves depend exclusively upon physical prowess; both are associated with ravens (Gallic *lugos* may mean 'raven'); both have a magic spear, and so on. Dagda is posited as the juridical (or Mitraic) counterpart (cf. Germanic *Tīwaz, or Týr); however, de Vries later substituted Nodens-Nuadu in this category.

This was followed in the next three years by a series of papers and monographs devoted, at least in part, to the tripartite structure of Celtic religion. One of these (de Vries, 1959) is concerned with manifestations of the number 3 in various Celtic materials. Another (de Vries, 1960a) is concerned with the *interpretatio romana*. Here, de Vries points out that Caesar's "Deorum maxime Mercurium colunt . . . post hunc Apollinem et Martem et Iovem et Minervam" was essentially a correct assessment of Gallic religion (though phrased, of course, in Latin terms) in that it included all the major divinities of the three functions, albeit not in the usual order. Mercurius and Jupiter are the two I-E "sovereigns" (that Caesar used the term Mercurius rather than Dius Fidius is only natural, considering the obscurity of the latter god in the first century B.C.); Mars indicates the presence of the warrior god, and Apollo and Minerva may be interpreted as indications of the presence of the two benevolent third-function deities (Quirinus, too, had become somewhat obscure in Caesar's day). Thus, de Vries concludes, Caesar was not ignorant or confused but presented in a nutshell a firm basis for a tripartite interpretation of the Gallic pantheon.

In 1961, in his *Keltische Religion*, de Vries summed up his thinking about the nature of the Gallic and other Celtic pantheons (cf. 1960c). In essence, it is as follows: Lug (or Teutates) and Nuadu correspond to Othinn and Týr, and the like, and represent the joint sovereignty (first function); Ogma (or Taranis) is the second-function figure; the third-function figures are still not wholly clear, though, from his preceding analysis of Caesar's interpretation, de Vries is sure that they are present (i.e., the Gallic "Apollo" and "Minerva"). The war between representatives of the third function and those of the first two is typified in Irish myth by the conflict between the *Tuatha Dé Danann* and the *Fomoire*, who collectively occupy a third-function position. De Vries cites here Dumézil's interpretation of the three *Machas* (cf. Dumézil, 1954*b*) and points to it as an important step in the understanding of Celtic religion. Finally, he disavows (1960*c*, p. 99) his former adherence (cf. 1953) to Dumézil's interpretation of Esus and *tarvos trigaranus* in terms of Indic tradition; the points of similarity, he now claims, are not clear enough to warrant the conclusions Dumézil draws. Despite this mild disagreement, de Vries' work is a most important augmentation of Dumézil's system. It brings the Celts much more clearly into focus and thus adds to the plausibility of the tripartite system as a whole.

In this connection, it is necessary to mention the work of Françoise Le Roux and Alwyn and Brinley Rees, who have also applied Dumézil's framework in their analyses of Celtic materials. Le Roux, among other things, has recently devoted a series of papers to the analysis of "le festiaire celtique" (1962*a*, 1962*b*, 1962*c*), in which she discusses various ancient Irish and Gallic festivals and ceremonial periods. *Imbolc* (celebrated in February) was the Celtic counterpart of the Roman Lupercalia, she asserts (1962*a*), and is clearly related to the third function, though its relative importance among the Celts seems to have been much less than among the Romans. *Beltaine*, the May festival, was a priestly (i.e., Druidic) affair; Bel(enus) is a surname of Lug in his illuminative aspects, and the festival (which still persists in parts of Scotland and Ireland) was centered on the exaltation of fire. *Samain*, the third great Celtic (Irish and Gallic) festival, celebrated November 1, is interpreted by her as the sacred transitional period between the old season and the new (the Celtic year seems to have begun in November), a time when the barriers between the natural and supernatural worlds are lifted. That this was a Pan-Celtic festival is evidenced by the fact that the Gallic calendar discovered at Coligny (cf. Le Roux, 1957) explicitly denotes a month named *Samon* and a period within that month as "the three nights of Samonios" (cf. the three-day duration of *Samain* in Ireland). A fourth festival, the *Lugnasad* (August 1), was also a first-function festival, Le

161

Roux claims, though here the focus is upon the king rather than upon the priesthood; in it the royal or sovereign aspect of the supreme god Lug was honored (cf. 1962c).

Perhaps Le Roux's most important contributions are her analyses of Druidism (1960, 1961a) and of the extent to which "le dieu borgne," the one-eyed figure, is present in Irish tradition (1961b). In her "Le dieu Druide et le Druide divin" (1960), and especially in her *Les Druides* (1961a), Le Roux pulls together from a variety of sources, both ancient and modern, all (or nearly all) that has been written about the Druids of ancient Gaul, Britain, and Ireland. Her premise is that the only fruitful way to approach the problems presented by this Celtic priestly class is to consider its social, ritual, and doctrinal aspects objectively and without recourse to the "romantic" speculations of earlier scholars.[13] The "hard" data exist, she feels, and it only remains for scholars to make judicious use of them. Her theoretical framework is basically Dumézilian. While the book cannot be labeled comparative in the strict sense, the author's orientation toward her subject is succinctly summed up in the first chapter. The Druids, she claims, "possédaient les deux aspects de la souveraineté: souveraineté guerrière et magique, souveraineté religieuse et juridique, et l'aspect 'Varuna' et l'aspect 'Mitra' selon les conceptions indiennes dans la terminologie fonctionnelle que nous empruntons à M. Dumézil" (1961a, p. 8). In Le Roux's work, then, the Druids are drawn definitively into the I-E system as a class corresponding to the Roman *Flāmines* and the Indic *Brahmans*. Although Dumézil had long since suggested this idea (cf. 1938a), and others had developed it (cf. Sjoestedt, 1940), it remained for Mlle. Le Roux to render it definitive.

Another aspect of Celtic religion, the relationship of blindness (or one-eyedness), is discussed by Le Roux in an article entitled "Le guerrier borgne et le Druide aveugle: La cécité et la voyance" (1961b). Drawing upon Dumézil's discussion (1948a and elsewhere) of the role of the "dieu borgne" in the first function, Le Roux attempts to point out in Irish tradition a connection between complete blindness and/or one-eyedness and the gift of prophecy and/or ability to perform feats of magic. One-eyed or blind Irish figures are Varunian in character, she asserts. The hero Cuchulainn, who is a second-function figure in most respects, nevertheless is

---

[13] Cf., for example, Frazer (1922, pp. 653-658).

often (though not constantly) described as having the ability to sink one eye into his head and at the same time to extend the other one to monstrous proportions. When this magical deformation occurs, Cuchulainn inevitably subdues his enemy in a Varuna-like fashion rather than by sheer physical force. Thus, a first-function characteristic, blindness, may, on occasion, devolve to a predominantly second-function figure, though when it does, that figure will act for the time being in a manner consistent with the magico-religious aspect of the first function: he will perform feats of either magic or clairvoyance. Although the chief god of the Druids, Dagda, is never described as either blind or one-eyed, blindness was indeed often a factor in the ability to prophesy, Le Roux claims, citing the many Druidic names that contain the element *dall-* ('blind'). In this connection, she also cites (1961*b*, p. 337) a remarkable instance wherein restoration of sight to a Druid (Dallan Forgaill) was a sign that he had lost his prophetic gifts and was soon to die (cf. the *Tromdamh Guaire*, or "Heavy Company of Guaire," an Irish text in which a number of examples of this sort may be found).

Dumézil, it will be recalled, has recently reevaluated his earlier position relative to "le dieu borgne" (cf. 1959*c*) and has asserted that "blindness" is not necessarily the same thing as "one-eyedness." Yet Le Roux's work here suggests that, as far as the first function is concerned, the difference between these two afflictions may not be so important, after all. The one-eyed and especially the blind person is at a disadvantage, certainly, when it comes to either physical combat or the management of food resources. Indeed, handicaps of this nature may well have been necessary preconditions to the assumption of certain priestly roles among the Proto-Indo-Europeans and their immediate descendants. That wisemen, or at least those who were in charge of the oral tradition, were characteristically blind in a variety of ancient I-E-speaking societies, may be seen in the tradition of Homer's blindness, the etymology of the word "bard" (which seems to have some connections with a form meaning "blind"), and in the fact that early Slavic storytellers were often intentionally blinded. In sum, it appears to me that Dumézil's (and Le Roux's) connection of *both* blindness and one-eyedness with an imputed ability to perform feats of clairvoyance and magic seems well founded, though whether this was a trait unique to I-E speakers is a moot point.

163

Disciples, Critics, and Assessment

The study by Alwyn and Brinley Rees, *Celtic Heritage: Ancient Tradition in Ireland and Wales* (1961) has also added to the Dumézilian interpretation of Celtic religion. In it Dumézil's scheme is judiciously applied, both to the several Irish mythological cycles (i.e., the "mythological" Ulster, Ossian, etc.), and to their Welsh counterparts (i.e., the "Four Branches of the Mabinogi," etc.). Unfortunately, the authors have limited themselves, for the most part, to Indic comparisons, although occasionally Italic and Germanic parallels are mentioned. The book is divided into three parts: (1) "The Tradition," in which the two Celtic traditions in question are outlined broadly; (2) "The World of Meaning," in which Dumézil's scheme is introduced and other interpretations are attempted (e.g., the importance of boundaries, both spatial and temporal; cf. Le Roux's [1957] discussion of the extent to which *Samain* involved a temporal boundary); and (3) "The Meaning of Story," in which specific categories of tales (e.g., "Births," "Wooings," etc.) are considered in more detail. In general, the Rees study correlates with those previously discussed, reaching essentially the same conclusions about the nature of the Celtic pantheon, the Druids, and so on, as have been drawn by Le Roux and de Vries. One important contribution here, as I see it, is that the two Welsh scholars present what is perhaps the best brief summary of Dumézil's system so far available in English (Rees and Rees, 1961, pp. 112–117); another is the extent to which the authors have conceived of their subject matter in ideological terms (cf. "The World of Meaning") rather than in purely taxonomic ones. Once again, there is a confirmation of Dumézil's basic assumption that social and mythological tripartition are manifestations of a unifying, deeply rooted I-E ideology.

THE IRANIANISTS

In addition to Benveniste and Wikander, a number of other Iranianists have found themselves, on occasion, partly or wholly in agreement with Dumézil's position relative to ancient Iranian religion. In 1947, following Dumézil's lead as set forth in *Naissance d'archanges* (1945), P. J. de Menasce attempted to prove not only that the Zoroastrian third-function figures Haurvatāt and Ameretāt were derived from Indo-Iranian (and ultimately I-E) prototypes (cf. the Nāsatyas), but also that under the names Hārūt and Mārūt they passed eventually beyond the borders of Iran proper and into

164

the realm of Judeo-Arab folklore, appearing in the Koran as a pair of angels. Citing an Indic myth wherein the Nāsatyas (or Aśvins) try to abduct Sukanyā from her ascetic husband Cyavana, but instead bring about the latter's rejuvenation and their own admission to the *soma* sacrifice through Cyavana's intercession with Indra, he points to the parallels contained in an Arab legend (Koran 2.96) of a young woman who escaped the attentions of the two angels in question and was raised to the heavens by Allah as the planet Zohra (or Venus). Even more interesting here is the fact that the woman is also referred to as Ānahid, a name that clearly recalls that of the ancient Iranian goddess Anāhitā. The latter was often associated with the stars, especially Venus (cf. *Yt.* 5.85). Although sublimated by Zoroaster into Spenta Armāiti, the cult of Anāhitā herself seems to have survived the Zoroastrian reforms almost intact, and hence the very name passed into Semitic folklore.

Another scholar who effectively utilized a Dumézilian framework is the late M. Molé. In 1951 he attempted to show that the *Vidēvdāt*, a set of ritual prescriptions against demons and techniques to counteract contamination from corpses, does indeed manifest functional tripartition, especially in the first chapter. In an enumeration of sixteen more or less mythical lands, one can see a concern not so much with geography as with the nature of the tripartite social universe. *Aryanam*, the first of these lands, is that once ruled by Yama Xšaita, the sovereign of the Golden Age, connected with Ahura Mazdah in much the same way as the Vedic Yama is connected with Varuna. The second is *Gava* of the Sogdians, a cattle land ruled by Mithra. The third through seventh lands are *Margiana*, called *sura*, or 'heroic'; *Bactria*, 'with raised banner'; *Nisaya*; *Harava*; and *Vaekereta*, meaning 'created by Vāyu,' a figure closely associated with the warrior hero Keresaspa. The eighth through thirteenth lands (e.g., *Urva*, called *pouruvastra*, 'rich in pasture') are clearly associated with third-function figures, while the remaining three are defined as non-Aryan. Thus, according to Molé, the tripartite world view is here applied to a conception of the earth and its component regions, each of which (save for the lands of the non-Aryans) is associated with one or more of the functionally differentiated divine beings.

Of more importance is a paper published by Molé in 1952, "Le partage du monde dans la tradition iranienne." Often cited by Dumézil (e.g., 1962*a*), it is an attempt to demonstrate some Iranian parallels to the Scythian origin myth. These parallels are to be found, Molé asserts, in several passages in the later Pehlevi texts (e.g., *Dēnkart* 7.1.28), in Firdausi (*Shāhnāmeh* 4.238), and in the writings of other post-Islamic Iranian poets. Although they differ somewhat in detail, these texts and writings suggest Feridun's division of the world among his three sons after submitting them to a test—either verbal or physical—which, as among the Scyths, only the youngest son passes. The eldest son, Salm, is awarded dominion over Rome and the West; the second son, Tōz, is given Turan (or Turkestan); and the youngest, Erič, is awarded Iran and sovereignty over all the rest. As among the Scyths, the latter lends his name to the Iranian people as a whole (cf. Kolaxaïs and the term *Skolotoi* as a designation for the Scyths as an ethnic group). Again, as in the Scythian example, each son is seen as a representative of one of the three functions: Salm chooses wealth; Tōz, valor; and Erič, law and religion.[14] Thus there is, in both instances, a combination of ethnic and social tripartition (Molé, 1952, p. 456).

Molé also points out (*ibid.*, p. 459) that the *Tura* originally (i.e., in the *Avesta*) had no connection with the Turks, and sees here a root (*tav-*) meaning simply 'strong.' Tōz is thus a representative of the second function, and the author cites the fact that most Iranian warrior figures (e.g., Garsasp, Kai Chosrau) are, in one way or another, likened to a *Tur*. The geographical regions mentioned in these late (Sassanid and later) texts reflect the political situation of the times; originally, Molé feels, "Turan" simply referred to a stratum in the social structure (*ibid.*, p. 460; cf. Molé, 1951).

Among Dumézil's most consistent Iranianist supporters is J. Duchesne-Guillemin, who, in two major works, *Zoroastre* (1948) and *The Western Response to Zoroaster* (1958), and a host of shorter ones, has done much to make precise Dumézil's ideas regarding the inherent I-E nature of Zoroaster's religion. In the 1958 book, largely concerned with a history of Zoroastrian studies and with an analysis of the impact of Zoroaster's religion upon Greek, Judaic, and Gnostic thought, Duchesne-Guillemin accords Dumézil a major place among those who, since the sixteenth century, have attempted to interpret the *Gāthās*, the *Yašts*, and other component

---

[14] Cf. the careers of Zoroaster's three sons as noted by Dumézil (1941*a*, pp. 92-103).

elements of the *Avesta*. Especially important is a summary of Dumé-zil's approach to the *Ameša Spentas* (Duchesne-Guillemin, 1958, pp. 38–51): that is, Aša and Vohu Manah as representative, re-spectively, of the magical and legal aspects of the first function; Xšathra as the representative of the second function; and Haurvatāt and Ameretāt, along with Armāiti, as representatives of the third function.

Although it contains nothing really new about the tripartite sys-tem, Duchesne-Guillemin's work provides yet another independent verification of Dumézil's position. After surveying the evidence—he is not unaware of Dumézil's critics—he aligns himself firmly with those who would see in the persons of the *Ameša Spentas* the repre-sentations of the three I-E functions, and who are certain that Zoroaster's reforms, sweeping as they were, were nevertheless basically consonant with the I-E ideological heritage. In an article published in 1960, "De la dicéphalie dans l'iconographie maz-déenne," Duchesne-Guillemin attempts to demonstrate the func-tional importance of bicephality. The Indic Aditi, the two-headed cow-bull, is compared to Ahura Mazdah's two-headed horse as de-picted on a coin from Kushana. Bicephality is interpreted as sig-nificant on a trifunctional level. In Duchesne-Guillemin's opinion, it is symbolic of omnivoyance (first function), swiftness (second function), and fertility (third function). The symbolic association of bicephality with omnivoyance is plausible enough, given Dumé-zil's delineation of the nature of the first function. Its association with swiftness and fertility is, however, less clear, though the third function does typically include twin figures (e.g., the Aśvins).

Other Iranianists who have generally accepted a Dumézilian framework include Kaj Barr (1952), H. Lommel (1954), J. C. Tavadia (1953*a*, 1953*b*), and G. Widengren (1960). Barr, like Duchesne-Guillemin, accepts with few reservations Dumézil's inter-pretations of the *Ameša Spentas*, especially as delineated in *Nais-sance d'archanges*. Lommel, though not explicitly one of Dumézil's disciples, has nevertheless arrived at an interpretation of the Indo-Iranian third-function female figure which is consistent with the tripartite scheme. According to Lommel, *Aredvi Sūrā Anāhitā*, 'humid, strong [or 'heroic'] immaculate' (i.e., elements of the third, second, and first functions; cf. the tendency, commented upon earlier, for the functions to be listed in inverse order) are three epithets of a **Harahvatī*. This postulated divine name (literally 'rich

Disciples, Critics, and Assessment

in waters') is actually attested in the Old Persian name of the province of Arachosia. Here, then, it can be seen that in the person of the third-function female (Armāiti-Anāhitā, Sarasvatī) are incarnated aspects of all three functions, despite the fact that the one that relates to fertility is dominant. Tavadia, though somewhat critical when it comes to technical points, nevertheless generally finds Dumézil's approach to Iranian matters useful. Widengren, in a discussion of the nature of ancient Iranian kingship, refers to Dumézil's views (cf. 1958a, pp. 32–33) about the connections of the I-E king with the third function. This raises some interesting and as yet unsolved problems. The exact nature of I-E kingship is a matter that still needs more research and analysis.

THE CLASSICISTS

Although some of Dumézil's most trenchant opposition has come from students of Greek and Roman religion, there are nevertheless a number of classicists who have found his ideas useful in interpreting their materials. Some, indeed, like Schelling, can almost qualify for the label "disciple." The latter, in an article (1960) dealing with the cult of Castor and Pollux at Rome, claims that "les travaux de Georges Dumézil ont incontestablement clarifié le problème [that of the origin of the Roman cult in question], en précisant le rôle des Jumeaux indo-iraniens, en les situant dans la hiérarchie fonctionnelle des dieux indo-iraniens" (p. 187). He also cites Wikander's (1957) argument that the Indic epic twins Nakula and Sahadeva are reflections of this I-E category of third-function Divine Twins, and concludes that Castor and Pollux must indeed be viewed from this trifunctional perspective. V. Basanoff, though critical of some of Dumézil's particular interpretations, has, on more than one occasion, utilized his general framework (cf. Basanoff, 1942). In an article published in 1947, "Note sur la triade 'indo-européenne' à Rome," Basanoff argues (on the basis of a passage in Festus [204 L]) that there is evidence for a triad consisting of Jupiter, Mars, and Janus, each with the epithet *quirīnus* (corresponding to the Umbrian epithet *Grabovius*; thus Vofion(o)- would correspond to Janus, not Quirinus). This was refuted in an appended note (Dumézil, 1947b).

F. Vian, in his "La triade des rois d'Orchomène: Étéoclès, Phlégyas, Minyas" (1960a), may also be classed as something of

168

a disciple. He attempts to demonstrate a trifunctional sequence in the mythical kings of Orkhomenos. Eteokles instituted the worship of the three *Kharites*, or 'Graces.' This term can mean either 'bodily grace' (third function), 'tribute due to a warrior' (second function), or 'majesty' (of or conferred by gods; first function).[15] Phlegyas, who follows Eteokles, was a crude warrior, the personification of *hybris*, whereas Minyas, who succeeded him, had large revenues and was the first to build a treasury (cf. Pausanias 9.36.4). After these symbolic trifunctional figures, the city was "complete"; it could bear its name and thus there ascended its eponym, King Orkhomenos. Thus one more fragment of Greek tripartition has come to light, rendering Dumézil's system that much more certain.

In another article (1960*b*), Vian turned his attention to the Typhon myth. His conclusions are interesting in light of Wikander's (1951, 1952*b*) suggestion that the kingship-in-heaven theme, in which the monster plays a most important role, is I-E in origin. As Vian sees it, Zeus's battle with the monster derived from an isolated story paralleling the typical fight between a second-function figure and a tricephalic monster so frequently encountered in other I-E traditions (cf. Horatius and the Curiatii; Indra and the son of Tvaṣṭar), which was later fused with a widespread, non-I-E Near Eastern dragon-slaying account (which had also diffused to the Hittites; cf. the Ullikumi and Illuyanka narratives) introduced by the Phoenicians in the early seventh century B.C. Thus, by the time of Hesiod, the story as it is generally known had fairly well crystallized. It is interesting in this connection that in later versions of the Typhon episode, notably those of Apollodorus (first century B.C.) and Nonnos (fifth century A.D.), the details undergo progressive elaboration, and become more and more similar to those of the Hurrian-Hittite version.

If Vian is right, some interesting possibilities present themselves. Perhaps the Hittites, too, grafted the dragon slaying onto an inherited three-headed monster tale and, like their Greek cousins a thousand years later, eventually fused this with another inherited I-E myth concerning the succession of three kings in heaven. The extent to which these three god-kings may reflect the three I-E

---

[15] According to Vian, Pindar's invocation (*Olympian Odes*, 14.3-7) of the three "Graces" at Orchomenos shows the same tripartition: Aglalia (second function), Euphrosyne (first function), and Thalia (third function). The same names appear in Hesiod in the same order.

functions is unclear,[16] though the fact that the one who finally attains perpetual sovereignty (e.g., Zeus) subsequently behaves in a fashion appropriate to the second function can perhaps be explained in Vian's terms, that is, as the result of a later admixture. In the original I-E protomyth (if there was such), the ultimate sovereign may well have had nothing to do with the monster, three-headed or otherwise.

Three other classicists who have, on occasion, expressed positive attitudes toward Dumézil and his work are Raymond Bloch (1946), J. Bayet (1947, 1957), and J. J. Orgogozo (1949). Bloch, in his *Origines de Rome* (1949), finds Dumézil's scheme very useful in analyzing early Roman social organization and religion (pp. 24–38), but asks whether the tripartite division into priests, warriors, and cultivators (i.e., *Ramnes*, *Luceres*, and *Titienses*) might not reflect a general organizational tendency on the part of late Neolithic and early Bronze Age communities, I-E-speaking as well as non-I-E-speaking. Dumézil was not slow to react to this suggestion (made originally in a review of *Naissance de Rome*) that socio-ideological tripartition might not be uniquely I-E; Bloch, he asserts (1947*b*, pp. 15–29), has neglected to review all the pertinent evidence. Despite this disagreement, I include Bloch among those who have supported rather than attacked Dumézil. Yet the point he raises has indeed been raised more than once by those who are clearly members of the opposition; I shall return to it shortly in my consideration of the criticisms of John Brough (1959).

Bayet, too, has often been critical of Dumézil's Roman interpretations, though, like Bloch, he readily gives credit to the brilliance of his overall system and the degree to which it renders intelligible otherwise obscure Roman data. Orgogozo, in a study of the Greek god Hermes, considers possible links between the latter and Loki, the Ossetic figure Syrdon, the Irish Bricriu, and other trickster figures, and, in doing so, draws heavily upon Dumézil's work, especially *Loki* (1948*c*). Yet Orgogozo concludes that the similarities are superficial: "Quand on examine le passé religieux d'Hermès, on s'asperçoit vite qu'il n'a rien d'indo-européen"—although he admits that "M. Dumézil garde à ce sujet [the existence of an I-E

---

[16] Following Wikander (1952), one would assume that in Iran, at least, *all three* were first-function figures. Cf. his analysis of Firdausi's king list discussed earlier.

trickster figure] la plus grande réserve" (Orgogozo, 1949, p. 168).

OTHER SUPPORTERS

In addition to those whose work has heretofore been summarized, Dumézil has received both implicit and explicit support from a variety of scholars, mythological and otherwise. One of these is Paul Arnold, who, in an introduction (1951) to the published version of Dumézil's inaugural lecture as a professor in the Collège de France (Dumézil, 1951*a*), clearly and most succinctly sums up the state of Dumézilian theory as of mid-century. Pointing out the difference between Dumézil's comparativism and that of the naturists, Arnold underlines the fact that "sans nier tout à fait la mythologie solaire, M. Dumézil porte l'accent sur une interprétation sociale et fonctionelle du mythe . . ." (p. 217). The author then proceeds to outline briefly the trifunctional approach, with emphasis upon the degree to which it renders early Roman historical materials intelligible. Arnold concludes that this approach "parvient à nous faire pénétrer profondement dans la préhistoire et la proto-histoire des peuples indo-européens" (pp. 220–221). Arnold has also published several other articles laudatory of Dumézil's efforts. One (1946) is concerned with the Roman *ius fetiale*, human sacrifices, the *devotio*, and other magical practices, and makes reference to Dumézil's early conception of Varuna, Ouranos, and Othinn as "binders" (cf. Dumézil, 1934); another (1950) is concerned with Mars and draws heavily upon both Dumézil and Wikander; a third (1952), entitled "La notion de souveraineté chez les Indo-Européens: En marge de l'oeuvre de Georges Dumézil," is concerned with an exegesis of Dumézil's theories regarding the Proto-I-E concept of sovereignty and the extent to which these theories can be validated in the several ancient I-E mythological traditions.

Among specialists in Germanic mythology, perhaps Dumézil's most consistent supporter, in addition to de Vries, has been E. Polomé. In 1953, following Dumézil's now discarded theory that Ouranos, Varuna, and Othinn were "binders" (cf. Dumézil, 1934), he attempted to demonstrate that the Proto-Germanic **ansuz*, 'sovereign god" (based upon Old Icelandic *æsir*, Old High German *ans-*, 'post, beam'), can be connected with the Sanskrit *asura-*.[17]

---

[17] The first to suggest this was H. Guntert (1923), who reconstructed Proto-I-E **an-s-u*; cf. Sanskrit *aniti*, 'breathe,' and *asu-*, 'life.'

Othinn, as chief of the *Aesir* (**ansuz*), is a "binder god," Polomé asserts, just as are Varuna (chief of the *Asuras*) and Ouranos.[18] The author sees the same root (as in **ansuz/asura-*) in a variety of other I-E words, including the Mitannian (Indic) name *Qalmaššura* (cf. Skt. *Kalma-asura*, 'bright lord'; for meaning, cf. Old High German *Berht-rich*) and the Hittite *ḫassus*, 'king' (presumably from 'lord'), which he detaches from *ḫas-*, 'beget', and ties to I-E **xen-s-y*, 'bind' (**xon-s-u-s*; cf. Greek ἡνία, Middle Irish *ēsi-*, 'reins'). The "binding" aspect of the foregoing is, of course, obsolete; but the extent to which the Germanic **ansuz*, the Sanskrit *asura-*, and perhaps the Hittite *ḫassus* all relate to the magical half of the first function suggests something regarding the nature of the function itself and that the concept of this function was widespread among I-E peoples.

In 1954 Polomé published two articles worthy of note. One (1954*a*) was concerned with the Germanic goddess Nerthus, who is closely associated with Njorðr. In analyzing this deity, whom he conceives of as a fertility figure, Polomé draws heavily upon Dumézil's ideas relative to the nature of the third function in general and upon the latter's interpretation of its Germanic manifestations in particular, such as Hadingus as a euhemerized transposition of Njorðr (cf. Dumézil, 1953*b*). The second work (1954*b*), entitled "La religion germanique primitive: Reflet d'une structure sociale," is an attempt to popularize Dumézilian interpretations of Germanic myth and society. In large measure, it is a survey of various conjectures about Germanic prehistory, religion, and society, most of which are phrased in terms of Dumézil's theories. For the most part, the author paints a balanced picture of these theories, though he does persist in his acceptance of the "binder-god" thesis then already largely, if not wholly, rejected by Dumézil himself (cf. Polomé, 1953).[19]

As has probably been evident from all that has gone before in

---

[18] From the supposed common root of *Ouranos* and *Varuna*, I-E **uer-*, 'to bind,' Dumézil had derived the term *runes* (believed to have been invented by Othinn); to this Polomé adds the Hittite *ḫurta-*, 'curse.'

[19] Another who persists in following this "binder-god" notion, despite Dumézil's rejection of it, is Montesi (1957), who (p. 14) claims to have isolated a "cosmic weaving" motif in various I-E mythologies. Eliade (1948), too, has drawn upon this theory in an attempt to develop a general theory of "le dieu lieur."

this and the preceding chapters, ancient Slavic myth and society have furnished little if any evidence one way or the other so far as Dumézil's thesis is concerned; but in 1961 a Russian, V. N. Toporov, sought to remedy the situation. After complaining of the sorry state of Slavic mythological scholarship, Toporov attempts a systematization of the ancient Russian pantheon along tripartite lines. As the first function representative he posits Stribog, referring to M. Vey's etymological analysis of *patri-bhagos* as meaning 'father-god' (cf. *Ju-piter*; cf. also the Old Persian *baga-*, 'god'). Perun, the thunder-god, represents the second function, while Volos, god of wealth and cattle, is the embodiment of the third function, as are a number of female figures such as Mokoš. Thus Toporov places a Slavic triad Stribog, Perun, Volos beside the Roman Jupiter, Mars, Quirinus, the Umbrian *Juu-*, *Mart-*, *Vofion(o)-*, the Norse Othinn, Thōrr, Freyr, and the Vedic Mitra-Varuna, Indra, Nāsatya. No attempt is made to interpret the balance of the old Russian divinities (e.g., Chors, Dažbog, Simarigl, Svarog), nor does the Russian scholar differentiate between the two aspects of the first function (is Stribog Varunian or Mitraic?). The twin aspects of the third function are also left unanalyzed (is Volos one of a pair of twins?). Nevertheless this represents a step in the right direction, for the distinction between Stribog and Perun (cf. Lith. Perkunas) does indeed seem to reflect the basic distinction between the first and second functions. As a "father-god," the former would certainly seem to be vested with sovereignty, while the latter's association with thunderbolts recalls Thōrr and Indra. Moreover, Volos' association with wealth and a source of sustenance does appear to have third-function implications. All in all, despite its shortcomings, I feel that Toporov's work may well prove to be a most important contribution to the overall pattern, and that it should be followed up.

An example of the limits to which one can go in applying, out of context, Dumézil's ideas may be seen in Przyluski's (1940) attempt to link lycanthropy with Wikander's (1938) conception of the I-E *Männerbund*. Other supposed aspects of this phenomenon (I-E werewolf tendencies), such as the bear disguise apparently underlying the Germanic designation *berserkir*, warlike *furor*, and ritual intoxication, are discussed with reference to Dumézil's work (cf. 1924a). The beverage (mead, *soma*, etc.) is assumed to have replaced a primeval cannibal meal. Needless to say, this thesis is untenable, especially in light of Dumézil's repudiation of the ambrosia cycle (cf. 1958*a*, p. 90).

Two other articles devoted to Dumézil and his efforts should be mentioned. In 1956 Brice Parain published an article in which he sought to introduce the layman to Dumézil's research. Entitled "Les dieux des Indo-Européens," it sketches the principles of the tripartite scheme and presents brief examples of the hierarchy as seen in Indic, Iranian, Italic, Celtic, and Germanic myth. Interestingly, Parain concludes with a discussion of the extent to which tripartition is still an important aspect of Western social organization and ideology (cf. Gerschel, 1956). I-E speakers are surrounded, he suggests, by a "ternary" rhythm that continually manifests itself in social patterns (e.g., the "three estates") and in habits of thought. This most important suggestion, that the tripartite ideology is an ongoing phenomenon, is discussed in chapter 7.

The second paper referred to above is by G. Turville-Petre, "Professor Dumézil and the Literature of Iceland," which appeared in the *Hommages à Georges Dumézil* (1960). Until recently, Turville-Petre points out, specialists in the study of Icelandic literature, especially of Snorri's *Edda*, found themselves in something of a cul-de-sac. It had apparently been demonstrated (by Mogk and others) that Snorri knew of few if any sources not presently known, and that he himself was the inventor of much that is contained in his work. As Turville-Petre puts it, "So long as Icelandic literature was studied solely by those who studied nothing else, the road was blocked" (1960, p. 210). Then came Dumézil and the new comparative method. Snorri, though a Christian and a euhemerist, can now be seen to have drawn on an inherited I-E source. For example, Snorri's elaborate discussion of Týr, elsewhere an obscure figure, gains new stature when viewed in terms of the tripartite ideology; the god emerges as a counterpart of Mitra, Vohu Manah, Scaevola, and other figures who represent the juridical half of the I-E concept of sovereignty. Although the author gives a good account of the degree to which Dumézil's research has affected Norse scholarship, it is perhaps unfortunate that, as this article is one of the few discussions of Dumézil available in English (cf. Gerschel, 1956; Tavadia, 1953*a*, *b*; Duchesne-Guillemin, 1958; Rees and Rees, 1961), it does not present a more general survey of Dumézil's system.

174

Other scholars[20] who have on occasion looked favorably upon Dumézil's work include Lindquist (1940, pp. 180–181), El'nickij (1947, p. 99), Ljungberg (1947), Devoto (1962, pp. 63–65), and Eliade (1948, 1961), who, though not principally concerned with I-E matters, has nevertheless often referred to Dumézil in his general works on the nature of religion, the sacred, and the like.

Finally, before concluding my discussion of the disciples, I should mention that as yet I have been unable to uncover any references to (let alone discussions of) Dumézil and his works by British and American anthropologists. The only anthropologist widely read in the United States and in England who appears to be aware of Dumézil is his colleague Lévi-Strauss, who has cited him on numerous occasions as a major contributor to the social anthropology of myth and religion and as one of the foremost contemporary students of structure (cf., for example, Lévi-Strauss, 1953, p. 535; 1964, pp. 23, 300). Unfortunately, however, Lévi-Strauss has not discussed the tripartite thesis in any detail, nor has he as yet attempted to contribute to it.

There are, nevertheless, some important similarities between the methods and assumptions employed by Dumézil and Lévi-Strauss. The latter (see especially 1955) has emphasized that all myths must be studied in terms of their underlying structure and that this structure can emerge only when one takes into account as many variant expressions of the same event as are obtainable. This point of view may be compared with Dumézil's insistence that he is primarily concerned with "système, explicite ou implicite." Moreover, to both scholars, *replication* is a key term. For example, Lévi-Strauss (1955, p. 59), in analyzing the Oedipus myth, points out that Zeus's rape of Europa, Oedipus' marriage to Jocasta, and Antigone's burial of Polynices (despite official prohibition), are all replications of a common structural element which he labels the "overrating of blood relations." Similarly, Dumézil underscores the extent to which the phenomena associated with each of the three functions is endlessly replicated (e.g., in the Indic tradition, Indra, Arjuna, exhortations to guard against foreign invasions, and the color red are all associated with the second function).

---

[20] Palmer (1960), too, should be mentioned here. In his *Achaens and Indo-Europeans* (1955), he attempted to demonstrate the presence of a tripartite, feudalistic social organization in Mycenaean Greece; cf. Dumézil (1958a, p. 94).

Disciples, Critics, and Assessment

THIEME

Perhaps the most intransigent of all Dumézil's critics has been the German Indologist and Indo-Europeanist Paul Thieme. While their disagreement has, in recent years, encompassed most of Dumézil's work, it began with, and has centered upon, the meaning of the Sanskrit root *ari-*, from which is derived the form *arya-*. In 1938 Thieme published a monograph entitled *Der Fremdling im Rigveda*. In it he suggested that *ari-* originally meant 'stranger,' and that it eventually evolved into both 'enemy' and 'host' (cf. Lat. *hostis* and *hospes*, and Eng. "guest"). Three years later, in his "Le nom des 'Arya' " (1941*c*), Dumézil criticized Thieme's interpretation and the battle was joined.

After complimenting the German scholar on his research ("Ces explications de textes font plaisir, pour le bon sens, pour la droiture de jugement ..." [Dumézil, 1941*c*, p. 37]), Dumézil goes on to point out several difficulties in Thieme's explanation of *ari-* as 'stranger, host,' and asks whether "sans en changer la direction, ne peut-on pas l'améliorer?" (p. 40). Dumézil claims that neither *ari-* nor its derivatives (*aryá-, árya-, āŕya-*) are used in contexts relating to persons "sans dieux" or "sans culte," as Thieme had suggested, and that if the term *aryá-* is indeed used to designate an enemy or rival (Thieme's secondary meanings derived from 'stranger'), it refers to one who is a member of the same ethnic group, if not the immediate social group, as the poet or speaker. In other words, it refers to one who does indeed worship the *same* gods (cf. *Rig Veda* 7.65.9, 10.12.1). Dumézil also points out that the Vedic language does not lack for terms specifically designating such concepts as 'guest' (*atithi-*) or 'enemy' (*śatru-*).

After surveying some of the passages where *arí-* and its derivatives are employed, Dumézil comes to the conclusion (1) that "au temps ou se rédigent les hymnes du *Rig Veda*, *arí* designe soit la 'communauté aryenne' soit le 'type aryen,' " (2) that "*arya*, adjectif dérivé d'*arí*, s'applique à tout homme (ou dieu, ou chose) appartenant à cette communauté ou repondant à ce type," and finally (3) that "*āŕya*, proprement adjectif dérivé de *arya*, tantôt signifie, adjectivement, 'concernant un être *aryá*,' " and is "pris substantivement pour désigner l'homme *arya* en toute circonstance et,

176

par opposition aux barbares—c'est à dire sensiblement la même chose qu'*aryá*" (1941*c*, p. 55). Dumézil also suggests that, as there is no common I-E word designating it, the generalized notion "stranger" is perhaps a "conquête ou un fantôme tardif de l'esprit humain" (p. 43), and that the idea in question was expressed in earlier times by much more specific terms such as "barbarian" and "rival."

This, then, was Dumézil's opening round in his still ongoing debate with Thieme. The argument over the meaning of *ari-* simmered steadily through the 1940's and into the early 1950's. In 1951 Benveniste joined the debate. In an article entitled "Don et échange dans le vocabulaire indo-européen," the Iranianist reviewed the controversy as it had developed up to that time and added some thoughts of his own with regard to the matter, especially as to the semantic ambivalence frequently encountered among I-E speakers relative to the forms in question (cf. Latin *hostis*, 'enemy'; *hostire*, 'recompense, requite'; *hostia*, 'propitiatory victim'; Gothic *gasts*, Old Slavonic *gostĭ*, 'guest').

Meanwhile, Dumézil published his *Le troisième souverain* (1949*b*). In it, it will be remembered, he incorporated the god Aryaman into his system as a "souverain mineur," as a specialized aspect of the benevolent or Mitra half of the first function as seen in Vedic India. This was in line with his previous thinking about the form *ari-*, for the name Aryaman is clearly derived from this root and, as such, can be viewed as a collective representation of the *arya-* as a community. As a result, the debate with Thieme escalated into a full-scale conflict, not merely over the validity of Dumézil's interpretation of *ari-*, but indeed over the validity of his theory as a whole, to say nothing of his methods.

In 1957 Thieme published two works severely critical of Dumézil's theory, especially as it relates to the nature of the sovereign Vedic gods. One (1957*b*), an article entitled "Vorzarathustrisches bei den Zarathustrien und bei Zarathustra" (see especially the section entitled "Ari 'Fremder,' " pp. 67–104), reasserts his original etymology of *ari-* and adds to it the assertion that Aryaman may best be conceived of as a god of hospitality. Here, Thieme constantly opposes his own linguistic methods to the "soziologische Ideologien" of Dumézil and Lommel (1954), who had supported Dumézil's interpretations of *ari-* and Aryaman. The idea that *ari-* meant originally "Volksgenosse" (as Lommel puts it) appears to Thieme to be

177

much too "soziologisch." In regard to Dumézil's suggestion that the generalized concept "stranger" may be a "fantôme tardif de l'esprit humain," Thieme asserts that "Ich kann nur wieder erstaunt fragen: Warum denn nur?" The concept "stranger" is, he feels, no more complex than that of "Volksgenosse" or "Mitglied der Volksgemeinschaft im weitesten Sinne" (i.e., member of the ethnic community as a whole; Thieme, 1957*b*, p. 99).

The other 1957 work, *Mitra and Aryaman* (1957*c*), was even more hostile to Dumézil and his theories. Here Thieme's avowed purpose is to call into question almost all Dumézil's ideas concerning the gods Mitra and Aryaman. While accepting Dumézil's (initially Meillet's) conception of Mitra as the personification of Contract, Thieme rejects his further assumptions that Mitra was also a personification of Friendship (i.e., Benevolence). He points out that these two concepts, while perhaps interrelated in that Mitra is a "friend" to those who keep contracts, are always quite distinct in the Vedic texts and thus cannot be traced back, as Dumézil suggests, to a single source. Thieme also rejects Dumézil's conception of Mitra as sharing in a joint sovereignty with Varuna; indeed, he appears to reject the whole idea of sovereignty (p. 58). Both gods are seen by him simply as personifications of abstractions, to be called upon should the need arise. Varuna, as the personification of True Speech (p. 61), is concerned with oath swearing in general; Mitra is more specialized, he claims, being concerned with those who enter into contractual relations. Their functions thus overlap, and neither god can be seen to exercise the kind of sovereignty claimed for them by Dumézil.

Turning to Aryaman, Thieme rejects Dumézil's contention that the latter god represents a specialized aspect of Mitra's friendship personification, and offers instead a conception of Aryaman as a personification of hospitality. This, of course, is in line with his rendering of the root *ari-* ('stranger'>'guest'). Many of Thieme's criticisms are directed toward what, in his opinion, are errors in Dumézil's reading of Vedic texts; for example (1957*c*, p. 12), he accuses Dumézil of making such gross grammatical mistakes as construing "(a) a dual as a plural, (b) a plural as a dual, (c) a singular as a dual" and of using the resulting mistranslation to prove his own ideas or to "disprove points correctly established by others." Finally, surveying Dumézil's interpretations of Roman texts, he finds what seem to be similar errors and issues a "warning to Latinists," suggesting that they guard against being misled by Dumézil into accepting false ideas about the nature of early Roman religion and society. Dumézil was not slow in replying to these attacks. In 1958, in answer to the charges leveled against him in Thieme's "Ari 'Fremder,' " he wrote an article entitled "Ari, Aryaman: à propos de Paul Thieme, '*Ari*, "Fremder" ' " (1958*d*). Here, once again, Dumézil points out that his antagonist's translation of *ari-* is misleading: "Parce qu'elle est très large, cette traduction—'l'étranger'—s'ajuste sans difficulté à presque tous les contextes, se colorant ici en étranger ami ou en hôte, là en étranger rival ou franchement ennemi ..." (p. 68). It is much more efficient, he asserts, to consider *ari-* simply as designating an ethnic community, that to which the derivative *arya-* refers. He also asks whether, even granting Thieme's tortuous chain of derivation (from 'stranger' to 'enemy' to 'host,' etc.), "est-il si naturel qu'un vaste ensemble d'hommes [the Indo-Iranians] se définisse, ethniquement, comme 'les hospitaliers'?" (p. 69). As far as Aryaman is concerned, Dumézil, of course, rejects Thieme's designation of him as the "god of hospitality" in favor of his own interpretation, "protector of the *arya*" (cf. Dumézil, 1949*b*). Dumézil concludes that if *ari-* must, as certain Rig Vedic contexts dictate, be translated as 'stranger,' the implication is one of "l'étranger non-barbare" (i.e., one who belongs to the same ethnic group as the speaker). In myth, he points out, Vr̥tra, who is truly a "foreign" demon, is *never* called *ari-* (1958*d*, p. 75).

Dumézil's reply to the charges in Thieme's other work, *Mitra and Aryaman*, appeared in an appendix to his *L'idéologie tripartie des Indo-Européens* (1958*a*), "Aryaman et Paul Thieme" (pp. 108–118). After citing two long passages from an article then in press in which he severely criticizes Thieme's interpretations, he proceeds to an examination of his opponent's charges that he had misconstrued pertinent Vedic texts. All are baseless, he asserts. Concerning the book as a whole, Dumézil concludes that some of Thieme's criticisms "m'ont paru justes et utiles et j'en tiendrai compte, sans qu'aucune change rien aux figures et aux rapports des dieux" (pp. 116–117); but, he adds, "Beaucoup [of these criticisms] sont, il faut le dire, du pur bluff, Thieme dénonçant comme antigrammaticale, ou erronée, ou dépourvue de sens, une traduction pourtant possible, mais qui n'a pas sa faveur, caricaturant mes exposés, inventant des contradictions pour avoir un grief de plus ..." (p. 117).

Meanwhile, another scholar intruded himself into the debate:

Disciples, Critics, and Assessment

Ilya Gershevitch, an Iranianist and an avowed anti-Dumézilian. In a joint review (1959) of Thieme's *Mitra and Aryaman* and Duchesne-Guillemin's *The Western Response to Zoroaster*, Gershevitch uncritically accepts Thieme's views of Mitra and Aryaman and lauds him for showing up "errors" in Dumézil's system. He asserts that the *Rig Veda* knows nothing of the distinctions Dumézil sees between Mitra and Varuna, claiming that "when Dumézil quotes Rigvedic passages in support of his theory he has either misunderstood them or pressed them to suit his views" (p. 54). Attacking, among other things, Duchesne-Guillemin's acceptance of the Dumézilian approach to the *Ameša Spentas*, Gershevitch claims that Dumézil views Aša and Vohu Manah "as if the Zoroastrian tradition provided no definition of the two entities and their names offered no clue to their character" (p. 155). He underscores the absence, in his opinion, of any Avestan evidence that would support Dumézil's (and Duchesne-Guillemin's) contention that Aša and Vohu Manah are, respectively, "more remote" and "closer" to mankind. "Varuna, too [Dumézil says], is more remote from man than Mitra. Hence Aša is Varuna in disguise and Vohu Manah is Mitra" (p. 155). Gershevitch claims that this interpretation is like defining the numbers represented by the symbols V and VI in terms of X and XI, simply because both pairs consist, respectively, of one and two signs. He concludes by stating that Dumézil's interpretations "constitute, in fact, not a doctrine which arises from the data as its defenders [i.e., Duchesne-Guillemin] claim, but one needlessly imposed on them from outside" (p. 156).[21]

This last is certainly a harsh criticism, too harsh, I feel, considering the vast scope of Dumézil's work; but, as I have noted elsewhere, it does indeed raise a point that must be considered in any evaluation of Dumézil's system (see chap. 7 for further discussion).

Dumézil's reply to Gershevitch, "Addendum à '*ari*, Aryaman' "

---

[21] In a note (p. 156), Gershevitch, commenting upon "Dumézil's lively reaction to criticism," quotes him as referring (1957c, p. 24) to anti-Dumézilians as "mongrels from every yard and of every color, yapping at our ankles." In a letter (1959i) to the *Bulletin of the School of Oriental and African Studies*, in which Gershevitch's review had appeared, Dumézil points out: "Mongrels is a wrong translation. The French word in my text is *roquets* literally 'pugdog,' which implies no such suggestion as to the paternal or maternal filiation of the special group of critics to whom it is applied. In its figurative sense according to the Hatzfield and Darmesteter dictionary the word *roquet* simply means 'un dédaigneur.' " This, incidentally, is the *only* item by Dumézil himself which has so far been published in English.

(1959*g*), appeared almost immediately. (It was on this article that Dumézil drew in his rejoinder to Thieme.) He begins by focusing upon what he terms Gershevitch's attempt to save Thieme's interpretation of *ari-* (in *Rig Veda* 9.79.3) by "comprenant *vṛka*, opposé à *ari*, comme 'l'animal loup' " (p. 171). This is most improbable, Dumézil claims. *Vṛka* cannot be established in the context as a species of animal: "... il s'agit, dans *ari* et dans *vṛka*, de deux variétés d'hommes" (p. 171). The opposition here, thus, is between two types of "enemies": "l'ennemi interne, de même race [*ari*], et l'agresseur barbare ou brigand [*vṛka*]" (p. 171). Dumézil also points out that Gershevitch (apropos of Duchesne-Guillemin) either fails to appreciate or ignores the many facts taken into consideration (e.g., *Yasna* 29.6) "par lesquelles j'ai mis en parallèle les couples Aša–Vohu Mana et Mitra-Varuna" (p. 173), and that a considerable number of Iranianists have long since publicly adopted his approach, including Benveniste, Barr, and Widengren, as well as Duchesne-Guillemin.

Thieme has continued to press his attack upon Dumézil and his theories. In 1960, in a significant article concerned with the Indic rather than Indo-Iranian character of the Mitanni deities, he credits Dumézil with first having pointed out the analogy between the list of Mitanni gods and that contained in *Rig Veda* 10.125.1 (cf. Dumézil, 1941*a*, pp. 11–15), and with having observed that, upon occasion, Indra functions to avenge bad faith in contractual relations (cf. *Rig Veda* 10.89.9), but goes on (pp. 309–310) to criticize him for failing to follow up the latter point. The failure, Thieme asserts, stems from Dumézil's attempt to fit the Mitanni data into his tripartite system. Claiming that any series of "men or gods" is easily divisible by three, he cites Brough's (1959) application of Dumézil's scheme to the Old Testament, as well as the fact that the *Rig Veda* contains numerous references to Indra as the slayer of the *amitra*, or "he who does not recognize the sacredness of contracts."

Dumézil's interpretation of *ari-* was bolstered in 1960 by an article by E. Laroche, "Hittite *arawa-* 'libre,' " which appeared in the *Hommages à Georges Dumézil*. Rejecting G. Neumannn's connection of the Hittite *arawa-* (Lycian 'Ερένα), 'free,' with the Lithuanian *arvas*, *ardvas*, 'free, independent,' Laroche shows that the Hittite *ara-* or *ari-* meant "propre au groupe social," hence 'communally acceptable, proper'; *ara-* as a person signified "individu appartenant à un groupe social," hence 'comrade, friend'; and *arawa-* was the derivative adjective characterizing an *ara-*, hence 'noble, free.' The author compares Dumézil's definition of Indic *ari-* as "celui qui appartient au groupe social exclusif," brushing aside Mayrhofer's derivation of *ari-* from I-E **ali-*, 'other,' and, by implication, Thieme's views that it connoted "stranger." This Hittite correspondence would, I feel, seem to tip the balance in Dumézil's favor, at least as far as his interpretation of *ari-* is concerned. I might add that the Greek ἄριστος, 'best,' might also perhaps be called to witness here. Its phonetic shape is broadly similar to the Hittite and Indic forms in question, and its derived meanings, 'noble,' and so on, would indeed seem to parallel those of *arawa-* and, to a lesser extent, *arya-*. It seems possible to me that the standard meaning of ἄριστος itself may ultimately have derived from the same sort of ethnic self-identification postulated by Dumézil, and that this was preserved in its connotations: the "best" man, the prototype of the "aristocrat," would originally have been one who was a member of the speaker's social group and not an outsider. The foregoing cannot, of course, be supported on a rigorous philological basis, but, in my opinion, it nevertheless lends further support to Dumézil's position.

Thus is the controversy between Thieme, Gershevitch, and Dumézil over the interpretation of *ari-*. While it seems likely that Dumézil is correct in his views here, the debate has developed into one involving far more than merely the meaning of a Vedic root and its derivatives. It concerns the whole of Dumézil's approach. Thieme's assertion that his opponent relies too heavily upon "soziologische Ideologien" sums up what seems to be at the heart of the matter: an objection to the use of sociological and social anthropological methods to explain I-E phenomena. This seems to me to be an invalid objection, for I believe with Dumézil that purely philological methods and assumptions are not alone sufficient when it come to the analysis of myth and the figures comprising it.

But Thieme and Gershevitch are not alone in their suspicion of "la méthode sociologique." Others, whose principal concern lies with Greek and especially Roman religion, have also taken Dumézil to task for his use of this method. These "others" include members of the so-called primitivist school, who, paradoxically, have sought to discredit Dumézil in terms of an anthropology now long since abandoned by most contemporary social anthropologists.

Decidedly antisociological, and abhorring the comparative method when it is applied to anything other than purely linguistic matters— an abhorrence that would, in large part, seem to stem from the failures of Müller and his school (cf. Rose, 1959, pp. 6–9)—the primitivists include those Latinists and the like who have sought to explain the religions of classical antiquity, especially Roman religion, in terms of the degree to which they were possessed of traits found among the religious beliefs of contemporary primitive peoples. Special emphasis has often been placed upon the concept of dynamism or mana, as delineated by R. R. Marett (1909), and Roman religious beliefs and practices have been compared to those of the Melanesians, Polynesians, and other peoples whose beliefs center in the existence of an impersonal supernatural force. Those among them who have stressed mana less heavily have indeed sought to find other primitive features in Roman religion and have drawn liberally upon Mannhardt, Frazer, and Harrison in their interpretations. Needless to say, this approach is very much at odds with that developed by Dumézil in his post-Frazerian period, and he has not been loath to say so. The result has been another running controversy.

Without doubt the most formidable spokesman for the primitivist approach to Roman religion has been the late Scots mythologist H. J. Rose. In a review of Dumézil's work published in 1947 he severely criticized the latter's reliance upon sociological assumptions and questioned the basis of his interpretation of Jupiter, Mars, Quirinus, citing what seemed to him more logical derivations. He also questioned the uniqueness of tripartition among I-E speakers and the degree to which the comparative method as developed by Dumézil could prove useful in solving problems of Roman religion. Dumézil has replied to this review on more than one occasion (cf. 1948b, pp. 12–16), pointing out the degree to which one's interpretations tend to be skewed if one does not attempt to isolate functional parallels among several related societies (e.g., Rome and Vedic India); the myths of one may well shed light on the rituals of another and vice versa.

Like Thieme, Rose has persisted in his opposition and has stimulated others to take up the cause. For example, in a review of Dumézil's *Rituels indo-européens à Rome* (1954*b*), Rose claimed that Dumézil had erred in not recognizing the manaïstic basis of such figures as Mater Matuta and Lua Mater. These and other Roman divinities, Rose suggests, can be understood only in terms of the concept *numen*, the Roman equivalent of what is termed "mana" in Melanesia and elsewhere. Dumézil responded to this criticism in the "Notes finales" of *Déesses latines et mythes védiques* (1956*a*, pp. 118–123), pointing out that the Scots classicist has not only misread him (e.g., only *one* Indic ritual, the "vache à huit pieds," not two, as Rose claimed, were seen as paralleling the *Fordicidia*; 1956*a*, p. 120), but has failed to understand the reason behind his use of Vedic and Roman parallels (e.g., Rose's remark [quoted by Dumézil, 1956*a*, p. 120] relative to the functional symbolism of colors in the *albati russati uirides*: "any attempt to trace them to an early source, Aryan or otherwise, is stultified in advance"). As for the term *numen*, Dumézil emphasizes that it was never used in the sense that a Melanesian might use the term "mana" (i.e., to refer to an *impersonal* force) but rather that it always appears in expressions such as *numen iovis*, *numina deorum*, and adds that "à aucun moment de leur développement, les Romains n'ont eu de mot pour exprimer ce mana d'où l'on [i.e., Rose and his colleagues] veut tirer toute leur religion" (*ibid.*, p. 119).

It should be emphasized that Rose and others who have criticized Dumézil for his supposed failure to consider the numinous or manaïstic aspects of Roman religion are also heavily biased against the methods and assumptions of structural analysis (i.e., Dumézil's "la méthode sociologique"). To Rose (1959, p. 10), for example, the most up-to-date methods of comparative mythology are those developed by Mannhardt and Lang. Nowhere does he mention, let alone discuss, the vast body of relevant theory developed by sociologists and social anthropologists since Durkheim. There is an irony in this, for the "anthropological" theories that Rose brings to bear in criticizing Dumézil (i.e., those of Mannhardt, Lang, Frazer, Marett, etc.) are precisely the ones that the latter was forced to reject as inutile for his purposes (cf. Dumézil, 1958*a*, pp. 91–92).

Perhaps the most manaïstic of the primitivists is H. Wagenvoort, a Dutch Latinist, whose *Roman Dynamism* (1947) sought to explain the whole of Roman religion in terms of this phenomenon. It goes without saying that this position has more than once been criticized by Dumézil. In 1952, for example, he published an article,

"Maiestas et *gravitas*: De quelques différences entre les Romains et les Austronésiens" (1952*d*), in which Wagenvoort's assumption that the two Roman terms mentioned in the title above had to do with mana (cf. the fourth chapter of *Roman Dynamism*) was castigated. Roman society, even in its earliest phases, cannot be compared with that of Melanesia, Dumézil asserts, and neither can its religion be compared with Melanesian religion.[22]

Among other critics who have insisted that Roman religion can be understood only on its own terms and that the only valid comparisons are with contemporary primitive religions, are the Italians U. E. Paoli and Angelo Brelich. The former has attempted on several occasions (e.g., 1950) to advance the thesis that Quirinus is not Latin but Sabine, that the name derives from **co-uirites*, and that Dumézil's delineation of him as a third-function figure is ambiguous. Dumézil responded to this statement (1955*c*), reiterating his stand concerning the origin of the name Quirinus and pointing to the fact that a similar ambiguity surrounds many third-function figures, who are at once at the bottom of the hierarchy yet primary in the sense that they tend to appear first and subsume in their persons traits of the other two functions (cf. the Norse Freyr). Brelich, in a review (1957), was critical of many points relating to Dumézil's interpretation of Roman religion. This was followed by a rejoinder (Dumézil, 1957*c*) and a surrejoinder (Brelich, 1958), and once again a controversy began.

Jan Gonda, a colleague of Wagenvoort's, has also entered the lists against Dumézil, though his criticisms have not been quite so polemical as those heretofore discussed. In an article entitled "Some Observations on Dumézil's Views of Comparative Indo-European Mythology" (1960*b*),[23] the Dutch scholar claims that, in reading Dumézil's often "fascinating" books, one can hardly escape the "conviction that his [Dumézil's] conclusions sometimes rest on too

---

[22] Cf. Wagenvoort's rejoinder in Latin (1952) and Dumézil's brief surrejoinder (1954*c*).

[23] See also Gonda (1960*a*), wherein the Dutch scholar offers a number of very specific criticisms. Dumézil's debate with Gonda began in 1950 as a result of the latter's attempt (Gonda, 1950) to uphold the connection of *Brahman* with the root *brh-,* 'be great,' and to discard the equation between it and the Latin *Flāmen*. In doing so, he criticized Dumézil's extralinguistic arguments for the equation (cf. Dumézil, 1935), especially the one concerning the extent to which *Brahmans* and the *Flāmen Diālis* were subject to similar sets of taboos.

small a basis, that some of the etymologies which he proposes are very doubtful, that he is sometimes carried away by his own hypotheses, constructions and formulations" (p. 4). Gonda then proceeds to offer a number of specific criticisms: for example, (1) Ouranos and Varuna cannot be equated simply on the basis that each might possibly be conceived as a "binder" (here, of course, he is kicking a long-dead horse); (2) Indra's three "péchés" and the three "sins" of Heracles (cf. Dumézil, 1956b) do not necessarily reflect an I-E tripartition and perhaps mirror, rather, a "widespread" tendency in popular literature toward a threefold characterization of "ancient heroes"; and (3) the concepts *Dharma*, *Kāma*, and *Artha* are not necessarily linked to the tripartite system, for he claims that Dumézil has not only mistranslated their respective meanings (i.e., 'morale,' 'passion,' and 'intérêt économique') but has also overlooked the fact that the traditional Indian order of presentation is *Dharma*, *Artha*, *Kāma* (i.e., first, third, and second functions).

Gonda's own point of view is perhaps best summed up in the following passage (1960b, p. 9): "What can be reasonably inferred is first that, already in prehistoric times, various I-E peoples had a predilection for classifications, and particularly for enumerative, and often tripartite formulations, and in the second place, that the elements of these enumerations are not rarely vaguely [*sic*], sometimes in a more evident way, co-ordinated with a socio-religious tripartition." Dumézil's "difficulty in arriving at exact definitions," Gonda notes "opens the door to mistakes and subjective interpretations."

I could continue almost indefinitely to discuss the various reviews, rejoinders, and surrejoinders that have characterized Dumézil's bouts with the primitivists and their "fellow travelers,"[24] but to do so would be to duplicate much of what has already been said. The essence of the position taken by Rose, Wagenvoort, Brelich, Paoli, Gonda, and others would seem to be that, as Gonda puts it, Dumézil is "carried away by his own hypotheses, constructions and formulations." This very well may be, but I do not feel that those

---

[24] For example, Dumézil has also responded (1961b) to critical reviews by the primitivists W. Pötshcer (1960) and M. van den Bruwaene (1959) of his *L'idéologie tripartie des Indo-Européens* (1958a), complaining that they have misread and misunderstood him, and have failed to appreciate the importance of his discoveries about the nature of I-E ideology.

who, ignoring the great mass of evidence clearly pointing toward a common I-E mythology, would substitute a manaïstic approach are any freer from the same criticism.

FRYE AND KUIPER

One who has indeed made a similar suggestion is R. N. Frye (1960), who, addressing himself to Thieme, Gershevitch, the primitivists, and others, has emphasized that criticism alone is not enough when it comes to Dumézil's theories about the nature of I-E myth and society. After outlining Dumézil's system, Frye neither accepts nor rejects the idea of a tripartition reflecting social forms; he grants that it is entirely possible that "ur-Indo-European" society might have been organized in the fashion Dumézil suggests. What he does criticize is the latter's insistence that this tripartition was the central feature of I-E ideology. He credits Dumézil with being the only one present to have a system by which I-E religion may be interpreted. To oppose him, Frye feels, one should have in mind another, more satisfactory system (*ibid.*, p. 166).

The first to pick up Frye's challenge to develop a new and better approach to I-E religion before taking Dumézil to task was F. B. J. Kuiper (1961). Concerning himself solely with Indic literature (especially the *Vedas* and the *Mahābhārata*), Kuiper feels he has found such a system in a progressive series of polar dichotomies based upon geographic orientations. The basic dichotomy, he suggests, is of north-east and south-west, the former two compass points being associated with the "upper world" (i.e., that of the *Devas*) and the latter two with the "lower world" (i.e., that of the *Asuras*). There are progressively more restricted dichotomies within each "world": for example, Mitra and Varuna are both associated with the west, and when any other quarter is compared with the west, they function as a unit (i.e., as Mitra-Varuna); however, within the western quarter, these two deities are opposed to each other, Mitra representing sunrise (or life) and Varuna representing sunset (or death).[25]

Kuiper sees these dichotomies carrying over into the *Mahābhārata* in the overall opposition between the Kauravas and Pānda-

---

[25] Can one perhaps detect in Kuiper's concern with sunrise and sunset a lingering trace of the solar school? Cf. Müller, *et al.*

vas, and in the composition of the Pāṇḍava group itself: north and east are represented, respectively, by Arjuna and Bhīma, west and south by Nakula and Sahadeva; the center (or totality) is represented by Yudhiṣṭhira. Thus, in Kuiper's opinion, Indic (and by extension I-E) religious ideology is fundamentally composed of a set of binary or polar oppositions. He admits that Dumézil's tripartition based upon social classes may indeed exist, but feels that it is probably a secondary rather than a dominant aspect of I-E ideology.

As I see it,[26] Kuiper's response to Frye's challenge falls considerably short of the mark. He ignores the vast amount of comparative evidence Dumézil has brought to bear relative to social and supernatural tripartition among the Iranians, Romans, Scandinavians, and Celts. That Kuiper may possibly have discovered a secondary (perhaps non- or even pre-I-E) aspect of Indic myth cannot be overlooked; it is possible to read certain geographical orientations into the relationship between Mitra and Varuna. It is even remotely possible that it is I-E in origin. (As Rees and Rees [1961] have demonstrated, the Celts were indeed fond of phrasing things in terms of the points of the compass; cf. the "four quarters of Ireland," etc.) But it seems extremely doubtful that these geographical polarities will ever be shown to be the dominant focus of I-E ideology as a whole or that of the Indians in particular. Until Kuiper is able to document their presence in all the areas wherein Dumézil has demonstrated the presence of tripartition, I must continue to agree with Frye that Dumézil is the only one at present to have a system by which to interpret I-E religion.

BROUGH

One of the most serious attacks so far launched against Dumézil has come from the British Indologist John Brough. It began in 1956 when, in the course of a BBC "Third Programme" (August 24), Brough sharply criticized the whole of Dumézil's interpretation of Indo-Iranian religion and, citing the recent criticisms of Rose and others, had many unkind things to say about his then recently published *Déesses latines et mythes védiques* (1956a). Shortly thereafter (1957c) Dumézil responded to this new attack,

---

[26] To my knowledge, Dumézil has yet to reply either to Frye or to Kuiper.

exhibiting considerable touchiness and bitterness, even going so far
as to paraphrase Mallarmé's "Après-midi d'un faune" in saying that
his reply to Brough "prouve hélas que bien seul il s'offrait / pour
triomphe la faute (idéale) de Rose."

But Brough has indeed continued to follow "la faute idéale de
Rose." His most important attack came in 1959 in an article entitled "The Tripartite Ideology of the Indo-Europeans: An Experiment in Method." Here, rather speciously, he offers a "Dumézilian"
analysis of some Old Testament data as a control experiment to test
the validity of Dumézil's repeated assertion that the Indo-Europeans were unique in their possession of a tripartite ideology. The
results of this experiment are, of course, seen by Brough to be
decisively negative.

Consciously applying Dumézil's methods, the British Indologist
feels he is able to discover a tripartite ideology in the Old Testament, exactly paralleling the one that Dumézil claims to have found
in early Roman history, the *Vedas*, and elsewhere. He gives as an
example the persons and events described in the Book of Judges:
Ehud and Deborah may be viewed as representatives of the first
function (cf. Mitra and Varuna, respectively); Gideon and Samson
may be seen as representing the chivalrous and brutish aspects of
the second function (cf. Indra and Vāyu, Arjuna and Bhīma); and
the "wives of the Benjamites" (Judges 31:16) would seem to belong to the third function. A second trifunctional scheme, Brough
asserts, occurs in the two Books of Samuel and the first book of
Kings with Eli and Samuel representing the first function; David
(as king) and Saul, the second; and David (as shepherd), the third;
Solomon is seen as a summation of all three.

On the basis of his analysis, Brough (1959, pp. 85–86) concludes
that "if any worker in this field still wishes to maintain that the
three 'fonctions' are significantly Indo-European, he should first
show that, in terms of the procedure, my analysis of the Old Testament material is incompetent and radically wrong; or, accepting my
results in principle, show that they are due to direct Indo-European
influence upon the Hebrews." Finally, he asks (p. 86) whether the
"nature of things," Dumézil to the contrary notwithstanding, does
not indeed everywhere dictate a tripartition of ideas, a division into
ideas concerning magic and the priesthood, defense and offense, and
sustenance.

Dumézil's rejoinder to Brough was almost immediate. In a 1959

189

article, "L'idéologie tripartie des Indo-Européens et la Bible" (1959*h*), he effectively shows up the speciousness in Brough's "experiment." Claiming that the latter has misapplied—or misunderstood—his method, Dumézil proceeds to a systematic examination of his critic's evidence. To cite an example, Dumézil points out (pp. 102–103) that, in extracting Ehud, Deborah, Gideon, and Samson from the list of Judges, and in labeling the first two as "first function" and the last two as "second function," Brough has conveniently overlooked such figures as Ontiel, Abimalek, and Japthet, "sur lesquelles le livre [of Judges] dit beaucoup." "Où," he asks, "ai-je donné l'exemple de cet arbitraire . . .?"

Dumézil's main point here seems to be that nowhere in Brough's evidence can one find a clear-cut trifunctional distinction *in the text itself*, such as one finds, for example, at Rome in the distinction between the *Ramnes*, *Luceres*, and *Titienses*. Dumézil himself supplies what might be such in a passage (Jeremiah 9:22–23) apparently overlooked by Brough. In it the prophet exhorts his people not to glorify, respectively, wisdom, valor, and wealth. Dumézil suggests that, given the period in which this was written (seventh century B.C.), it could be understood as an exhortation to the Israelites not to follow a "voie étrangère" in an attempt to overcome the calamities then befalling them. This interdicted "voie," he argues, could indeed be the I-E "voie" or ideology, which, by this late date, had affected Egyptian society and was undoubtedly well known throughout the Near East.

There is a great deal of cogency in what Dumézil says here. Almost without exception, from Genesis on, the Old Testament was composed at a time long after the first I-E speakers appeared in the Near East; indeed, an Indo-Iranian- (or Indic-) speaking warrior class had gained political hegemony in northern Syria and Babylonia several centuries before the traditional date of the Exodus (*ca.* 1200 B.C.), and there is some evidence that I-E speakers had penetrated Palestine at a time when Hebrew society as generally conceived of had not yet crystallized.[27] That Hebrew culture of 1000 B.C. had assimilated some I-E ideas is by no means inconceivable, and thus Brough's examples of Hebraic tripartition, even if correct, are not conclusive. Moreover, Dumézil himself suggests that the I-E

---

[27] Indeed, Professor Marija Gimbutas informs me that there are sound archeological reasons for assuming an I-E penetration of Palestine as early as 2300 B.C.

pattern may well have been known and conceived of as a "voie étrangère" by Jeremiah.

Yet, despite the weakness of the evidence with which he supports it, Brough's central point—that a tendency to divide phenomena into those associated with magic and religion, offense and defense, and the gaining of sustenance, is part of the "nature of things"— remains a crucial one (see chap. 7 for further discussion).

OTHER CRITICS

The examples of anti-Dumézilian sentiment discussed in the preceding pages are merely those that, in my opinion, are representative of the several directions the reaction to Dumézil's thesis has taken. Indeed, the list of scholars who, for some reason or other, have found fault with Dumézil's theories, methods, and interpretations is well-nigh endless. For example, P. Lambrechts (1946) objects to the classification of Mars as a representative of the second function, and likewise to the assignment of Quirinus to the third. To Lambrechts, Quirinus is the Sabine pendant of Mars (a point often raised by the primitivists), and both seem to belong to the sphere of rural divinities (cf. Dumézil, 1957b). C. Koch (1953), though agreeing that "die altindische Kastenordnung liefere den Schlüssel zum Verständnis der römischen Verhältnisse" (p. 6), nevertheless takes exception to certain of Dumézil's ideas concerning the origin and character of Quirinus (cf. Dumézil's rejoinder, 1953e). And K. Helm (1955) doubts whether the "soziologische" approach espoused by Dumézil, Arnold, de Vries, Polomé, and Wikander is any more efficient than his own "geschichtliche" method; he also considers the tripartite character of I-E mythology far from proven. In a rejoinder (1956f), Dumézil politely rectifies some of Helm's factual errors and misconceptions and asserts that he has no "school" or "disciples," as the latter had suggested. Arnold, he claims, is a popularizer for whom he is not responsible.

I have already noted that Bloch and Basanoff, who may be broadly characterized as "neutrals" rather than as either "disciples" or "critics," have, on occasion, taken stands at odds with those of Dumézil. In each instance, Dumézil has responded vigorously, claiming that his erstwhile supporters have fallen into error. There is, however, one thing that separates the latter two (and others like them; cf. Koch) from the rest of the critics heretofore discussed:

they accept in principle the kind of research Dumézil has done and find fault with its details rather than its general objectives.

These, then, are the critics. For the most part specialists in one or another branch of I-E studies (Indology, Iranian studies, Roman studies, etc.), they have among them criticized almost every major theory or interpretation Dumézil has promulgated. Yet, despite the range of their attacks and the often very specific bones of contention involved, two underlying themes can be discerned. The first is a distrust (based perhaps in large part upon misunderstanding) of the sociological approach, especially when it is coupled with the comparative method as practiced by linguists; the result is often either a partial or a total rejection of the *idea* of the three functions as expressive of a common, inherited ideology that underwent differential development among various I-E-speaking peoples. The second, typified by Brough but implicit in most of the others, is a rejection of the unique character of I-E social and mythological patterns, let alone those of any all-encompassing ideology. That these are indeed the major axes upon which opposition to Dumézil's theories has turned can be seen quite clearly in the character of his rejoinders, which inevitably stress the efficiency of "la méthode sociologique" and the uniqueness of "l'idéologie tripartie des Indo-Européens."

7

An Anthropological Assessment

As the present state of Dumézil's system has been summarized and both the contributions made to it by his disciples and the objections raised against it by his critics have been reviewed, it is time to evaluate the "new comparative mythology" from the standpoint of social anthropology, for, rightly or wrongly, Dumézil and his colleagues are making what are essentially anthropological observations. In the last analysis they are concerned with the extent to which a common linguistic heritage is necessarily accompanied by a common social and cultural heritage. Despite their tendency to become involved in minutia, they are concerned with the discovery of, as Dumézil (1951a, p. 223) puts it, "le système, explicite ou implicite," inherent in the myths, social forms, religions, and, above all, ideology characteristic of communities whose members spoke (and/or still speak) languages classifiable as belonging to the I-E family. In short, though necessarily predicated in large measure upon the assumptions of historical linguistics, Dumézil's system is by nature an anthropological one, and it is in anthropological terms that it can best be assessed.

THE VALIDITY OF THE SYSTEM

Before attempting to assess some of the theoretical implications of Dumézil's thesis, it is necessary to comment upon the validity of the "système" he claims to have isolated; for if it is invalid, as many of his critics have asserted, then there would be no reason to attempt such an assessment. Therefore, it is necessary to ask to what extent Dumézil is correct in his conclusion that the several ancient I-E-speaking communities shared a common, tripartite social organization, and that the latter was reflected in a common set of supernatural beliefs; and to what extent this conclusion is firmly grounded in the data (cf. the three questions posed earlier on pp. 64–66).

To answer these questions, a brief review of the early history of Dumézil's concern with tripartition is in order. Initially, it will be recalled, his approach to comparative I-E mythology, while perhaps unconventional, was not sociologically oriented. He came to recognize the social basis of I-E religion only after exhausting, in the course of a decade or so, several other avenues of approach to this subject. Obviously, the naturistic approach had failed, and it was necessary to find a new theoretical foundation upon which to build a new and sounder comparativism. At first he attempted to apply a Frazerian framework, and the result was, among other things, the now long since discarded "ambrosia cycle." Later, the equally abortive "binder-god" hypothesis emerged out of an attempt to link Ouranos and Varuna. Gradually, however, as he became more and more sensitive to the importance of social organization in the study of religious phenomena—a sensitivity that, as noted elsewhere, seems to have been due in no small measure to his association with Mauss and Granet—he began to see a correlation between Indic and Iranian stratification patterns (cf. Dumézil, 1930b) and arrived at the then still tentative conclusion that Proto-Indo-Iranian social organization was composed of the now familiar "three functions": priests, warriors, and food producers. He was supported in this conclusion by the independent but parallel conclusions reached by Benveniste (1932, 1938). Only later did he come to recognize the extent to which the major gods of the *Rig Veda* were personifications, "réprésentations collectives," of this tripartite social structure. Once this had been determined, he began to probe deeper and to examine other ancient I-E-speaking societies to see if a similar pattern could be found. By the mid-thirties he had found in the French school of sociology, as developed by Durkheim, Mauss, Granet, and others, the theoretical basis he had been seeking; and, as more evidence was obtained, especially from the Latin and Norse regions, the system rapidly began to crystallize.

Thus, Dumézil's initial discovery of I-E social and supernatural tripartition emerged slowly and painfully out of the data. It was

194

only after this pattern had been fully documented in the Indo-Iranian area, and after he had begun to see that it was present elsewhere, that he came to the conclusion (1938–39) that it was I-E. There is no evidence to suggest that he began with a preconceived hypothesis. Indeed, Dumézil has been quite emphatic on this point; it will be remembered that one of his chief criticisms of Brough's attempt to isolate tripartite patterns in the Old Testament is that the latter was *selective* in the figures cited as representative of the three functions. Nowhere, Dumézil asserts, is he able to find tripartite patterns in the texts themselves. Of no small importance here is the fact that Dumézil has refrained from reading into Greek, Slavic, Baltic, and Hittite myth patterns that are not present in the relevant texts. The result has been that Greece has provided only marginal examples, and the other three have yielded almost nothing that would support his position. If, indeed, he was merely attempting to validate a preconceived scheme, he could easily have selected data from those traditions which would support it.

This is not to imply that I agree with every example of tripartition which Dumézil and his colleagues claim to have uncovered; far from it. Admittedly seeking to discover "le système, explicite *ou implicite*" (italics mine), he has often interpreted specific phenomena in such a way as to preclude alternate, albeit less favorable, interpretations. And, like many scholars who have made a basic discovery of this sort, he seems to have succumbed, on more than one occasion, to the temptation to select for emphasis those data that support his system (i.e., clear-cut tripartite formulas, etc.) and to deemphasize those that do not. Examples of this emphasizing of data compatible with the system, both by Dumézil and by his disciples, have been noted repeatedly. Thus, despite his protestations to the contrary, Dumézil has on occasion been as narrow in his interpretations as Rose and as selective in his data as Brough.

It is also possible to impeach certain aspects of his theory per se. For example, his suggestion that certain divinities such as Vāyu, Janus, and Heimdallr stand outside the system and serve, as it were, as its "épine," is certainly less well founded than his conclusions concerning the tripartite identification of most of the basic I-E divinities. As suggested earlier, this may indeed reflect a residual category of otherwise unclassifiable gods (i.e., in terms of the tripartite scheme). Also, the canonical order of the functions, as represented in myth and saga, is often ambiguous, to say the least. In

195

some instances, the first function heads the list; in others, the third function appears first. Dumézil asserts that the latter situation may perhaps be the more archaic, in that the agricultural stratum necessarily stands at the base of the social pyramid. Perhaps he is correct. The ultimogeniture pattern encountered in Scythian and Iranian myth, as well as in the modern Germanic folktales cited by Gerschel, in which the firstborn represents the third function, the second, the warrior function, and the youngest, the sovereign first function, may be a reflection of the priority of the food producers and perhaps harks back to a primeval, undifferentiated Neolithic pattern of life. But what of the "war between the functions"? If the third function is indeed the primeval one, how can the implication that it was the last to be admitted to the system be explained? Earlier I suggested a possible explanation of this phenomenon: perhaps the formation of what may be termed Proto-I-E society (*ca.* 3000 B.C.) involved the superimposition of a warlike, nonagricultural people upon a weaker but technologically more advanced agricultural one. This, of course, is sheer speculation and is offered only in lieu of any better explanation by Dumézil and others. If, by some chance, it could be proven to be correct, it might possibly account for the ambiguity in which the functions are listed; but, in the absence of any clear evidence one way or the other,[1] I must continue to regard this matter as one of the weakest elements in Dumézil's system.

As far as specific problems of interpretation are concerned, perhaps none are more troublesome than those raised by the figures of Zeus and Mithra. Both are important divinities who are clearly I-E but who nevertheless subsume in their personalities traits characteristic of at least two or, in the case of Mithra, all three functions. Zeus is, in many respects, the Greek counterpart of Indra, Thōrr, and other divine representatives of the second function. He is a fighter, a wielder of the lightning bolt, and a leader of a band of vigorous companions (cf. the war against the Titans); yet he is also a sovereign figure not unlike Varuna and Jupiter. He has recourse to spells as often as he does to the thunderbolt. Dumézil, of course, has refrained from classifying the chief of the Olympians, but has, in at least one instance, viewed Hera, his consort, as a first-function figure (cf. 1953a). It is possible, perhaps, to suggest that the classic

---

[1] If Trubetzkoy (1939) is correct in his view of the origin of the I-E language family (see above, p. 13), this speculation might be more plausible.

definition of Zeus (i.e., that of Hesiod) dates from a time when the Greeks had ceased to think in terms of a clear distinction between the first and second functions (cf. Dumézil, 1958*a*, p. 91).[2] But the problem remains unsolved and is one of the major reasons Greece has yielded so little evidence in support of Dumézil's thesis. Mithra, who managed to survive the Zoroastrian reforms, is manifestly the Iranian variant of Mitra; there can be no question of this from a purely philological standpoint. Moreover, his association with things judicial is clearly attested in his role as judge of those souls seeking entry into Paradise. Yet, like Zeus, he appears as a virile young man, an animal slayer who depends more upon his physical prowess than upon his ability to cast spells. His association with the regenerative principle, so clearly attested in the Mithraic cult that became popular in the Roman world (cf. Cumont, 1956), may be seen to conform to the third function. Thus, the Iranian figure, along with Zeus, presents a major problem to those who would interpret the various I-E pantheons in terms of a tripartite ideology.

Despite these problems, errors, biased interpretations, and inconsistencies, there remains in each of the regions upon which Dumézil has concentrated his attention a solid core of unimpeachable evidence pertaining to the existence of social and supernatural tripartition. The Iranian tradition is a case in point here, regardless of the problems posed by Mithra, as is Dumézil's interpretation of Norse myth and saga. In Norse myth and saga, for example, while it is indeed possible to question Dumézil's suggestion that Hadingus reflected, sequentially, the third, second, and first functions, it nevertheless does seem clear that the legendary Danish king bears some striking resemblances to the third-function figure Njorđr (cf. Dumézil, 1953*b*). And his assessment of the basic distinctions among the chief Norse divinities (Othinn and Týr, Thōrr, the *Vanir*, etc.) does indeed seem to be correct. The same can be said for his analysis of the Iranian *Ameša Spentas*, early Roman "history" and religion, the major Vedic divinities, the Scythian origin myth, and so on. What is more, despite the absence of supportive evidence in Hittite, Slavic, and Baltic myth, the common I-E character of the system is evident in its widespread geographic distribution.

---

[2] But it should be remembered that Dumézil (1958*a*, p. 97) sees a clear example of I-E tripartition in Plato's ideal city (see above, pp. 72–73).

Disciples, Critics, and Assessment

It is a fundamental axiom of historical linguistics (cf. Bloomfield, 1933, pp. 350–360) that, other things being equal, the presence of a correspondence between two languages that are geographically remote from each other is far more significant for purposes of reconstruction than one between several languages that are contiguous; in the former case, the possibility of intrafamilial borrowing is greatly reduced. The same thing would seem to hold true for the kinds of correspondences with which Dumézil is concerned. If tripartition were limited to the Indo-Iranian area, or to the Italo-Celtic area, then its I-E character would by no means be certain; but the fact that it occurs in both the Roman and Indo-Iranian traditions, to say nothing of the Celtic and Germanic traditions, would appear to preclude much intrafamilial borrowing and to establish it as Proto-I-E.

If, indeed, Dumézil's assessment of the extent to which the ancient I-E-speaking communities were characterized by an inherited, tripartite ideology—an ideology manifesting itself in social structure, religious beliefs, and overall world view—is substantially correct, and I believe that it is, the question remains as to whether this ideology was (or is) uniquely I-E. Discounting the primitivist attempt to substitute a universal mana theory, it is necessary to take cognizance of Brough's suggestion that a division of phenomena into three is part of the natural order of things. On this point Piggott, by no stretch of the imagination classifiable as a disciple or supporter of Dumézil, has made a most interesting observation. In commenting upon the basic character of Aryan social organization and the extent to which it may reflect a common I-E pattern, he observes (1950, pp. 259–260):

The *Rigveda* hymns reflect the aspirations and life of members of the upper classes of a society which, in common with other Indo-European communities, was formally divided into a threefold grading of warriors, priests, and artisans—*Kṣatriyas*, *Brahmans*, and *Vaiśyas*, comparable with the *milites*, *flamines*, and *quirites* of Roman society or the *equites*, *druides*, and *plebes* of the Celts of Gaul as recorded by Caesar in the first century B.C. But it is important to realize that the concept of *caste*, as known in later literature, is quite unknown in the *Rigveda*. The tripartite arrangement is perhaps an obvious enough division of responsibilities within a community, but its formal recognition is characteristically Indo-European.

Although Piggot does not proceed to an analysis of Vedic religion in terms of the three social strata, it is highly significant that this Brit-

198

ish archeologist, after covering much the same ground as Dumézil, should arrive at the same general conclusion regarding the nature and uniqueness of I-E social tripartition, for it is just such a "formal recognition" of a tripartite division of functions which would seem to set the ancient I-E speakers apart from their neighbors. Almost any society that has evolved beyond a simple horticultural level can be analyzed in terms of a functional interrelationship between priests, warriors, and food producers; even the presence of a priest class is not uncommon (cf. the Levites). But it was only among the I-E speakers that these "natural" distinctions achieved formal recognition and served, initially at least, as the basis for a societal stratification system.

The role of the I-E king or chief is an important factor. Dumézil has insisted that one of the central characteristics of Indo-Iranian, to say nothing of Celtic and Germanic, society (that of ancient Rome is less clear in this respect) was a clear distinction between the king and the priest, between the leader of the *Männerbund* and the spokesman for the sovereign gods. Such a distinction is met with nowhere else among the ancient civilizations of the Near East, or even China, for that matter. For example, among Egyptians, Sumerians, and Akkadians, the pharaoh, lugal, and so on, were originally both chief-priest (or god incarnate) and ruler (Jacobsen, 1949; Kramer, 1959). The temple was the center of both religious and secular authority; and the basic Mesopotamian concept that the temporal ruler was, in effect, the earthly steward of his city's proprietary divinity (cf. Jacobsen, 1949), to say nothing of the Egyptian and later Mesopotamian "god-king" concept, is vastly different from anything encountered among most ancient I-E speakers.

Among the Hebrews, whose kingdom arose long after I-E penetration of this region, the distinction between king and priest (e.g., Solomon) was by no means so clear as in Iran, India, or ancient Ireland. Even among the New World civilizations, distinctions between sacred and secular authority were generally absent: The Inca was, at the same time, both the chief-priest—indeed, the incarnation —of Viracocha and the supreme military commander of the empire; the Maya city-states were almost certainly theocratic in character, as was the Aztec empire, though in the latter there existed, to be sure, a somewhat wider cleavage between priestly and military authority.

By the middle of the second millennium B.C., changes began to occur in the nature of Near Eastern society, changes that seem to

Disciples, Critics, and Assessment

be correlated with the rise of Hittite power and the appearance of the Indo-Iranians.[3] The fusion of sacred and secular authority, so clearly evident in the most ancient Egyptian, Sumerian, and Akkadian texts, begins to break down. Standing armies, in all probability patterned after the I-E *Männerbunde* that had established themselves in Mitanni and Babylonia, make their appearance. In short, it is only *after* the impact of the otherwise far less civilized Indo-Iranians and Hittites that a defined military stratum, divorced from the temple, begins to take shape in the Near East. The institution of kingship becomes more and more secular in character, though never, even in the last stages of the Assyrian Empire (seventh century B.C.), is a full transition made to the I-E pattern. The Assyrian king remained the earthly representative of the sovereign god Asshur, just as the kings of Babylon had been representatives of Marduk a thousand years earlier.

On the other hand, the Near Eastern god-king pattern seems to have influenced the later I-E concept of the kingship, especially among Hittites, Greeks,[4] and Romans. Even Proto-I-E society, at the far end of a long chain of diffusion from the southwest, was probably affected to some extent by this most ancient Near Eastern pattern. This, perhaps, would account for what Dumézil has called "le problème du roi" (cf. 1958a, pp. 32–33) among I-E speakers everywhere, including India. This problem can be seen in the nature of the structural opposition, discussed earlier, between representatives of the first two functions. The warlike leader, personified by such figures as Indra, Mars, Thōrr, and, indeed, Heracles, is in an ambiguous position. Ultimate sovereignty, resting in the persons of the two sovereign gods—again, a uniquely I-E pattern—and interpreted by the priests, is denied him, yet at the same time he possesses the physical power to challenge the judicial and religious authority of the priesthood. Thus, kings are often associated with

---

[3] Fairservis (1959, pp. 130-140) has suggested that Shang Dynasty China (early Bronze Age) seems to have borrowed a number of material traits elsewhere associated with I-E speakers, such as the light battle chariot. That this diffusion (there is no evidence to suggest that I-E speakers themselves ever penetrated the Hwang Ho Valley) could also have involved some non-material I-E traits, e.g., the standing army concept, is not inconceivable. See also Eberhard (1942).

[4] According to Palmer (1960), the Linear B texts indicate a concept of kingship, at Pylos and elsewhere in Helladic Greece, not far removed from the Mesopotamian and Egyptian god-king pattern.

200

the first function (e.g., Romulus and Numa) as well as with the second (cf. Tullus Hostilius, the Iranian Kai Gursasp, etc.). The uneasy relationship between pope and emperor in medieval times may well be a reflection of this inherent I-E ambiguity in regard to kings.

As for the third function, though all ancient civilizations were necessarily founded upon an agricultural base, it is again only the I-E speakers who seem to have set the food-producing class apart, at least in theory, from the class that was ordinarily called upon to wage war. Undoubtedly, in times of great peril, herders, cultivators, and the like bore arms and assisted in the defense of the society. That this was so may be seen in the Roman conception of the *arma quirini*. But their role in military activities would seem to have been secondary, as they participated in military conflict only when an invading army threatened the physical well-being of the community. They do not seem to have formed part of the *Männerbund*, which appears to have been the primary offensive as well as defensive arm of the community. An illustration is provided by the Roman figure Cincinnatus, who was primarily a farmer and only secondarily a military leader. In the *Mahābhārata,* Nakula and Sahadeva parti-cipated in battles but only in addition to their roles as groom and herdsman. Another difference between the I-E communities and those upon whom they intruded would seem to be that the food-producing class, while distinct from that of the warriors, was never-theless a much more integral part of the total society. The semi-autonomous peasant village, which was so characteristic of the Near East from Neolithic times on and has become typical of India, Iran, and other I-E-speaking regions in the last several millennia, does not appear to have been typical of the earliest I-E societies. Collectively represented by their own special class of divine beings, the ancient I-E herdsmen and cultivators—and perhaps the artisans as well—would seem to have played a part in the total ritual and social life of their communities undreamed of by the ancestors of the Egyptian *fellahin* and their counterparts in Mesopotamia.

Even if it is acknowledged that the fundamental elements (if not configuration) of Proto-I-E social organization were ultimately derived from Mesopotamian prototypes, it is still possible to make a strong case for the uniqueness of the I-E ideology strictly from the standpoint of myth and religion, especially when the picture presented by the ancient Near Eastern religions (cf. Kramer, 1961) is considered. Among the Sumerians, for example, such major divinities as Enlil, Enki, and Inanna cannot be neatly pigeonholed into functional classes, tripartite or otherwise. The same may be said for the Babylonian figure Marduk, and for such Egyptian deities as Amon, Ra, and Ptah. Although triads of gods do occur in Near Eastern texts (e.g., the Babylonian triad Ea, Tiamat, Marduk, as delineated in the *Enuma-Elish*), never do they conform to the threefold functional pattern delineated by Dumézil; nor are the tripartite formulas (colors, ritual injunctions, exhortations, etc.) so characteristic of Indic and other early I-E texts found here. If, indeed, the Babylonians were to have possessed a tripartite religious ideology similar to that of the Indo-Europeans, it would almost certainly have appeared in the Gilgamesh epic. Yet, search as one will, neither an explicit nor an implicit manifestation of such an ideology can be uncovered in this most important of all Mesopotamian epics. The Semitic- (or perhaps Sumerian-) speaking authors of the epic just did not think in these terms.

In sum, the I-E pattern of tripartition, though indeed "natural" in the sense that Brough uses the term, would nevertheless appear to be unique. Its ideological character is apparent in the wide range of phenomena so organized, from triads of functionally interrelated classes, castes, estates, and orders and their respective collective representations, to triads of calamities, colors, talismans, cures, and celestial and geographical regions, all (or perhaps most) of which are clearly discernible in the relevant texts. The fact that the three functions are almost endlessly replicated (even if some of Dumézil's more obscure examples are discarded) in each of the several I-E traditions concerned is a clear indication of the degree to which this unique, inherited ideology seems to have shaped the ancient (and perhaps not quite so ancient) I-E speakers' *Weltanschauung*, of the degree to which it was embedded in the earliest I-E-speaking cultures of India, Italy, and elsewhere.

A final point relating to the validity of the system, one that bears on the more theoretical side of things, concerns the extent to which Dumézil's background in sociological theory is limited to what he absorbed from the French school. Throughout this volume I have asserted that Dumézil's theories reflect a thorough awareness of "la methode sociologique." It should be emphasized that I refer specifically to the sociological tradition founded by Durkheim and carried on by Mauss, Granet, and others. There is no clear evidence that Dumézil has sought to utilize, or is even aware of, the advances in sociological theory which have been made in the course of the last several decades by Parsons, Merton, and other American sociological theorists. With the possible exception of Dumézil's colleague Lévi-Strauss, the same thing holds true for contemporary anthropological theory. Admittedly, the theories and methods developed by Durkheim and his school are of fundamental importance to modern social theory, especially the theories (if not methods) that bear on the relationship between social and supernatural phenomena. The idea that society is necessarily the stuff of the supernatural is still valid, in my opinion, and there is no reason to criticize Dumézil for having made judicious use of it. Nor does his failure to take into account other theories—those of Max Weber, for example— necessarily render his system suspect.

I do feel, however, that certain points of possible confusion, at least for sociologists and anthropologists, might have been avoided had Dumézil been more familiar with contemporary theory, or even taxonomy. For example, had he been familiar with Merton (1957), he might well have reserved the label "function" for the role played by each stratum relative to the others and/or for the consequences of such role behavior,[5] and have avoided the ambiguity wherein the term in question is used to refer both to the strata themselves and to their respective roles in the system. This is, as noted elsewhere, a minor point, and I do think I understand the logic behind his use of the term. Nevertheless, even if he were to continue to follow his own definition of terms like "function," at least some reference to modern sociological and social anthropological theory, if only in passing, might well enhance the possibility of a wider appreciation of his work among British and American social scientists.

SOME THEORETICAL IMPLICATIONS

It should be emphasized that the theoretical framework evolved by Dumézil is, in itself, as unique as the I-E ideology it has brought

---

[5] Cf. Merton's (1957, p. 51) definition of *manifest functions* as "those objective consequences contributing to the adjustment or adaptation of the system which are intended and recognized by participants," and of *latent functions* as "those [consequences] which are neither intended nor recognized."

to light. Combining as it does the fundamental assumptions of Durkheimian sociology and the methods and postulates of historical linguistics, this framework may indeed prove to have important implications for the study of the relationship between language and culture in general. The essence of Dumézil's theory is that there is necessarily a genetic relationship between the ideologies of those who speak genetically related languages. In many respects, it is quite similar to the "genetic model" developed by Vogt (1964) and others for the analysis of Middle American materials.

To assess this theory, it is necessary first to inquire into the validity of Dumézil's conception of *ideology*. Unlike his use of the term "function," Dumézil's conception of the nature of ideology is indeed congruent with contemporary anthropological usage. For example, Goldschmidt's (1959, p. 100) assertion that an ideology "provides the basic metaphysical assumptions, tying the observed and observable phenomena of the natural and human environment into a kind of unity, filling in the voids of knowledge with religious and magical beliefs, and ultimately supplying a system of justification of the circumstances of existence" comes close to approximating Dumézil's suggestion (1958*a*, p. 92) that "tout système théologique signifie quelque chose, aide la société qui le pratique à se comprendre, à s'accepter, à être fière de son passé, confiante dans son présent et dans son avenir." An ideology inevitably forms the core of a culture;[6] it provides the basic framework in terms of which phenomena are categorized and thus rendered meaningful. It is in terms of its ideology that a society structures its religious beliefs, validates its social organization, and generally conceives of its relationship to the phenomena surrounding it. This conception of ideology, implicit in Dumézil's work, is paralleled in most contemporary sociological and anthropological works[7] that have dealt with the subject (cf., for example, Mannheim, 1949; Rousseas and Farganis, 1965, p. 272).

Moreover, it has become increasingly clear that there is a fundamental relationship between the language spoken by, and the ide-

---

[6] Goldschmidt (1959, p. 101) asserts that "ideology is the quintessence of culture."

[7] What I, following Goldschmidt and Dumézil, have labeled "ideology" is often referred to in contemporary anthropological works as "world view" (cf., for example, Jacobs, 1964, pp. 366-367; Mandelbaum, 1955, p. 223). As I see it, these two terms are synonymous.

ology characteristic of, a given people. The first modern scholar to recognize this relationship[8] was, of course, Sapir (1921, p. 7). Later, the idea that the basic patterns underlying the morphology and syntax of a language necessarily reflect the ideology shared by its speakers (and vice versa) was developed by Whorf (1956) into the well-known "Sapir-Whorf hypothesis." In the last twenty-odd years an increasing number of anthopologists, including Hoijer (1954), Lee (1959), and Hockett (1954), have followed up this general line of research; but so far all attempts at metalinguistics, ethnolinguistics, and the like have been synchronic in character. They have concentrated upon the relationship at a given time between the language and the thought of a given community (cf. Lee's work with the Wintu). Where comparison has entered the picture, as it certainly does in Whorf's attempt to contrast "Standard Average European" (SAE) with Hopi, it has been synchronic rather than diachronic.

Neither Dumézil nor his disciples can be strictly classed as "Whorfians," but by implication Dumézil's thesis carries this idea a step further. The evidence that at least the ancient I-E-speaking community shared a common ideology as well as a set of related linguistic forms, and that, in both instances, the relationship was clearly genetic, would seem to indicate that there is indeed an intrinsic relationship between ideology and language, and that this relationship persists *through time*; that, as the various daughter languages diverge from a common ancestor (e.g., Proto-I-E), the ideology of the ancestral, undifferentiated speech community will also diverge, and that, just as the protophonemes, morphemes, and syntactical patterns of the protolanguage can be reconstructed through the application of the comparative method, so can the character of the protoideology.

Dumézil does not attempt to analyze the specific correlations between the morphological and syntactical patterns of Proto-I-E and the ideology shared by its speakers, nor does he attempt to account for variations in later manifestations of this ideology in terms of

---

[8] The idea that there is necessarily a link between the structure of a language and the ideology of its speakers was first articulated by the pioneer nineteenth-century philologist Wilhelm von Humboldt. Cf. Jespersen (1921, p. 57), who points out that, to Humboldt, a language was "characteristic of one nation's psyche, and indicates the peculiar way in which that nation attempts to realize the ideal of speech."

differential developments in the various I-E daughter languages. The reason lies perhaps in the fact that the morphological and syntactical evidence for Proto-I-E does not present a clear-cut pattern of tripartition. For example, although most modern I-E languages have evolved a three-tense system (past, present, and future) which, at first glance, might seem to be somehow connected with ideological tripartition, one cannot reconstruct such a system for Proto-I-E. It appears certain that the future tense evolved out of what may be termed the "desiderative" aspect of the verb in Proto-I-E. Both the present and the past tenses seem to have emerged ultimately out of the unmarked or aorist aspect. In short, the kind of temporal organization so clearly demonstrated by Whorf as a central characteristic of SAE does not appear to hold for the parent language.[9] Yet the drift toward such a pattern, so evident in the Germanic, Italic, and other Western I-E substocks, may itself be significant, for it may indicate that a tendency toward such tripartition was implicit (and thus perhaps undetectable philologically) in Proto-I-E, or at least the major dialects thereof, and that, for some reason or other, it became explicit only after the breakup of the parent community. Even if this were to be substantiated, however, the connections, if any, between the three functions and a tendency to divide actions into those that have occurred, are presently occurring, and will at some future date occur would remain obscure.

Other aspects of Proto-I-E syntax appear to be equally unrewarding when it comes to some reflection of tripartition. The replication[10] of tripartite formulas in Old Norse, Sanskrit, and so on may possibly point to a generalized I-E tendency to group morphemes into clusters of three. Such a pattern, if it existed, might well have conditioned or at least reinforced the manifest tendency among ancient I-E speakers (and perhaps not-so-ancient I-E speakers) to divide social and other phenomena into three hierarchically ranked categories. Nevertheless, given the overall picture of Proto-I-E morphology and syntax as revealed by the comparative method, it is impossible at present to make a case for the presence of a "linguistic microcosm," to use Whorf's term, of the three functions. Yet

---

[9] Whorf's construct is based primarily upon patterns common to the Western branch of the I-E family and thus is not wholly equatable with "Indo-European," modern or ancient.

[10] The extent to which Dumézil's emphasis upon replication approximates that of his colleague Lévi-Strauss (1955) has been noted previously.

if Whorf and others who have asserted that a language and the culture of those who speak it necessarily reflect each other are correct, and I believe that, in the main, they are, then it is indeed possible that such a microcosm may eventually be isolated, the current picture of Proto-I-E to the contrary notwithstanding. Its presence is certainly implied by the evidence compiled by Dumézil, and I strongly suggest that this area of comparative I-E studies is worthy of much more research and analysis than has heretofore been devoted to it.

Leaving aside these metalinguistic considerations, the fact that a common ideology manifest in myth, social organization, and elsewhere does indeed seem to be correlated with the presence of languages classifiable as I-E is in itself a most important matter. As Wikander and Gerschel, to say nothing of Dumézil himself, have amply demonstrated, this ideology seems to have persisted long after these several communities had undergone profound transformations. In India, for example, it seems to have persisted well into the Hindu (as opposed to the Vedic) phase, which appears to have developed as a result of a syncretism between the indigenous religious patterns, examples of which can be seen at Harappa and Mohenjo-daro, and those characteristic of the I-E-speaking Aryan invaders.[11] The *Mahābhārata* is manifestly a different sort of document from the *Rig Veda*; in it patterns that are still characteristic of Hindu thought and belief can be clearly seen in the figures of Krṣṇa and others. Yet the inherited I-E ideology, though disassociated from Mitra, Varuna, and the rest, is nevertheless present in the figures of Pāṇḍu and his sons. Indeed, it is possible to assert that the basic patterns of Indian social organization continue to reflect this ideology, despite the proliferation of castes and subcastes. In Iran, as Wikander has shown, it not only survived the Zoroastrian reforms, but was still present in the post-Moslem period and is manifested in Firdausi's *Shāhnāmeh* (tenth century A.D.).

---

[11] There is good reason to believe that many elements of Hinduism (as opposed to the religion of the *Vedas*) are ultimately derived from the Indus Valley civilization. E.g., the horned figure surrounded by beasts who so often appears upon stamp seals found at Harappa and Mohenjo-daro is very probably a prototype of Śiva. Also, the prominent position of the humped cow in Indus Valley iconography may be significant in the later Hindu sacred attitude toward cattle. Cf. Piggott (1950, p. 203), who observes that "it is even possible that early historic Hindu society owed more to Harappa than it did to the Sanskrit-speaking invaders." See also Littleton (1965, pp. 24-25).

Disciples, Critics, and Assessment

In the West, it would appear that the ideology in question was drawn upon when the Roman augurs sought to account for the variation in the fortunes of Rome and Carthage. It appears to have colored the early Christian Scandanavian "historical" literature (e.g., Saxo Grammaticus), and, as Gerschel has attempted to demonstrate, appears to have survived until the nineteenth century in certain regions of South Germany and Switzerland. That it may have played a more important role in the last few millennia of Western history is a distinct possibility. As noted elsewhere, it seems possible to suggest that the three estates of medieval and later European society were manifestations of this ideology (cf. Batany, 1963), and that the conflict between pope and emperor may perhaps reflect the inherent I-E antagonism between the priest and the warrior. The ideology of tripartition could have profound implications for the basic patterns of modern European culture. Despite the introduction of Christianity and the subsequent centuries of at least formal adherence to a non-I-E ideology, it would appear that the I-E pattern of categorizing phenomena did not give way. Indeed, it is quite possible that the nature of Christianity itself was affected by the presence of this ideology: the idea of the Trinity, so central to Christian dogma, took shape only *after* the religion had penetrated the Greek- and Latin-speaking communities[12] (cf. Albright, 1957; Potter, 1962).

That tripartition is still a factor as far as European (and American) thought is concerned is clearly evident. Indeed, the history of sociology and anthropology, to choose but one area of thought, is replete with tripartite schemes: for example, Hegel's thesis, antithesis, and synthesis; Comte's "law of three stages"; Morgan's "Savagery," "Barbarism," and "Civilization"; and the almost universal tendency of archeologists (to say nothing of geologists) to divide their phenomena into three successive stages or periods. Even anecdotes, as usually told, seem to contain three segments: the first incident, the second incident, and the punch line. In short, it seems clear that Europeans and Americans are conditioned to think and categorize in three's; whenever they set out to organize phenomena, they seem to do so most naturally in terms of a tripartite arrangement.

---

[12] Cf., for example, the common iconographic theme of "Christ the Warrior" and the extent to which symbols associated by the Greeks with the Holy Ghost (e.g., the dove, an old symbol of Aphrodite) bespeak the I-E third function.

208

Whether or not this tendency toward classificatory tripartition carries with it still the implications of the three functions is less clear. Europeans and Americans are, however, I-E speakers; and if, as suggested above, there is a link between language and ideology, it is quite possible that the three functions linger on. Dumézil himself (1949*b*, p. 242) has suggested that Soviet Russian society and the German Third Reich might possibly be analyzed in terms of them. It is even possible to suggest, perhaps, that the American system of government, often considered by historians to be a wholly new phenomenon, is itself a manifestation of the ideology in question: the judiciary, especially the Supreme Court, would seem to reflect the idea of sovereignty, of ultimate decision; the executive branch, as the seat of legitimate force, would seem to suggest the second function; and the legislative branch, associated as it is with the population as a whole, would perhaps reflect the third function. The idea that the framers of the United States Constitution, like Zoroaster, were heirs to an inherited I-E ideology is thus not wholly out of the question. Admittedly, I am perhaps guilty of some of the things I and others have criticized in Dumézil; and, like many other suggestions in the present chapter, this one is offered merely as an example of some of the possible implications of Dumézil's system.

The foregoing comes into focus when the patterns of non-I-E speakers are considered, especially those of communities far removed from contact with the ancient I-E-speaking communities. For example, would a Crow Indian be as apt to tripartize, or would he be more apt to think in terms of a quadripartite set of categories? As has long been recognized (cf., for example, Lowie, 1956, pp. 256–257), the Crow, like many other American Indians, are conditioned to think in terms of four, and it would appear extremely doubtful whether a Crow savant would arrive at a "law of three stages." Crow ideology is thus, in many ways, a quadripartite one; and it is in terms of this quadripartite ideology that the Crow justifies his own existence and the existence of things around him. Quadripartition, sequences of four, whether in myth, social organization, or in the categorization of natural phenomena, are to the Crow what tripartitions were (and perhaps still are) to the German, the Celt, or the Indo-Iranian.

Like the German, the Celt, and the Indo-Iranian, the Crow speaks a language belonging to a historically related stock of languages, in this instance the Siouan. Given the genetic model implicit in Dumézil's I-E research, might it not be possible to elicit the same sort of

209

model for the language family of which Crow is a part? Might it not be possible to delineate a quadripartite Siouan ideology, an ideology that could be traced back to a Proto-Siouan ideology and could be seen to have undergone differential development as the several Siouan daughter languages diverged from their common ancestor? Of course, one could not attempt this solely on the basis of the Crow evidence, any more than Dumézil was able to speak of a tripartite Indo-European ideology solely in terms of the Indo-Iranian data. Moreover, it would be much more difficult to apply this method to a nonliterate (or recently literate) community, as there would be no datable texts for comparison. Yet, in many ways, the Indic texts fall into this category, for they were preserved orally for many generations, perhaps millennia, before being committed to writing; nor were the Norse materials committed to writing until a very late date. Nevertheless, they do yield the kind of social and mythological data required by this approach. Thus, through judicious use of oral materials (cf. Jacobs, 1959), one might well be able to isolate ideological systems analogous to the one that Dumézil sees as characteristic of the I-E speakers in a large number of the world's language families, including those of the New World, sub-Saharan Africa, and Oceania. That the approach in question could also be profitably applied to the other language families of the Old World for which there are ancient texts, such as the Afro-Asiatic (Semitic, Hamitic, etc.) and the Sino-Tibetan, goes without saying.

It should be emphasized that no single ideology (i.e., one that is characteristic of a given culture localized in time and space) will ever be wholly determined by inherited patterns.[13] Greece is a good example, for it appears to have lost most of its I-E ideological inheritance long before it reached the threshold of written history. The level of technological and economic sophistication, the impact of ideological patterns characteristic of neighboring cultures, to say nothing of innovation or the particular historical circumstances in which every society finds itself, will necessarily ensure the uniqueness of particular ideological configurations. Moreover, the degree of overall cultural difference between two communities speaking related languages (e.g., between Rome and India, or, technolog-

---

[13] I should emphasize that my use of the term "inherited," when applied to an ideology or elements thereof, has no connection whatsoever with any biological process and is meant in its customary linguistic sense: i.e., an inherited form is one that did not enter a language through borrowing.

ically and economically speaking, between Rome and Scandinavia) will inevitably affect the extent to which these communities will manifest ideological similarities. Yet, if Dumézil is correct, it is indeed possible to assert that no matter how wide the differences in technology, size, and so on, if no other ideology has intruded itself to the degree that it has wholly obliterated all earlier habits of thought—a condition rarely if ever encountered—there will remain a common core of ideological similarity. Even Greece, despite the extent to which it was indebted to the non-I-E-speaking communities of the Near East, presents some evidence of such a core.

I should point out that there are a number of recorded instances wherein a conquering population has been able to impose its language upon the communities it has conquered; examples of such "imposed languages" include Spanish in the New World and Latin in ancient Gaul and elsewhere. When this occurs, the ideology linked to the new language will gradually replace the ideology that previously held sway, though probably never *in toto*. Indeed, it seems quite probable that this is what happened during the I-E migrations. Almost everywhere, it would appear, the initial wave of I-E speaking invaders constituted a relatively small elite that superimposed itself upon an indigenous population. The Mitanni, the Kassites, and the Hittites are good examples of this, though in none did the language manage to persist. Indeed, among the Hittites, the ideology seems to have given way long before the language. Elsewhere, in northern India, Iran, and Europe, the language spoken by the invading elite triumphed over that spoken by the indigenous population (in western Europe, Basque alone has survived from the pre-I-E period), and eventually the whole region became and has remained I-E in both language and ideology. It must be noted, however, that the pre-I-E ideology probably had its effect upon the particular mythological and social manifestations of the I-E ideology in each area. This can be seen perhaps most clearly in India, where many of the religious traits characteristic of the Indus Valley civilization seems to have carried over into and affected profoundly the evolution of Hinduism. That a similar, though perhaps less clearly identifiable, pre-I-E influence helped shape the several Western manifestations of the I-E ideology would seem quite likely.

A word is perhaps in order here concerning the differences between the kinds of phenomena amenable to analysis in terms of the genetic model, as developed by Dumézil, and those that lend them-

211

selves to explanation in terms of the more conventional generic models, that is, those predicated upon diffusion, independent invention, common ecological adaptation, and so on. Where technological and, to a large extent, fundamental economic parallels are concerned, it is usually much more efficient to attempt an explanation in generic terms than it is to postulate a common inheritance. The role of common ecological adaptation in producing such parallels has been amply demonstrated by Steward (1955) and his colleagues. Yet when it comes to parallels in language, ideology, and, to a lesser extent, the fundamental configuration of the social order, it is by no means possible to rely solely upon generic explanations. Such parallels can and do exist despite wide differences in economy, technology, and ecological adaptation; and it is clear, at least among the ancient I-E speakers, that these parallels are correlated with the presence of a common linguistic inheritance. In short, it is to the analysis of phenomena most closely associated with language, especially ideology, that the genetic model can be most fruitfully applied.

In conclusion, from the anthropological perspective—or at least from the perspective of this anthropologist—Dumézil has made and, I think, will continue to make a significant contribution to scholarship, a contribution that has implications far beyond the immediate realm of I-E studies. Any errors, any faulty etymologies and hasty interpretations, would seem in large measure to result more from overenthusiasm on the part of Dumézil and his colleagues than from any fatal flaw in methodology. The confrontation of Dumézil by his critics is as old as the history of scholarship itself. It is the opposition between the generalist and the specialist; it is the opposition between those who move out ahead of the data and seek to establish new relationships and those who become so enmeshed in a web of particulars that they shun the making or accepting of broad generalizations. Both types of scholar are, of course, necessary, especially in the search for new knowledge. Yet when all is said and done, after all due credit is given to those who correct inaccuracies, rectify faulty etymologies, and ameliorate hasty interpretations, one cannot help but applaud the generalist just a bit more loudly than one applauds his critics. Without the Georges Dumézils, there would be little new knowledge, and therefore little need of the specialists.

212

References Cited

ABBREVIATIONS

AA	*American Anthropologist*
BSOAS	*Bulletin of the School of Oriental and African Studies* (University of London)
CS	*Cahiers du Sud*
JAF	*Journal of American Folklore*
JA	*Journal Asiatique*
NC	*La Nouvelle Clio*
O	*Ogam*
PUF	Presses Universitaires de France
REL	*Revue des Études Latines*
RHR	*Revue de l'Histoire des Religions*
SMSR	*Studi e Materiali di Storia delle Religioni*
ZDMG	*Zeitschrift der Deutschen Morgenländischen Gesellschaft*

REFERENCES CITED

Aiken, Henry
1956 The age of ideology. New York: Mentor Books.
Albright, William F.
1957 From the Stone Age to Christianity: monotheism and the historical process. New York: Doubleday Anchor Books.
Alpert, Harry
1939 Emile Durkheim and his sociology. Chicago: University of Chicago Press.
Arnold, Paul
1946 Magie guerrière dans la Rome antique. CS 25:449-459.
1950 Le mythe de Mars. CS 31:93-108.
1951 Civilisation indo-européenne (avant-propos). CS 34:216-220.
1952 La notion de souveraineté chez les Indo-Européens: en marge de l'oeuvre de Georges Dumézil. CS 36:3-8.
Bacon, Elizabeth
1958 Obok: a study of social structure in Eurasia. New York: Wenner-Gren Foundation for Anthropological Research. Viking Fund Publications in Anthropology, no. 25.
Barr, Kaj
1952 Irans profet som τέλειος ἄνθρωπος. In Festskrift til L. L. Hammerich, pp. 26-36. Copenhagen.
Basanoff, V.
1942 Les Dieux des Romains. Paris: PUF.
1947 Notre sur la triade "indo-européenne" à Rome. RHR 132: 110-114.
Bascom, William
1957 The myth-ritual theory. JAF 70:103-114.
Batany, Jean
1963 Des "trois fonctions" aux "trois etats"? Annales Economiques Sociétés Civilisations 18:933-938.
Bayet, J.
1947 Nouveaux aspects de la recherche sur les siècles légendaires de Rome. REL 25:54-55.
1957 Histoire politique et psychologique de la religion romaine. Paris: Bibliothèque historique.
Bender, Harold H.
1922 The home of the Indo-Europeans. Princeton: Princeton University Press.

References Cited

Bendix, Reinhard
  1960 Max Weber: an intellectual portrait. New York: Doubleday and Company.
Benveniste, E.
  1932 Les classes sociales dans la tradition avestique. JA 221:117-134.
  1937 Expression indo-européenne de l'éternité. Bulletin de la Société de Linquistique de Paris 38:103-112.
  1938 Traditions indo-iraniennes sur les classes sociales. JA 230: 529-549.
  1945a La doctrine médicale des Indo-Européens. RHR 130:5-12.
  1945b Symbolisme social dans les cultes gréco-italiques. RHR 129: 5-16.
  1951 Don et échange dans le vocabulaire indo-européen. L'Année Sociologique (3ème série), 1948-49:7-20
Bloch, Raymond
  1946 Origines de Rome. Paris: PUF.
Bloomfield, L.
  1933 Language. New York: Holt and Company.
Bopp, Franz
  1886-1874 Grammaire comparée des langues indo-européennes: comprenant le sanscrit, le zende, l'arménien, le grec, le latin, le lithuanien, l'ancien slave, le gothique, et l'allemand. Trans. M. Bréal. Paris: Imprimerie impériale.
Bosch-Gimpera, P.
  1961 Les Indo-Européens: problèmes archéologiques. Trans. from Spanish by R. Lantier. Paris: PUF.
Brelich, Angelo
  1957 Review of Georges Dumézil, Idéologie tripartie des Indo-Européens (1958). SMSR 28:113-123.
  1958 Surrejoinder to Dumézil, Religion indo-européene: examen de quelques critiques récentes, RHR 152:8-30 (1957). SMSR 29:109-112.
Brinton, Daniel
  1896 The myths of the New World: a treatise on the symbolism and mythology of the red race of America (3d ed.). Philadelphia: American Philosophical Society.
Brough, John
  1959 The tripartite ideology of the Indo-Europeans: an experiment in method. BSOAS 22:68-86.
Brown, W. Norman
  1942 The creation myth of the *Rig Veda*. Journal of the American Oriental Society 62:85-97.
Carnoy, A.
  1921 Les Indo-Européens. Louvain: Editions Universitas.
Chase, Richard

1949   Quest for myth. Baton Rouge: Louisiana State University Press.

Childe, V. Gordon
   1926   The Aryans. London: Kegan, Paul.
   1929   The Danube in prehistory. Oxford: Clarendon Press.
   1947   The dawn of European civilization. London: Kegan, Paul.

Cornford, Francis M.
   1912   From religion to philosophy: a study in the origin of Western speculation. New York: Longmans, Green.

Cox, Sir George W.
   1887   Mythology of the Aryan nations. London: Kegan, Paul.

Creuzer, Friederich
   1819   Symbolik und Mythologie der alten Völker, besonders der Griechen. Leipzig and Darmstadt: Heyer and Leske.

Cumont, F. V. M.
   1956   The mysteries of Mithra. Trans. from French by Thomas J. McCormak. New York: Dover Publications.

Curtius, Georg
   1873   Zur Chronologie der indogermanischen Sprachforschung. Leipzig: S. Hirzel.

Dandekar, R. N.
   1942   Twenty-five years of Vedic studies. Progress of Indic Studies 1917-1942. Poona, India.

Darmesteter, James
   1902   Selections from the Zend-Avesta. *In* Sacred books of the East, ed. Epiphanus Wilson. New York: Colonial Press.

Davies, A. Powell
   1956   The meaning of the Dead Sea Scrolls. New York: Mentor Books.

De Menasce, P. J.
   1947   Une légende indo-iranienne dans l'angélologie judéo-musulmane: à propos de Hārūt et Mārūt. Asiatische Studien 1:10-18.

Detter, Ferdinand
   1899   Edda Saemundar, Voluspa, herausgeben und erklärt. Vienna: Carl Gerold's Sohn.

Devoto, G.
   1962   Origini indeuropee. Florence: Instituto Italiano de Preistoria e Prostotoria.

De Vries, Jan
   1942   Rood, wit, zwart. Volkskunde 2:1-10.
   1951   Der heutige Stand der germanischen Religionsforschung. Germanisch-romanische Monatsschrift 2:1-11.
   1952   La valeur religieuse du mot germanique *irmin*. CS 36:18-37.
   1953   A propos du dieu Esus. O 5:16-21.
   1958   L'aspect magique de la religion celtique. O 10:273-284.

References Cited

1959 Note sur la valeur religieuse du nombre trois. O 11:305-306.

1960a Kelten und Germanen. Bibliotheca Germanica, vol. 9. Bern.

1960b Quelques réflexions sur la nature des dieux gaulois. O 12:321-334.

1960c Die Interpretatio Romana der gallischen Götter. *In* Festschrift für Wolfgang Krause, pp. 204-213. Heidelberg: Indogermanica.

1961 Keltische Religion. Die Religionen der Menschheit, Band 18. Stuttgart.

Dillon, Myles
    1948 The archaism of Irish tradition. The Sir John Rhys Memorial Lecture, 1947. Proceedings of the British Academy, vol. 32. London.

Dorson, Richard
    1955 The eclipse of solar mythology. *In* Myth: a symposium, ed. Thomas Sebeok. Bibliographic and Special Series of the American Folklore Society 5:15-38. Philadelphia.

Duchesne-Guillemin, J.
    1948 Zoroastre. Paris: PUF.
    1958 The Western response to Zoroaster. Oxford: Clarendon Press.
    1960 De la dicéphalie dans l'iconographie mazdéenne. *In* Festgabe für Herman Lommel, pp. 32-37.

*Dumézil, Georges
    1924a Le festin d'immortalité: étude de mythologie comparée indo-européenne. Annales du Musée Guimet, vol. 34. Paris.
    1924b Le crime des Lemniennes: rites et légendes du monde egéen. Paris: Geuthner.
    1925 Les bylines de Michajlo Potyk et les légendes indo-européennes de ambroisie. Revue des Études Slaves 5:205-237.
    1926 Les fleurs Haurot-Maurot et les anges Haurvatât-Amĕrĕtât. Revue des Etudes Arméniennes 6:43-69.
    1929 Le problème des Centaures: étude de mythologie comparée indo-européenne. Annales du Musée Guimet, vol. 41. Paris.
    1930a Légendes sur les Nartes, suivies de cinq notes mythologiques. Bibliothèque de l'Institut Français de Leningrad, Vol. II. Paris: Institut d'Études Slaves.
    1930b La préhistorie indo-iranienne des castes. JA 216:109-130.
    1934 Ouranos-Varuna: étude de mythologie comparée indo-européenne. Collection d'Études Mythologiques, ed. Sylvain Lévi, vol. 1. Paris: A. Maisonneuve.
    1935 Flāmen-Brahman. Annales du Musée Guimet, vol. 51.
    1936 Temps et mythes. Recherches Philosophiques 5:235-251.
    1938a La préhistoire des flāmines majeurs. RHR 118:188-200.

* For an almost complete bibliography of Dumézil's works to 1960, see Hommages à Georges Dumézil, Collection Latomus, vol. 45, pp. xi-xxii (Brussels, 1960).

1938*b* Jeunesse, éternité, aube: linguistique et mythologie comparée indo-européenne. Annales d'Histoire Économique et Sociale 10:289-301.

1938*c* Le plus vieux nom arménien du jeune homme. Bulletin de Société de Linguistique de Paris 39:185-193.

1939*a* Deux traits du monstre tricéphale indo-iranien. RHR 122:5-20.

1939*b* Mythes et dieux des Germains: essai d'interprétation comparative. Collection "Mythes et Religions," ed. P.-L. Couchoud, vol. 1. Paris: PUF.

1940*a* Mitra-Varuna: essai sur deux représentations indo-européennes de la souveraineté. Bibliothèque de l'École des Hautes Études, Section Religieuse, vol. 46. Paris: PUF.

1940*b* La tradition druidique et l'écriture: le Vivant et le Mort. RHR 122:125-133.

1941*a* Jupiter, Mars, Quirinus: essai sur la conception indo-européenne de la société et sur les origines de Rome. Collection "La Montagne Sainte-Geneviève," vol. 1. Paris: Gallimard.

1941*b* L'étude comparée des religions indo-européennes. La Nouvelle Revue Française 29:385-399.

1941*c* Le nom des "Arya." RHR 124:36-59.

1942 Horace et les Curiaces. Collection "Les Mythes Romains," vol. 1. Paris: Gallimard.

1943*a* Servius et la Fortune: essai sur la fonction sociale de louange et de blâme et sur les éléments indo-européens du *cens* romain. Collection "Les Mythes Romains," vol. 2. Paris: Gallimard.

1943*b* "O fortunatos nimium. . . ." La Nouvelle Revue Française 31:270-286.

1943*c* Les débuts de la religion romaine. *In* Memorial des Études Latines, pp. 316-329. Paris: PUF.

1943*d* Légendes sur les Nartes: nouveaux documents relatifs au héros Sosryko. RHR 125:97-128.

1944 Naissance de Rome (Jupiter, Mars, Quirinus II). Collection "La Montagne Sainte-Geneviève," vol. 3. Paris: Gallimard.

1945 Naissance d'archanges: essai sur la formation de la théologie zoroastrienne (Jupiter, Mars, Quirinus III). Collection "La Montagne Sainte-Geneviève," vol. 4. Paris: Gallimard.

1946*a* "Tripertita" fonctionnels chez divers peuples indo-européens. RHR 131:53-72.

1946*b* Les "énarées" scythiques et la grossesse du Narte Hamyc. Latomus 5:249-255.

1947*a* La tripartition indo-européenne. Psyché 2:1348-1356.

1947*b* Tarpeia: cinq essais de philologie comparative indo-européenne. Collection "Les Mythes Romains," vol. 3. Paris: Gallimard.

1947*c* La triade "Jupiter, Mars, Janus"? RHR 132:115-123.

References Cited

1947d Mitra-Varuna, Indra, les Nāsatya, comme patrons des trois fonctions cosmiques et sociales. Studia Linguistica 1:121-129.

1948a Explication de textes indiens et latins (Jupiter, Mars, Quirinus IV). Bibliothèque de l'École des Hautes Études, Section Religieuse, vol. 62. Paris: PUF.

1948b Mitra-Varuna: essai sur deux représentations indo-européennes de la Souveraineté. 2d ed. Collection "La Montagne Sainte-Geneviève," vol. 7. Paris: Gallimard.

1948c Loki. Collection "Les Dieux et les Hommes," ed. G. Dumézil, vol. 1. Paris: G.-P. Maisonneuve.

1948d Religion et mythologie préhistorique des Indo-Européens. In L'histoire Générale des religions, ed. A. Quillet, pp. 443-453. Paris: PUF.

1948e A propos de latin jus. RHR 134:95-112.

1949a L'héritage indo-européen à Rome: introduction aux séries "Jupiter, Mars, Quirinus" et "Les Mythes Romains." Paris: Gallimard.

1949b Le troisième souverain: essai sur le dieu indo-iranien Aryaman et sur la formation de l'histoire mythique d'Irlande. Collection "Les Dieux et les Hommes," ed. G. Dumézil, vol. 3. Paris: G.-P. Maisonneuve.

1950a Les archanges de Zoroastre et les rois romains de Cicéron. Journal de Psychologie 43:449-465.

1950b Dieux cassites et dieux védiques: à propos d'un bronze du Louristan. Revue Hittite et Asianique 11:18-37.

1951a Civilisation indo-européenne. CS 34:221-239.

1951b Mythes romains. Revue de Paris, December:105-115.

1951c L'inscription archaïque du forum et Cicéron, De divinatione, II, 36. Recherches de Science Religieuse 34:17-29.

1952a La bataille de Sentium: remarques sur la fabrication de l'histoire romaine. Annales, Économies, Sociétés, Civilisations 7:145-154.

1952b Les dieux des Indo-Européens. Collection "Mythes et Religions," ed. P.-L. Couchoud, vol. 29. Paris: PUF.

1952c Sur quelques expressions symboliques de la structure religieuse tripartie à Rome. Journal de Psychologie 45:43-46.

1952d Maiestas et gravitas: de quelques différences entre les Romains et les Austronésiens. Revue de Philologie 26:7-28.

1953a Les trois fonctions dans quelques traditions grecques. In Hommage à Lucien Febvre, vol. 2, pp. 25-32. Paris: Armand Colin.

1953b La saga Hadingus (Saxo Grammaticus, I, v-viii); du mythe au roman. Bibliothèque de l'École des Hautes Études, Section Religieuse, vol. 66. Paris: PUF.

1953c Le iuges auspicium et les incongruités du taureau attelé de Mudgala. NC 5:249-266.

References Cited

1953*d* Viṣṇu et les Maruts à travers la réforme zoroastrienne. JA 241:1-25.

1953*e* Rejoinder to Carl Koch, Bemerkungen zum römischen Quirinuskult, Zeitschrift für Religions und Geistesgeschichte 5: 1-25 (1953). REL 31:189-190.

1954*a* Le trio des Macha. RHR 146:5-17.

1954*b* Rituels indo-européens à Rome. Collection "Études et Commentaires," vol. 19. Paris: Klincksieck.

1954*c* À propos de H. Wagenvoort, *Gravitas et maiestas*. Revue de Philologie 28:19-20.

1955*a* Les "enfants des soeurs" à la fête de Mater Matuta. REL 33: 140-151.

1955*b* Remarques complémentaires sur les six premiers noms de nombres du turc et du quéchua. Journal de la Société des Américanistes 44:17-38.

1955*c* À propos de Quirinus. REL 33:105-108.

1956*a* Déesses latines et mythes védiques. Collection Latomus, vol. 24. Brussels.

1956*b* Aspects de la fonction guerrière chez les Indo-Européens. Bibliothèque de l'École des Hautes Études, Section Religieuse, vol. 68. Paris: PUF.

1956*c* Les pas de Krsna et l'exploit d'Arjuna. Orientalia Suecana 5: 183-188.

1956*d* Remarques sur le *ius fetiale*. REL 34:93-108.

1956*e* Structure du quéchua (dialecte cuzquénien). Travaux de l'Institut de Linguistique de l'Université de Paris 1:125-134.

1956*f* L'étude comparée des religions des peuples indo-européens. Beiträge zur Geschichte der deutschen Sprache und Literatur 78:173-180.

1957*a* Remarques sur *augur, augustus*. REL 35:126-151.

1957*b* Remarques sur les armes des dieux de "troisième fonction" chez divers peuples indo-européens. SMSR 28:1-10.

1957*c* Religion indo-européenne, examen de quelques critiques récentes (John Brough, I; Angelo Brelich). RHR 152:8-30.

1958*a* L'idéologie tripartie des Indo-Européens. Collection Latomus, vol. 31. Brussels.

1958*b* La *Rigsþula* et la structure sociale indo-européenne. RHR 154:1-19.

1958*c* L'idéologie des trois fonctions dans quelques crises de l'histoire romaine. Latomus 17:429-446.

1958*d* *Ari, Aryaman*, à propos de Paul Thieme, *"Ari,* Fremder," ZDMG 107:96-104 (1957). JA 256:67-84.

1959*a* Les dieux des Germains: essai sur la formation de la religion scandinave. 2d ed., rev. Collection "Mythes et Religions," ed. P.-L. Couchoud, vol. 38. Paris: PUF.

1959*b* Loki. German ed. trans. Inge Köck, with introduction by O.

References Cited

Höfler. Darmstadt: Wissenschaftliche Buchgesellschaft.

1959c La transposition des dieux souverains mineurs en héros dans le *Mahābhārata*. Indo-Iranian Journal 3:1-16.

1959d Remarques comparatives sur le dieu scandinave Heimdallr. Études celtiques 8:263-283.

1959e Le *rex* et les *flāmines maiores*. Studies in the History of Religions: The Sacral Kingship. Supplements to Numen 4:407-417.

1959f Quaestiunculae Indo-Italicae 7. REL 37:94-101.

1959g Addendum à *"Ari*, Aryaman," JA 146:67-84 (1958). JA 147:171-173.

1959h L'idéologie tripartie des Indo-Européens et la Bible. Kratylos 4:97-118.

1959i Letter. BSOAS 22:627.

1960a Quaestiunculae Indo-Italicae 4-6. *In* Hommages à L. Herrmann. Collection Latomus, vol. 44, pp. 315-329. Brussels.

1960b Les trois "trésors des ancêtres" dans l'epopée Narte. RHR 157:141-154.

1960c Carna (déesses latines et mythes védiques, 5). REL 38:87-98.

1961a Quaestiunculae Indo-Italicae 8-10. Latomus 20:253-265.

1961b Idéologie tripartie des Indo-Européens, MM. Walter Pötscher et Martin van den Bruwaene. Latomus 20:524-529.

1962 La société scythique avait-elle des classes fonctionelles? Indo-Iranian Journal 5:187-202.

1965 À propos de la Plainte de l'Ame du Boeuf (*Yasna*, 29). Académie royale de Belgique: Bulletin de la classe des Lettres et des sciences morales et politiques (5e série) 51:23-51.

Dumézil, Georges, and Pierre Sipriot
1961 Dialogue avec Georges Dumézil. La Table Ronde, no. 157: 66-74.

Dupont-Sommer, E.
1954 The Jewish sect of Qumran and the Essenes. London: Vallentine, Mitchell.

Durkheim, Émile
1961 The elementary forms of the religious life. Trans. from French by Joseph Ward Swain. New York: Collier Books.

Durkheim, Émile, and Marcel Mauss
1903 De quelques formes primitives de classification: contributions à l'étude des représentations collectives. L'année sociologique 6:1-72.

Eberhard, Wolfram
1942 Lokalkulturen in alten China. Vol. 1. Leiden: E. J. Brill.

Eggan, Fred
1955 Social organization of North American tribes. Chicago: University of Chicago Press.

Eliade, Mircea
1948 Le "dieu lieur" et le symbolisme des noeuds. RHR 134:5-36.
1961 The sacred and the profane. New York: Harpers.

References Cited

Elkin, A. P.
1954   The Australian aborigines: how to understand them. Sydney: Angus and Robertson.

El'nickij, L. A.
1947   Nekotorye problemy istorii skifskoj kul'tury. Vestnik Drevnej Istorii (Kiev) 2:95-101.

Evans-Pritchard, E. E.
1940   The Nuer. Oxford: Clarendon Press.

Fairservis, Walter A., Jr.
1959   The origin of Oriental civilization. New York: Mentor Books.

Feist, S.
1913   Kultur, Ausbreitung und Herkunft der Indogermanen. Berlin: Weidmann.
1924   Indogermanen und Germanen. Halle: M. Neimeyer.

Firth, Raymond
1956   Elements of social organization. 2d ed. London: Watts.

Fisk, John
1888   Myths and myth makers: old tales and superstitions interpreted by comparative mythology. Boston and New York: Houghton, Mifflin.

Fox, Sir Cyril
1947   A find of the Early Iron Age from Llyn Cerrig Bach. Oxford: Clarendon Press.

Frazer, Sir James G.
1910   Totemism and exogamy. London: Macmillan. 2 vols.
1922   The golden bough: a study in magic and religion. Abridged ed. New York: Macmillan.

Freud, Sigmund
1950   Totem and taboo: some points of agreement between the mental lives of savages and neurotics. Trans. James Strachey. London: Routledge and Kegan Paul.

Frye, Richard N.
1960   Georges Dumézil and the translators of the *Avesta*. Numen 7:161-171.

Fustel de Coulanges, N.
1958   The ancient city. New York: Doubleday Anchor Books.

Gaster, T. H.
1950   Thespis: ritual, myth, and drama in the ancient Near East. New York: Shuman.

Gehlke, Charles E.
1915   Émile Durkheim's contribution to sociological theory. New York: Columbia University Press.

Gerschel, Lucien
1950   Saliens de Mars et Saliens de Quirinus. RHR 138:145-151.
1952   Structures augurales et tripartition fonctionnelle dans la pensée de l'ancienne Rome. Journal de Psychologie normale et pathologique 45:57-78.
1953   Coriolan. *In* Hommage à Lucien Febvre, vol. 2, pp. 33-40.

References Cited

Paris: Librairie Armand Colin.
1956 Sur un schème trifonctionnel dans une famille de légendes germaniques. RHR 150:55-92.
1957 Georges Dumézil's Comparative Studies in Tales and Traditions. Trans. Archer Taylor. Midwest Folklore 7:141-147.
1958 Varron logicien. Latomus 17:65-72.
1960 Un épisode trifonctionnel dans la saga de Hrolfr Kraki. In Hommages à Georges Dumézil. Collection Latomus, vol. 45, pp. 106-116. Brussels.

Gershevitch, Ilya
1959 Joint review of Paul Thieme, Mitra and Aryaman (1957), and J. Duchesne-Guillemin, The Western response to Zoroaster (1958). BSOAS 22:154-157.

Gimbutas, Marija
1952 On the origin of north Indo-Europeans. AA 54:602-11.
1961 Notes on the chronology and expansion of the Pit-grave Kurgan culture. In Europe à la fin de l'âge de la pierre, pp. 193-200. Prague: Éditions de l'Académie Tchécoslovaque des Sciences.
1963 The Indo-Europeans: archeological problems. AA 65:815-836.
1964 Comments on Indo-Iranians and Tokharians: a response to R. Heine-Geldern. AA 66:893-898.

Goldschmidt, Walter
1959 Man's way. New York: Holt-Dryden.

Gonda, Jan
1950 Notes on Brahman. Utrecht: J. L. Beyers.
1960a Die Religionen Indiens. Vol. I, Veda and älterer Hinduismus. Die Religionen der Menschheit, Band 11. Stuttgart.
1960b Some observations on Dumézil's views of Indo-European mythology. Mnemosyne 4, no. 13:1-15.

Grantovskij, E.
1960 Indoiranische Kastengliederung bei den Skythen. Papers presented by USSR delegation, XXV International Congress of Orientalists. Moscow.

Grimm, Jakob
1822 Deutsche Grammatik. Göttingen: Dieterichsche Buchhandlung.
1883 Teutonic mythology. Trans. J. S. Stallybrass. London: George Bell and Sons.

Güntert, H.
1923 Der arische Weltkönig und Heiland, bedeutungs-geschichtliche Untersuchungen zur indo-iranischen Religionsgeschichte und Altertumskunde. Halle: M. Niemeyer.

Güterbock, Hans G.
1948 The Hittite version of the Hurrian Kumarbi myths: Oriental

forerunners of Hesiod. American Journal of Archeology 52:122-134.

Harrison, Jane Ellen
1903 Prolegomena to the study of Greek religion. Cambridge: Cambridge University Press.
1912 Themis: a study of the social origins of Greek religion. Cambridge: Cambridge University Press.

Hegel, G. W. F.
1900 The philosophy of history. Trans. J. Sibree. Rev. ed. New York: Colonial Press.

Heine-Geldern, Robert
1964 Comment on Gimbutas' "The Indo Europeans: archeological problems." AA 66:889-893.

Helm, K.
1955 Mythologie auf alten und neuen Wegen. Beiträge zur Geschichte der deutschen Sprache und Literatur 77:333-365.

Hencken, Hugh
1955 Indo-European languages and archeology. American Anthropological Association Memoir no. 84.

Herzfeld, Ernst
1947 Zoroaster and his world. Princeton: Princeton University Press.

Hockett, Charles F.
1954 Chinese versus English: an exploration of the Whorfian thesis. In Language in Culture, ed. Harry Hoijer. American Anthropological Memoir no. 79, pp. 106-123.
1958 A course in modern linguistics. New York: Macmillan.

Höfler, O.
1934 Kultische Geheimbünde der Germanen. Vol. I. Frankfurt am Main: M. Diesterwez.

Hoijer, Harry
1954 The Sapir-Whorf hypothesis. In Language in Culture, ed. Harry Hoijer. American Anthropological Association Memoir no. 79, pp. 92-104.

Hyman, Stanley Edgar
1955 The ritual view of myth and the mythic. In Myth: a symposium, ed. Thomas Sebeok. Bibliographic and Special Series of the American Folklore Society 5:84-94. Philadelphia.

Hymes, Dell
1960 Lexicostatistics so far. Current Anthropology 1:1-20.

Jacobs, Melville
1959 The content and style of an oral literature: Clackamas Chinook myths and tales. Chicago: University of Chicago Press.
1964 Pattern in cultural anthropology. New York: Harper and Row.

Jacobsen, Thorkild

References Cited

1949 The cosmos as a state. *In* H. and H. A. Frankfort, *et al.*, Before philosophy, the intellectual adventure of ancient man, pp. 137-199. Harmondsworth: Pelican Books.

Jespersen, Otto
1921 Language, its nature, development, and origin. New York: Holt.

Keith, A. B.
1937 New theories as to Brahman. *In* Jha Commemoration Volume, pp. 208-217. Poona, India.

Koch, Carl
1953 Bermerkungen zum römischen Quirinuskult. Zeitschrift fur Religions- und Geistesgeschichte 5:1-25.

Kossinna, Gustav
1914 Die Deutsche Vorgeschichte. Würzburg: Kapitzsch.

Kramer, S. N.
1959 History begins at Sumer. New York: Doubleday Anchor Books.
1961 Mythologies of the ancient world. New York: Doubleday Anchor Books.

Kuhn, Adalbert
1859 Die Herabkunft des Feuers und des Göttertranks. Berlin: F. Dümmler.

Kuiper, F. B. J.
1961 Some observations on Dumézil's theory (with reference to Professor Frye's article). Numen 8:34-45.

Lambrechts, P.
1946 Mars et les Saliens. Latomus 5:111-119.

Lang, Andrew
1897 Modern mythology. London: Longmans, Green.

Laroche, E.
1960 Hittite *arawa-* 'libre'. *In* Hommages à Georges Dumézil. Collection Latomus, vol. 45, pp. 124-128. Brussels.

Latte, Kurt
1960 Römische Religionsgeschichte. Handbuch der Altertumswissenschaft. Munich.

Lee, Dorothy
1959 Freedom and culture. New York: Prentice-Hall.

Le Roux, Françoise
1957 Le calendrier gaulois de Coligny (Ain) et la fête irlandaise de Samain. O 9:337-342.
1960 Le Dieu Druide et le Druide divin. O 12:349-382.
1961a Les Druides. Paris: PUF.
1961b Le guerrier borgne et le Druide aveugle: la cécité et la voyance. O 13:331-342.
1962a Études sur le festiaire celtique. O 14:174-184.

References Cited

1962b Études sur le festiaire celtique, II: La fête irlandaise de février, Imbolc; III: Beltaine, la fête sacerdotale. O 14:174-184.

1962c Études sur la festiaire celtique, IV: Lugnasad ou le fête du roi. O 14:343-372.

Lessa, William A.
1961 Tales from Ulithi Atoll: a comparative study in Oceanic folklore. Folklore Studies: 13. Berkeley and Los Angeles: University of California Press.

Lévi-Strauss, Claude
1949 Les structures élémentaires de la parenté. Paris: PUF.
1953 Social structure. In Anthropology today, ed. A. L. Kroeber, pp. 524-553. Chicago: University of Chicago Press.
1955 The structural study of myth. In Myth, a symposium, ed. Thomas Sebeok. Bibliographic and Special Series of the American Folklore Society 5:50-68. Philadelphia.
1964 Le cru et le cuit. Paris: Plon.

Liljeblad, Sven
1963 Review of Anna Birgitta Rooth, Loki in Scandinavian Mythology, Lund, C. W. K. Gleerup (1961). AA 65:144.

Lindquist, Ivar
1940 Religiösa runtexter, II: Sparlösa-stenen, ett svenskt runmonument från Karl den Stores tid upptäckt 1937; ett tydningsförslag. Skrifter utgivna av Vetenskaps-societeten i Lund 24.

Linton, Ralph
1955 The tree of culture. New York: Alfred A. Knopf.

Littleton, C. Scott
1962 Anthropological influences on Freud and psychoanalysis. Unpublished MS. Department of Anthropology, University of California, Los Angeles.
1964 The comparative Indo-European mythology of Georges Dumézil. Journal of the Folklore Institute (Indiana University) 1:147-166.
1965 A two-dimensional scheme for the classification of narratives. JAF 78:21-27.
In press Is the "kingship in heaven" theme Indo-European? In Indo-European and the Indo-Europeans: Proceedings of the Third Indo-European Conference, ed. Henry M. Hoenigswald. Chicago: University of Chicago Press.

Ljungberg, H.
1947 Tor: Undersökningar i indoeuropeisk och nordisk religionshistoria. Uppsala Universitets Årsskrift 9.

Lommel, H.
1939 Der Arische Kriegsgott. Religion und Kulter der Arier, vol. 2. Frankfurt: Klostermann.
1954 Anahita—Sarasvati. In Asiatica: Festschrift Friedrich Weller, pp. 405-413. Leipzig.

References Cited

Lowie, Robert H.
  1956 The Crow Indians. New York: Holt, Rinehart, and Winston.
Malinowski, Bronislaw
  1955a Magic, science, and religion. New York: Doubleday Anchor Books.
  1955b Sex and repression in savage society. New York: Meridian Books.
  1960 A scientific theory of culture. New York: Meridian Books.
Mandelbaum, David
  1955 The world and the world view of the *Kota*. *In* Village India: studies in the little community, ed. McKim Marriott. Chicago; University of Chicago Press.
Mannhardt, W.
  1877 Antike Wald- und Feldkulte. Strassburg: H. Patzig. 2 vols.
Mannheim, K.
  1949 Ideology and Utopia: an introduction to the sociology of knowledge. Trans. Louis Wirth and Edward Shils. New York: Harcourt Brace.
Marett, R. R.
  1909 The threshold of religion. London: Methuen and Company.
Mauss, Marcel
  1954 The gift: forms and functions of exchange in archaic society. Trans. of "Essai sur le don" by Jan Annison. Glencoe: Free Press.
Meillet, Antoine
  1907 Le dieu indo-iranien Mitra. JA, series 10, 9:143-159.
  1922 Introduction à l'étude comparative des langues indo-européennes. Paris: Librairie Hachette.
  1925 Review of Georges Dumézil, Le Festin d'immortalité (1924). Bulletin de la Société de Linguistique de Paris 25:42.
Merlat, P.
  1960 Orient, Grèce, Rome, un exemple de syncrétisme? Les "Castores" dolichéniens. *In* Éléments orientaux dans la religion grecque ancienne, pp. 77-94. Paris.
Merton, Robert K.
  1933 Durkheim's division of labor in society. American Journal of Sociology 40:319-328.
  1957 Social theory and social structure. Glencoe: Free Press.
Molé, M.
  1951 La structure du premier chapitre du Vidēvdāt. JA 239:283-298.
  1952 Le partage du monde dans la tradition iranienne. JA 240:455-463.
Mongait, Alexander
  1959 Archeology in the USSR. Academy of Sciences of the USSR. Moscow: Foreign Languages Publishing House.

References Cited

Montesi, G.
1957   Uṣāsānaktā: mitologia vedica della notte. SMSR 28:11-52.

Müller, F. Max
1869   Lectures on the science of language. New York: Scribner, Armstrong & Co.
1872   Chips from a German workshop. Vol. II. New York: Scribner, Armstrong & Co.

Müller, Otfried
1845   Introduction to a scientific system of mythology. Trans. J. Leitch. London: Longmans, Brown, Green, and Longmans.

Müller, W.
1886   Zur Mythologie der greichischen und deutschen Heldensage. Heilbronn: Henninger.

Murray, Gilbert
1907   The rise of the Greek epic. London: Oxford University Press.

Orgogozo, J. J.
1949   L'Hermès des Achéens. RHR 136:10-30, 139-179.

Palmer, L. R.
1955   Achaeans and Indo-Europeans. Oxford: Clarendon Press.
1960   Mycenaeans and Minoans. London: Faber and Faber.

Paoli, V. E.
1950   La signification du sigle NP dans les calendriers romains. REL 28:252-279.

Parain, Brice
1956   Les dieux des Indo-Européens. La Nouvelle Nouvelle Revue Française 4, part 3:694-702.

Parsons, Talcott
1951   The social system. Glencoe: Free Press.

Pettazzoni, Raffaele
1954   Essays on the history of religion. Trans. H. J. Rose. Leiden: E. J. Brill.

Piganiol, André
1939   L'histoire de Rome. Paris: PUF.

Piggott, Stuart
1950   Prehistoric India. Harmondsworth: Penguin Books.

Poisson, Georges
1934   Les Aryens. Paris: Payot.

Polomé, E.
1953   L'étymologie du terme germanique *ansuz "dieu souverain." Études germaniques 8:36-44.
1954a A propos de la déesse Nerthus. Latomus 13:167-200.
1954b La religion germanique primitive: reflet d'une structure sociale. Le Flambeau 37:437-463.

Pötscher, W.
1960   Review of Dumézil, L'idéologie tripartie der Indo-Européens (1958). Gymnasium 67:255.

References Cited

Potter, Charles Francis
  1962 The lost years of Jesus revealed. New York: Mentor Books.
Powell, T. G. E.
  1948 Celtic origins: a stage in the enquiry. Journal of the Royal Anthropological Institute 78:71-79.
Przyluski, J.
  1940 Les confréries des loups-garous dans les sociétés indo-européennes. RHR 121:128-145.
Puhvel, Jaan
  1955 Vedic *aśvamedha-* and Gaulish IIPOMIIDVOS. Language 31:353-354.
  1964 The Indo-European and Indo-Aryan plough: a linguistic study of technological diffusion. Technology and Culture 5:176-190.
Radcliffe-Brown, A. R.
  1953 Structure and function in primitive society. Glencoe: Free Press.
Raglan, Fitzroy Richard Somerset, Lord
  1937 The hero: a study in tradition, myth, and drama. London: Methuen.
Rapp, K. M.
  1841 Die vergleichende Grammatik als Naturlehre dargestellt. Stuttgart: Cotta.
Rask, Rasmus
  1818 Undersøgelse om det gamle nordiske eller islanske sprogs oprindelse. Copenhagen: Gyldendal.
Rees, Alwyn, and Brinley Rees
  1961 Celtic heritage: ancient tradition in Ireland and Wales. London: Thames and Hudson.
Reinach, Salomon
  1941 Orpheus: a history of religion. Trans. Florence Simmonds. New York: Liveright.
Rose, H. J.
  1947 Review of Georges Dumézil, Jupiter, Mars, Quirinus (1941) and Servius et la Fortune (1943). Journal of Roman Studies 37:183.
  1955 Review of Georges Dumézil, Rituels indo-européens à Rome (1954). Classical Review 69:307-308.
  1959 A handbook of Greek mythology. New York: E. P. Dutton.
Rousseas, Stephen, and James Farganis
  1965 American politics and the end of ideology. *In* The new sociology: essays in social science and social theory in honor of C. Wright Mills, ed. Irving Louis Horowitz. New York: Oxford University Press.
Sapir, Edward
  1921 Language. New York: Harcourt, Brace.

References Cited

Schelling, Robert
    1960   Les Castores romains à la lumière des traditions indo-euro-
            péennes. *In* Hommages à Georges Dumézil. Collection
            Latomus, vol. 45, pp. 177-192. Brussels.
Schlegel, Friedrich von
    1859   Lectures on the history of literature, ancient and modern.
            Trans. H. G. Bohn. London: H. G. Bohn.
Schleicher, August
    1871   Compendium der vergleichenden Grammatik der indoger-
            manischen Sprachen. Weimar: H. Böhlan.
Schmidt, Johannes
    1872   Die Verwandtschaftsverhaeltnisse der indogermanischen
            Sprachen. Weimar: H. Böhlan.
Schräder, Otto
    1890   Sprachvergleichung und Urgeschichte. Jena: H. Constenoble.
Sjoestedt, Marie-Louise
    1940   Dieux et héros des Celtes. Paris: Leroux.
Smith, William Robertson
    1889   Lectures on the religion of the Semites. New York: Appleton.
Spence, Lewis
    1921   An introduction to mythology. London: G. G. Harrap and
            Company.
Spencer, Robert F.
    1965   The nature and value of functionalism in anthropology. *In*
            Functionalism in the social sciences, ed. Don Martindale.
            American Academy of Political and Social Science, Mono-
            graph no. 5. Philadelphia.
Steward, Julian H.
    1955   Theory of culture change: the methodology of multilinear
            evolution. Urbana: University of Illinois Press.
Sturtevant, E. H.
    1947   An introduction to linquistic science. New Haven: Yale
            University Press.
Swadesh, Morris
    1953   Archeological and linguistic chronology of Indo-European
            groups. AA 55:349-352.
    1955   Towards greater accuracy in lexicostatistical dating. Interna-
            tional Journal of American Linguists 21:121-137.
Tavadia, J. C.
    1953a   From Aryan mythology to Zoroastrian theology: a review of
            Dumézil's researches. ZDMG 103:344-353.
    1953b   Zoroastrian and Pre-Zoroastrian: à propos the researches of
            G. Dumézil. Journal of the Bombay Branch of the Royal Asi-
            atic Society 28:171-186.
Thieme, Paul
    1938   Der Fremdling im Rigveda. Heidelberg.

References Cited

1953 Die Heimat der indogermanischen Gemeinsprache. Wiesbaden: Akademie der Wissenschaften und der Literatur.
1957a Review of Hugh Hencken, Indo-European Languages and Archeology (1955). Language 33:180-193.
1957b Vorzarathustrisches bei den Zarathustrien und bei Zarathustra. ZDMG 107:67-104.
1957c Mitra and Aryaman. Transactions of the Connecticut Academy of Arts and Sciences 41:1-96. New Haven.
1960 The "Aryan" gods of the Mitanni treaties. Journal of the American Oriental Society 80:301-317.

Thompson, Stith
1946 The folktale. New York: Dryden Press.

Thomsen, V.
1903 Sprogvidenskabens historie. Copenhagen: J. H. Schultz.

Timasheff, Nicolas S.
1955 Sociological theory: its nature and growth. New York: Doubleday.

Toporov, V. N.
1961 Fragment slavjanskoj mifologii. Akad. Nauk SSSR, Institut slavjanovedenija, Kratkie soobščenija 30:14-32.

Trager, George L., and Henry L. Smith
1950 A chronology of Indo-Hittite. Studies in Linguistics 8, no. 3:61-70. New Haven.
1953 The chronology of North Indo-European: a rejoinder. AA 55:295-298.

Trubetzkoy, N. S.
1939 Gedanken über das Indogermanenproblem. Acta Linguistica 1:81-89. Copenhagen.

Turville-Petre, G.
1960 Professor Dumézil and the literature of Iceland. In Hommages à Georges Dumézil. Collection Latomus, vol. 45, pp. 209-214. Brussels.

Tylor, Edward Burnett
1871 Primitive culture. London: John Murray. 2 vols.

Unbegaun, B. O.
1958 Sybaris. In Festschrift Hans Krahe, pp. 173-176. Wiesbaden.

Van den Bruwaene, Martin
1959 Review of Georges Dumézil, L'idéologie tripartie des Indo-Européens. L'Antiquité Classique 28:488-490.

Vendryes, Joseph
1921 Le langue: introduction linguistique à l'histoire. Paris: Renaissance du Livre.

Verner, Karl
1902 Afhandlunger og breve udgivne af Selskab for germansk filologi. Copenhagen: J. Frimodt.

References Cited

Vian, F.
1952   La guerre des géants, le mythe avant l'époque hellénistique. Paris: PUF.
1960a   La triade des rois d'Orchomène: Étéoclès, Phlégyas, Minyas. *In* Hommages à Georges Dumézil. Collection Latomus, vol. 45, pp. 215-224. Brussels.
1960b   Le mythe de Typhée et le problème de ses origines orientales. *In* Éléments orientaux dans la religion grecque ancienne, pp. 17-37. Paris: PUF.

Vogt, Evon Z.
1964   The genetic model and Maya cultural development. *In* Desarrollo cultural de los Mayas, ed. Evon V. Vogt and Alberto Ruz L. México: Universidad Nacional Autónoma de Mexico, Facultad de Filosofia y Letros, Seminario de Cultura Maya.

Wagenvoort, H.
1947   Roman dynamism. Oxford: B. Blackwell.
1952   Gravitas et maiestas. Mnemosyne 5:287-306.

White, Raymond C.
1957   A Luiseño theory of knowledge. AA 59:1-19.

Whorf, B. L.
1956   Language, thought, and reality: selected writings. Ed. John B. Carroll. Cambridge: Technology Press of Massachusetts Institute of Technology.

Widengren, G.
1960   La légende royale de l'Iran antique. *In* Hommages à Georges Dumézil. Collection Latomus, vol. 45, pp. 225-237. Brussels.

Wikander, Stig
1938   Der arische Männerbund. Lund: Ohlsson.
1947   Pāṇḍava-sagan och Mahābhāratas mytiska förutsättningar. Religion och Bibel 6:27-39.
1950   Sur le fonds commun indo-iranien des épopées de la Perse et de l'inde. NC 1:310-329.
1951   Hethitiska myter hos greker och perser. Vetenskaps-societeten i Lund, Årsbok, pp. 35-56.
1952a   Mithra en vieux-perse. Orientalia Suecana 1:66-68.
1952b   Histoire des Ouranides. CS 36:8-17.
1957   Nakula et Sahadeva. Orientalia Suecana 6:66-96.
1960a   Från Bråvalla till Kurukshetra. Arkiv för nordisk filologi 75:183-193.
1960b   Germanische und indo-iranische Eschatologie. Kairos 2:83-88.

Zaehner, R. C.
1961   The dawn and twilight of Zoroastrianism. London: Weidenfeld and Nicholson.

233

Index

INDEX

Ādityas, 90, 96, 106, 117
Aesir, 12, 18, 70–71, 83, 89, 106, 130, 155, 160
Agni, 15–16, 52, 82, 105, 149
Ahura Mazdah, 10, 51, 74–75, 77, 82, 88, 102, 137, 145, 165, 167
Akkadians, 199
Ameretāt, 11, 46, 75–76, 107, 164, 167
Ameša Spentas, 10, 46, 74–75, 82, 93, 167, 180, 197
Amṛta, 45, 62
Amśa, 91
Anāhitā, 11–12, 16, 74, 76–77, 82, 148, 165, 168
Andronovo culture, 29–30
Angra Mainyu, 74, 82
Arjuna, 18, 107, 123, 128, 175, 188–189
Armāiti, 11, 75–77, 82, 165, 167–168
Arnold, P., 171, 191
Arya, 7, 90, 94, 176–177
Aryaman, 8, 90–92, 104–105, 117–118, 134, 159, 177, 179; seen by Thieme as personification of hospitality, 178
Aša, 10, 75, 84, 136–137, 167, 180; as one of pair of joint sovereigns, 84
Aṣṭāpādī, 111–112
Aśvamedha, 113
Aśvins, 9, 11–12, 15, 40, 67–68, 76, 88, 97, 104, 107, 114, 147, 164, 167; as collective representations, 9; consulted by Indra, 120; as prototypes of Nakula and Sahadeva, 123, 129, 148–149; compared with Russian Volos, 173
Atharva Veda, 53, 91, 96, 116. See also *Vedas*
Athena, 14–16, 72
Avesta, 11, 16, 50, 51, 77–78, 84, 90, 110, 148, 166–167. See also *Vidēvdāt*

Aži Dahāka, 84. *See also* Zohak

Balts, 30
Barr, K., 6, 167, 181
Basanoff, V., 168, 191
Bayet, J., 170
Behistun, 18
Bellator equus, 113
Benveniste, E., 50–53, 56, 60, 67, 75, 95, 136–137, 143–146, 153, 164, 177, 181
Bhaga, 8, 90–92, 104–105, 118, 134
Bhīma, 148–149, 188–189
Bloch, R., 170, 191
Boas, F., 2, 45
Boghazköy, 9, 14
Bopp, F., 23–24, 33
Brāhmanas, 8, 67–68, 112
Brahmans, 7–8, 17, 55–56, 59, 68, 89, 91, 113, 119, 121, 123, 162, 185, 198
Brávellir, battle of, 150
Brelich, A., 185–186
Brough, J., 7, 66, 143, 181, 188–191, 195, 198, 202
Buddha, 121, 123
Bylinas, 46, 49

Carnoy, A., 36
Carthage, Roman interpretation of, 18–19
Celts, 13, 16–17, 29, 80, 97, 102, 157–158, 161, 188
Centaurs, 47
Chariot, I-E, 26
Childe, V., 25–26, 28
Christianity, influenced by I-E ideology, 208
Collective representations, 4, 39, 52, 87, 122, 127, 131, 194
Coriolanus, 133, 153
Cox, G., 34–35
Croesus, 15
Crow Indians, 209–210

237

Index

Index

239

Index

Index